My Dearest Louise

Marie-Louise
by Gérard

MY DEAREST LOUISE

Marie-Louise and Napoleon
1813–1814

UNPUBLISHED LETTERS FROM THE EMPRESS
WITH PREVIOUSLY PUBLISHED REPLIES FROM NAPOLEON

Collected and annotated by
C.-F. PALMSTIERNA
Private Secretary to H.M. the King of Sweden

Translated by
E. M. WILKINSON

METHUEN & COMPANY LIMITED
36 Essex Street, Strand, London W.C.2

First published in France as
Marie-Louise et Napoléon 1813–1814
in 1955 by Librairie Stock
First English edition 1958
Copyright in all countries signatory
to the Berne Copyright Convention
English translation © 1958 by Methuen & Co. Ltd.

CATALOGUE NO. 6020/U

PRINTED IN GREAT BRITAIN
BY WESTERN PRINTING SERVICES LTD. BRISTOL

Acknowledgements

The majority of the illustrations used in this edition have been kindly lent to the Publishers by Baron Palmstierna, from the Swedish Royal Archives.

Napoleon's letter of 23rd March 1814 is reproduced by kind permission of the Director, Bibliothèque Nationale, and the United Feature Syndicate.

The portrait of Marie-Louise by Baron Gérard and the bust by Dalaistre are both reproduced by kind permission of Son Excellence Maximo Sciolette.

Contents

Illustrations

INTRODUCTION

The Letters exchanged between
Napoleon and Marie-Louise, 1813-1814

Napoleon and Marie-Louise, during the first twenty-seven months of their married life, were seldom parted. In 1812 the Emperor left his young wife in order to assume command of the Grand Army and saw her again only seven months later, when the Russian winter had defeated him. In 1813 he was obliged to leave Paris, to which he returned only on 9th November after his defeat at Leipzig. On 25th January 1814 he took reluctant leave of his family and hastened away into Champagne to check the invasion; during the three months which elapsed between his departure and the day when, having abdicated from the throne, he embarked for the isle of Elba, he was not once to meet his wife—they were, in fact, never to see each other again.

Throughout these separations, husband and wife wrote to each other almost every day, loving and intimate letters of which only eight from Napoleon and one or two from Marie-Louise were known when, in 1934, it was learned that Prince Ferdinand Montenuovo had in his possession in Austria all the letters from Napoleon written during the years 1810–14. Their subsequent history is explained by the following events.

By September 1814, and before they returned to Vienna, General Adalbert von Neipperg had already become the lover of the ex-Empress. From this liaison two children were born, in 1817 and 1819 Albertine and Guillaume. Widowed by the death of Napoleon, Marie-Louise, henceforth Duchess of Parma, contracted a morganatic marriage with Neipperg in 1821. Already during her lifetime the Duchess of Parma

had undoubtedly given away some of her possessions to her illegiti-
mate children, who had assumed the titles of Comte and Comtesse de
Montenuovo.[1] In a piece of furniture which had belonged to her were
found the letters from Napoleon to Marie-Louise. General Guillaume,
who became Prince Montenuovo in 1864, bequeathed them on his
death in 1897 to his son Alfred, Grand Master of Ceremonies at the
Court of Austria, who died in 1927. He had a son Ferdinand, born in
1888, who died as a Russian prisoner after 1945. This great-grandson
of Marie-Louise resolved, in 1934, to offer for auction in London the
letters written by Napoleon to his great-grandmother. Thanks to the
efforts of French historians, they were acquired by the French Government. In the following year they were published by the Bibliothèque
Nationale in Paris, with an Introduction and Notes by Louis Madelin
which have been followed in the present volume.

These 318 letters, often quoted by historians, obviously made it possible to study, in fairly close detail, the relations between the imperial
couple, but they supplied only half the dialogue (admittedly the more
interesting half), since Marie-Louise's replies were missing. Some attempt should surely be made to discover the answering letters of the
one who, from 1810 onwards, was 'the woman behind Napoleon'. In
an endeavour to win back both her and his son, Napoleon, in 1815,
made his great resolve to leave the isle of Elba. Thus Marie-Louise,
although herself a very ordinary person, played a decisive rôle in history—a woman who, in part at least, was responsible for the Hundred
Days, is deserving of some interest and attention.

From the numerous works of Frédéric Masson it is clear that he was
acquainted with a considerable number of original letters from Marie-
Louise; not those she had sent to Napoleon, of which he had been able
to trace only a single one, but letters he had gleaned from various col-
lections. In 1912, in *Marie-Louise intime*, Edouard Gachot revealed
the existence of 243 letters from the Empress to her close friend and
confidante the Duchesse de Montebello, whose descendants had informed him of the existence of the collection. To the works of Masson
and Gachot have recently been added the biographies of Jean de Bourgoing, in which appear, in addition to a number of other letters from
that inveterate scribbler the Empress, several hitherto unknown letters
to Napoleon.

But where could all the other letters from Marie-Louise be lying

[1] The Italian translation of the name Neipperg (Neuberg).

Document dated 11th June 1815 (see p. 16)

hidden? Could it be, as Masson and even Madelin seemed to imagine, that in the month of March 1814, Napoleon had caused them all to be burnt? In 1941, Albert Ciana gave it as his opinion that they 'were still buried in the deepest depths of some archives or other'. Had every possible clue really been followed up? The search had been confined to France and Austria. One possibility had been overlooked—the trail leading to the north, towards the Bernadottes.

From this hitherto neglected source it has been possible to fill a part, and the most important part, of that 'terrible gap' of which French scholars have so long complained. In Stockholm, in the archives of the Royal Family, in a folder labelled *Letters to Queen Désirée written by her relatives and members of the Royal House*, is a document dated Paris, 11th June 1815, which states, '*The Emperor is sending Prince Joseph a sealed portfolio, containing the letters of the Empress Marie-Louise, and a notebook, containing the King's official report. The Emperor begs the Prince to keep these documents for him.*'

This text, which furnished the main clue to the whereabouts of this collection, was found in 1945 by the archivist Nils F. Holm.

Dictated in the Elysée Palace, probably after the family dinner on Sunday, the eve of his departure for the campaign which was to end in Waterloo, this document proves that Napoleon entrusted to the ex-King of Spain, amongst other papers, a portfolio containing the letters from his wife, written during his absence in 1813 and 1814 and brought back by him from the isle of Elba in 1815. After Waterloo, on his way through Paris, Napoleon also dispatched to Joseph yet another small box containing precious papers. The presence of our document amongst the papers of Queen Désirée proves, moreover, that in 1815, before leaving for America, and in order to put them out of reach of the Allied powers, Joseph had deposited certain papers—amongst them the letters entrusted to him by the Emperor—with his sister-in-law Désirée Bernadotte, who for several years had been Princess Royal of Sweden. In spite of the actively hostile part played by her husband, Désirée was living quietly in Paris in her town house, 36 Rue d'Anjou. The affectionate regard felt by Napoleon ever since 1795 for this kindly Marseillaise, whose family was later to be linked with his by ties of marriage, is a matter of common knowledge—eloquent proofs of it are contained in the letters at the end of this volume. We know, furthermore, that Désirée returned his regard by giving a home, on several occasions from March 1815 onwards, to her much-loved sister

Julie, Joseph's wife; and that after Waterloo she did everything in her power to supply the needs of her unfortunate relatives. Désirée, indeed, once she had become Princess Royal, and later Queen of Sweden, ceaselessly importuned the Allies to hasten her brother-in-law's return from the United States.

What was Bonaparte's former fiancée to do with so unexpected a present as that of the Empress Marie-Louise's letters? To return them to Marie-Louise, in other words to Metternich, would certainly have been repugnant to her. The prisoner of St Helena, for his part, remained inaccessible. The death of Napoleon and the morganatic marriage of Marie-Louise in 1821 solved this delicate problem; returning once and for all to Sweden, Désirée took with her all the papers entrusted to her by her brother-in-law, who was still on the other side of the Atlantic. The Queen's return to Sweden took place in 1823, and with her went her son Oscar and her daughter-in-law, the young Princess Joséphine, daughter of the ex-Viceroy of Italy, Eugène de Beauharnais, Duc de Leuchtenberg. On her death in 1860, Désirée bequeathed all her papers to Joséphine, who for the past year had herself been Queen Dowager.

So it comes about that, in the Bernadotte Archives in Stockholm, amongst a miscellaneous assortment of documents belonging to Joseph Bonaparte, are to be found 127 letters from Marie-Louise to Napoleon, covering the years 1813–14. In default of a catalogue listing the treasures contained in these archives, the originals of these letters remained more or less inaccessible, although they were not unknown to Swedish historians. It is only recently, thanks to the interest shown by His Majesty King Gustaf VI Adolf of Sweden, the great-great-grandson of Désirée, and to the kind help and co-operation of the Keeper of the Archives, Professor Torvald Höjer, that these deposits have finally been made available to serious research workers. The distinguished humanist who now occupies the throne of Sweden has been graciously pleased to give his unhesitating consent to the publication of the present volume.

The editor's warm and most sincere thanks are due to the Directors of the Bibliothèque Nationale and to the United Feature Syndicate for their kind permission to reprint here a selection of Napoleon's letters already published in 1935. A debt of gratitude is owing also to Baron Jean de Bourgoing of Vienna for permission to include three letters from Marie-Louise, published in 1953 in his biography *Marie-Louise von Österreich* (Nos. 190, 191 with the health bulletin of 10th May 1814, and 206). These are copied from the original MSS in the State Archives in Prague.

The commentaries which give continuity to the letters in this edition have been composed in part from the texts of Masson, Madelin, Bainville, de Bourgoing, Jules Bertaut, Raymonde Bessard and Jean Savant.

THE DOCUMENTS

The letters from Marie-Louise during the years 1813–14 are generally longer than those from Napoleon, which are really no more than brief notes. They vary little, although there are several of 6 to 8 lines and others of 70 or more, the longest being that of 20th April 1814 which runs to 88 lines. Often they consist of about 40 lines, filling approximately two and a half pages. The paper on which they are written is fairly uniform in appearance and shape; for the most part it is thick, with a gilt edge. The watermarks which appear in 37 letters are not all the same; only one, that dated the evening of 1st April 1814, shows the Emperor's head with an exergue below, a mark already known from one of Napoleon's letters of 30th May 1812 (Madelin, *Lettres inédites*, pp. 29, 32). Others bear as watermark the imperial eagle crowned, in a double circle; others again an 'M L' over the imperial crest, covered with bees and surmounted by a crown, or incomplete armorial bearings, a conch shell, and even, as in Napoleon's letter of 11th August 1813, a flower (perhaps a lily?). There are also the watermarks of F. Johannot, Pot et Co., H. Renoz and Jan [. . .]. Most of the letters however bear no watermark at all, and several are written on odd scraps of paper. The gilt edge which decorates almost all of them is a feature of Napoleon's letters also; it has remained exceedingly bright.

On the paper, which has yellowed only slightly, and which, except for the last letters of 10th and 18th August 1814 (which must have been torn a little as they were being unsealed), has remained uncrumpled, the ink has faded very little. Only one letter is written in pencil; it is undated, but may be assigned to the night of 12th–13th April 1814, when Marie-Louise was compelled to move from Orleans to Rambouillet. Written in haste and without the knowledge of the Austrian escort, it was folded very small, to be entrusted to the officer mentioned by the Empress. By its outward appearance alone, this letter bears eloquent testimony to the situation in which Marie-Louise found herself on the day after Fontainebleau.

The Empress's written French is evidence of the care with which she was educated; it is, in short, good governess-French, although, naturally, Germanisms and spelling mistakes are not infrequent, especially where place-names are concerned. The letters could almost be compared to present-day telephone conversations. The Empress's handwriting is very legible and there are few erasures; in all probability she made a rough copy first. The arrangement of her material is almost always the same: first an acknowledgement of the letter just received, then a few words of anxiety or affection, a description of some function or other which the Empress has been obliged to attend, news of the little King and of her own health. The letters generally end with repeated assurances of love and devotion. The editor has thought it advisable to divide them into paragraphs corresponding to this basic plan of composition.[1] In addition, the punctuation, but not the literary style, has been brought into line with modern usage. Marie-Louise, in error, continued to date her letters 1813 up to 11th February 1814— an instance of her casual ways! From the moment when Napoleon left for exile in Elba, she began, as a precautionary measure, to number her replies; from the series 1–15, letters 6, 7, and 10 are missing—they were probably intercepted. From the letters published here, it has been possible to ascertain that six notes from Napoleon are missing also, three of 27th and 30th January, and three of 1st, 14th, and 27th February 1814.

The envelopes in which most of the letters were apparently enclosed have not, as a rule, been preserved; only a single one remains, that of 29th September 1813, decorated with a seal of red wax and bearing the joint coat of arms of the imperial pair. It is addressed to: 'His Majesty the Emperor and King—The Empress.' On two notes, 31st March and 10th August 1814, the address has been written on the back. The first has a green wax seal on which the crown is still visible, the second —and the modification is significant—bears the direction: 'His Majesty the Emperor Napoleon—at Porto Ferrajo.'

Several letters are accompanied by enclosures, some of which are of great historical interest. To that of 27th February 1814, for example, is attached the copy of a letter from Marie-Louise to her father the Em-

[1] It has also been thought more convenient, in the English edition, to transfer the date from the end to the beginning of the letter in each case.

peror Francis, dated the 26th, and drafted in rough by Napoleon on the previous day (cf. Madelin, p. 209). The original was in German, as was Francis's reply of 6th March, received or intercepted at Chavignon on 10th March and sent by Napoleon to Marie-Louise for translation. The Empress returned it to her husband the following day with a translation, together with her reply in French. This reply from his wife was forwarded by Napoleon to the Austrian Emperor as promptly as 12th March. Another enclosure gives the list of people who ought to accompany the Empress on the journey she was planning on 10th April to Leghorn, from which place she hoped to rejoin her husband who was about to start his journey to the isle of Elba. A third enclosure is a bulletin on her health composed at Aix-les-Bains on 31st July 1814 by the doctor Jean-Nicolas Corvisart—a document which must be considered as a deed of justification for her stay in Aix. A letter from Corvisart to Napoleon, written at Rambouillet on 22nd April 1814, of which the original has also emerged from the papers of Joseph Bonaparte in Stockholm, proves how deeply the conscience of this 'family oracle' was troubled.

To this collection of letters have been added, besides the three already published by Baron Bourgoing, a letter published by Jean Hanoteau (No. 169) and another (No. 130) borrowed from Masson, which in 1902 he believed to be 'the only one yet discovered from that daily correspondence which alone can throw light on the events of the time, this letter in which, indeed, a whole character is laid bare, a whole mind is delineated, a whole way of life is caught and held'. The rest lay in the Bernadotte Archives. There they were put in order and dated, towards the end of her life, by the Dowager Queen Joséphine, led to undertake the task by her interest in Marie-Louise to whom, when she herself was seven, she had been presented on the occasion of the ex-Empress's journey from Vienna to Aix in 1814. The young Joséphine at that time bore the Napoleonic title of 'Duchesse de Galliéra'. Proof of her labours is to be found in the note written on an envelope at the beginning of the collection: *Letters from the Empress Marie-Louise to the Emperor Napoleon I in 1814. No. 16.*[1] The small dossier has in recent times been bound together in morocco leather, except for one letter of 26th March lent by Queen Joséphine to her lector Joseph

---

[1] Queen Joséphine has added in pencil: '*The portrait of M[a]d[ame] Bonaparte Empress Joséphine is in the Collection of Miniatures [in the Royal Palace in Stockholm].*'

Müller, and which was returned to the Royal Archives only in 1936, after his death.

As for the letters written by Marie-Louise before 1813–14, that is from the month of May 1812, their fate is unknown, together with that of the letters written between 29th September and 9th November 1813. It is possible that before leaving the Tuileries Marie-Louise commanded the Emperor's official archivist, Bary, to burn them along with the other 'documents relating to the Bonaparte family' which were thrown into the fire on 20th March 1814. Judging from the Emperor's replies, published by Madelin, they must have numbered about 125, including several letters from the years 1810–11. Probably about one half remain to us, and doubtless the more interesting half. It may be that amongst these are to be found the seventeen letters which Napoleon, at the moment of his attempted suicide in April 1814, had entrusted to Caulaincourt, who may have returned them later to his master. It is quite possible that the portfolio which, in 1815, contained the letters from Marie-Louise, is the same as that mentioned by Caulaincourt in 1814, but both this portfolio and the official report (of 3rd April 1814) have as yet eluded discovery.

C.-F. PALMSTIERNA

The Historical Background

If these letters shed light on this one question only—the extent to which Napoleon's love for Marie-Louise influenced the course of events —they would, for that reason alone, rank as documents of the first importance in the history of the Empire. They may also, perhaps, by their very nature, incline public opinion more favourably towards this Empress who was still only twenty-two when the whole story came to an end. Her critics, surely, will judge her less harshly when they realise that it took the events of the Hundred Days to convince her once and for all that she must resign herself to a new way of life. Her artless chatter, just because it has no claim to literary merit, makes interesting reading. Her anxious fears lest Napoleon should catch cold on his campaigns are not without a certain appeal. 'I hate to think of you on military operations in this cold, wet weather', she writes on 15th March. 'I am sure your clothes must often be soaking wet when you can't possibly change them, and it makes me very worried and uneasy.'

'The *Corsican Lady*', wrote her young uncle the Archduke Rudolph, 'tells you a whole lot of news and tittle-tattle, but cannot always reduce her tale to order; all the same she is a mine of information and sometimes gives us a good laugh.' Her early correspondence makes insipid reading. Only Napoleon's letters break vividly in, announcing the astonishing victories of his wonderful French campaign. But the 'Corsican Lady' was indeed a mine of information.

In the latter half of the correspondence, written as the Allies were marching on Paris, followed at a prudent distance by the Emperor of Austria, the Empress's letters become absorbingly interesting. Her flight, the utter confusion of her entourage, her uncertainties, torn as she was between husband and father, her 'imprisonment' at Rambouillet and in Vienna, the gradual, painful separation of husband and wife—all are related in generous detail. Like eavesdroppers at a keyhole, we listen to the fallen Emperor and his unhappy wife talking together. In spite of the machinations of Metternich and of the Tsar Alexander, and the shuffling evasions and contradictions of the turncoat Emperor of Austria—for at one and the same moment Francis I was assuring his son-in-law of his devotion, and admitting to his Chancellor that he would like to see him, 'God willing, a good long way away from Europe'—there was no Machiavellian plot to separate Napoleon and Marie-Louise. It was the force of circumstances, and of unpredictable events, which parted them.

*

Let us glance briefly at the historical background.

Divorced on 15th December 1810, Napoleon had at once cast about for a second marriage which would best further his interests. The Russian alliance having fallen through, the Austrians offered him their princess, intending thereby to win the favour of the master of destiny. He took them at their word. Wasting no time, the Emperor wrote on 6th February 1810 to Vienna requesting the hand of the Archduchess Marie-Louise.

This 'lovely heifer offered up to the Minotaur', to quote the Prince de Ligne, was born on 12th December 1791. Her parents were Francis, then Emperor of Germany, and Marie-Thérèse, a Bourbon of Naples. For this, his eldest child, Francis had always felt the liveliest affection; she, for her part, had repaid him from earliest childhood, and was to do so always, with an almost fanatical devotion and a boundless trust. After the death of Marie-Thérèse in 1807, the Emperor, within a short space of time, had married as his second wife Maria-Ludovica-Béatrice of the Modena Habsburgs, whom General Bonaparte had formerly driven from their Italian principality. Towards her step-daughter Marie-Louise, who was also her first cousin, the new Empress of Austria was never other than cool, and so, inevitably, it was always and wholly towards 'Papa François' that his daughter's affections turned.

Her tastes were simple and domesticated; at Schönbrunn she was happiest with her geese, her chickens, her turtle-doves, her rabbits, and her dog Thisbe. She loved to dabble in cookery and to make dainties, preserves, and pastries. She was impressionable and romantic, dreaming of the young Duke of Modena, Francis IV, with whom she could perhaps have led a life of homely comfort. Generally believed to be strong and healthy—though she always had a slight tendency to consumption—she fussed over trifling disorders, mistook the slightest stomach-ache for an illness, called for physic though suspicious of doctors, and was to spend her life moaning over imaginary illnesses, exasperated because no one would take them seriously. Cotton knickers and drawers, that revolution in feminine underwear, owed their introduction into French life to Marie-Louise. She was in perpetual, mild revolt against her doctor, 'the family oracle' Dr Corvisart. Whenever she announces that her health is 'fairly good' we can take it for granted that she is really 'feeling marvellous'. Beneath her sentimentality, side by side with bourgeois tastes and quite unsuspected by the world at large, there lay hidden a strongly sensual nature, probably inherited from her father. Once aroused—as it was so violently—it was to shape her destiny.

On the arrival of Marie-Louise in France, Napoleon chose to greet her as so importunate a lover that the young girl, after her first startled surprise, was fascinated. Christine de Mathis was sent away. He was delighted to discover in this 'daughter of the Caesars' a perfect simplicity which put him completely at his ease. He found her naïve, good-natured, trusting, amiable, and noted above all that 'rose-freshness' which was her greatest charm. He was captivated by her ignorance of the world, by her touching readiness to yield to his wishes, for at times her compliance reached the point of self-sacrifice, and especially by her 'sweetness', to which in his more expansive moments the Emperor refers again and again. 'I have been thinking about you so much today,' she writes to him on 20th March 1814, the King of Rome's birthday, 'it is three years since you gave me so moving a proof of your love that the tears come whenever I think of it. . . .' The Empress had never forgotten Napoleon's attitude during her difficult labour in 1811, when, asked for his opinion, he had resolved to sacrifice the child rather than the mother.

She, for her part, though bored with victories, would listen dutifully to stories of the prowess of her *sehr böser Galant,* told with an almost childish glee, sometimes treating him rather like a schoolboy who has done well and earned his mother's indulgent approval. The Marie-Louise of these letters was no longer the young bride of 1811; the first freshness had gone—they had been married now for four years. Voltaire was bold enough to define marriage as 'selfishness for two'; in the case of Marie-Louise the selfishness, even though unconscious, was none the less considerable. A certain lack of tact sometimes revealed in difficult situations is its noticeable and inevitable consequence.

In order to understand Marie-Louise more fully, some knowledge of the young Empress's entourage is essential. Wherever she went, whether at Saint-Cloud or at the Tuileries, she was closely guarded and waited on only by attendants of the Emperor's choosing. Out of doors his equerries stood guard around her; indoors, 'at home', the chamberlains and palace ladies did the same. Napoleon was anxious to show that in strictness of protocol the Court of France was by no means inferior to the Court of Vienna. The Empress's private apartments became a holy of holies, to which no one was admitted who had not first been presented to the Emperor.

'Born to the purple', Marie-Louise soon grew accustomed to this isolation, from which she emerged only for ceremonies, festivals, or drives. She had scarcely a single close friend apart from her Lady-in-Waiting the Duchesse de Montebello, widow of the celebrated Lannes. Next to the Duchess came the Lady of the Bedchamber, the Comtesse de Luçay, who was responsible for every detail of the Empress's toilet. The Lady of the Bedchamber, moreover, appointed the staff of the private apartments. At their head were six 'first ladies', known as the 'red ladies', from their gowns of crimson silk, and they alone had the right to give orders to the maids in charge of the bedroom; they went in early in the morning, supervised the lighting of the fires, helped the Empress to rise and dress, and continued to wait on her as she breakfasted alone in her small drawing-room. To one were entrusted her jewels, another acted as her secretary, two more looked after her musical instruments and her paintings.

Below the 'red ladies' were the 'black ladies', who wore black silk aprons. They were the real chambermaids. Then came the 'white ladies', who did the heavy work and must never be found in Her Majesty's presence.

The cloistered seclusion imposed upon her placed Marie-Louise at the mercy of the small company of people who surrounded her. The Duchesse de Montebello, her link with the outside world, made no attempt to combat her mistress's prejudices, and divulged to her, not without a certain pleasure, news of any petty quarrels and the latest society gossip. On the other hand, she rendered to the Empress a multitude of small services which bound her ever more closely to her royal mistress; she became indispensable and all-powerful. In essentials, the life led by Marie-Louise at this time had much in common with that of the last years of her girlhood. She had her music and painting lessons; her tutors were Isabey, the water-colourist, and Fernando Paer, with whom she played pieces on the harp or the harpsichord. Lastly there was her embroidery mistress, Madame Rousseau, who taught her to make silk purses, belts, and even tapestries for the furniture.

Distinct from the Court of the Empress was the 'Household' of the King of Rome. At its head was the governess, the Comtesse de Montesquiou, wife of the Grand Chamberlain, warm-hearted, loving, with a passionate devotion to duty. The easy-going Empress let her have her own way. . . . Between the Comtesse de Montesquiou and the Duchesse de Montebello raged a relentless feud; jealous of her position, the Lady-in-Waiting soon influenced Marie-Louise against the governess, and soon we shall hear the repercussions of these battles, which, moreover, were not without consequences. The little King's entourage included, in addition, two under-governesses, the Comtesses de Boubers and de Mesgrigny. Then came 'red ladies' and 'black ladies', nurses, maids of the wardrobe, gentlemen ushers, and footmen.

The Empress's letters, naturally, are full of details about 'the little King'. He is learning La Fontaine's Fables—'Maman Quiou' is teaching him—and they are telling him tales from Berquin and stories from the *Magazin des Enfants* and, most important, from the military history of all the nations. Already at the age of three he is a typical small boy playing with lead soldiers; he rides along the terrace of the Tuileries in his little carriage drawn by sheep, but is just as interested in the drums and capes of the guard of honour. At the parade he hates to keep his bonnet on under his National Guard hat, because 'the little King doesn't want to look like a baby'. Sometimes he amuses himself with a set of Russian and French soldiers, 'the kind you buy on the embankment', or astride his hobby-horse stages superb cavalry charges against Cossacks and Baschkirs. 'I have never seen a child so military-minded at such an early age', sighs his mother. 'He says some really astonishing things for his age', she adds later, and does not hide her fears that 'children who are so forward for their years don't live long'.

THE LETTERS

Before the Invasion

Turning his back on the Russian disasters, Napoleon had wasted no time in re-creating an army. Levying men in still greater numbers in France, he was preparing himself for a struggle which he foresaw would be extremely severe. Prussia was already flouting the alliance, but his greatest source of worry was Austria. Officially an ally, Francis I continued to protest his loyalty by offering to mediate with Russia in an attempt to secure 'a good peace'. The very moment such armed mediation was allowed, Austria would use it as an excuse for detaching herself from the alliance. Eagerly hoping that a fresh conflict was preparing which would allow the House of Austria the fullest possible retaliation, Metternich was holding out the most dazzling prospects. In the name of the new Coalition, he would submit to Napoleon peace proposals of such a nature that he would refuse to agree to them, whereupon Austria would declare her adherence to the enemies of France in order to destroy the usurper at one fell blow.

The Corsican, on the other hand, had an intensely strong sense of family loyalty; to him it was unthinkable that a father might strive to overthrow his daughter's throne, or that a grandfather might willingly deprive a grandson of his inheritance. He held to the conviction that the Austrian marriage had forged such bonds between himself and the Court of Vienna that he need have no fear of being abandoned. 'Papa François', he believed, would never bring himself to betray his own flesh and blood.

In February 1813, however, this actually happened. On the 13th of that month a secret treaty was signed between the Tsar Alexander and King Frederick William. With the Russians in Berlin, Prussia threw aside all pretence; the whole of Germany was seething with revolt.

Making ready to abandon the alliance, Metternich allowed Schwarzenberg to regain Galicia, and only then did Napoleon realise that he was being duped. His anger centred on Metternich who, he was convinced, would never succeed in enticing the Austrian Emperor into opposition against his son-in-law and daughter. Deliberately to enhance the brilliance of the favours which he was heaping upon the Empress, Napoleon endeavoured to arrange that both she and the King of Rome should be crowned by the Pope, and as he was about to leave for the battlefield, established a Regency of which Marie-Louise could be head. The measure might also prevent a recurrence of the Malet incidents of 1812. This proof of trust and affection was, in his eyes, merely a political act intended to bind Francis more closely to him.

This accession to the Regency drew Marie-Louise abruptly out of her exclusively feminine world. In her new capacity of Empress-Regent she was obliged to attend every inaugural ceremony, every social festivity. She acquiesced in all the demands made on her, remaining as passive as on the first day of her arrival in France, for Napoleon left her not the slightest opening for initiative. Her natural mentors were the Arch-Chancellor Cambacérès, Champagny, Duc de Cadore (Secretary of the Regency Council), and Méneval, her private secretary. They prompted her replies and indicated what documents were to be signed. She presided at Councils: 'Every time I see these Gentlemen involved in a heated argument, I get into such a panic that I long to run away', she confesses to Napoleon. 'You see just how brave I am.' Every morning she had to send the Emperor a most detailed account of the events of the preceding day, and at the same time she was strictly forbidden to pass on to the Court any military information she might hear. She did, however, confide some of the news to her 'dear Duchess' (de Montebello).

With delighted relief Marie-Louise allowed the Arch-Chancellor to take decisions, give orders, and attend to matters of which she knew nothing. Governing bored her—as Napoleon was soon to find out. 'I wish', she admitted to him, 'that I could find a way of shutting myself up in some quiet little corner of the world where I could live unknown until the moment of your return, or until I could be of some use to you and prove the measure of my love.' That moment came; she was able to act as go-between in his dealings with his Austrian father-in-law, and to pass on, when commissioned to do so, artful hints about French victories and about the strength of his armies. Thanks to his wife,

Napoleon was able to keep in touch with the Court of Vienna—a fact by which he set great store—for if by chance he should be defeated, his wife and son would be dependent on Francis for their safety.

So Napoleon departed, and in the correspondence between husband and wife can be heard echoes of the mighty blows being struck in Germany, and of the sensational reappearance of the lion already wounded to death—or so it had generally been believed. Perceiving, after Poischwitz, that the armistice was merely furthering the aims of the Coalition, the Emperor made up his mind to tempt fate once more, and summoned Marie-Louise to meet him at Mainz on 24th July 1813. The homage paid him there was to be the last accorded to the 'Emperor of the West' and his wife. This was no longer the 'mob of crowned heads' of Erfurt in 1808, at which he had hurled his famous, 'Silence, Kings!'; Napoleon knew now that the Congress was no more than play-acting, in which Austria was merely seeking a pretext to break with him, that Spain was lost and Italy faithless, that Bernadotte had thrown Sweden into the arms of Russia and was about to join the armies of the Coalition. As early as 1st August, Napoleon took leave of the Empress, to cross the Rhine—for the last time.

Whilst Napoleon was inspecting his auxiliary troops in Bavaria, Marie-Louise returned to France, where she took up residence at Saint-Cloud. Her life resumed its habitual routine; drives in an open carriage, riding, visits to Queen Hortense at Saint-Leu, private receptions in the evenings, on Thursdays theatricals in the royal apartments, and on Sundays a formal audience and the family dinner-party. War having been formally declared on Austria, the Emperor forced his way into Bohemia, whilst the corps commanded by Oudinot were halted at Gross Beeren by Bülow and Bernadotte. Then came the brilliant victory of Dresden, which disconcerted the Allies. Having held Schwarzenberg's counter-offensive, Napoleon resumed his march against the army threatening him from the north.

Now the curtain rises, and we hear the first exchanges between the imperial pair in the autumn of 1813.

*

Napoleon spent the 23rd September 1813 at Hartau, which he left early the following day.

[1]

Harta[u], 24*th September* [1813]

My Dearest, I have received all your letters down to that of 17th September, our communications having been opened up and the irregulars driven off. My health is very good. My affairs are in good shape. Adio, mio bene. A kiss to the little King.

Nap

Marie-Louise had resumed her life at Court in an atmosphere heavy with depression. Returning to Saint-Cloud on 5th September, the Empress, in her capacity of Regent, held a Council there on the 29th. Current problems were discussed: the pay and clothing of the Spanish troops, destined later for the army of Lyons, commanded by Augereau.

[2]

St. Cloud, 29*th September* 1813

My Darling, This morning I received your letter of the 24th addressed from Hartau, I am delighted to see that you are still keeping well and that communications have been restored, I was so afraid you might no longer be able to get my letters, and it would upset me if you had been worrying about it. As for me, I can give you only the faintest idea of the intense pleasure your letter has brought me. I was really rather cross at not hearing from you yesterday, especially as a courier had come in, but don't imagine it was you I was angry with. I realise you can't possibly write to me when you are on horseback and have a great deal to do.

I held the Council of Ministers this morning; it didn't last very long in spite of the discussions that raged between several of those Gentlemen about the pay and clothing of the Spanish troops, serving with your army in Spain. You will laugh at me when I tell you that every time I see these Gentlemen involved in a heated argument, I get into such a panic that I long to run away. You see just how brave I am.

Your son sends you a kiss, he is wonderfully well and very lively. He has made me promise to give him a hat like those worn by the Mamelukes in the Guard, he has a passion for everything Military and we shall soon be seeing his room crammed with all kinds of military equipment instead of toys.

Napoleon

From a miniature by Isabey. (Royal Palace, Stockholm)

Marie-Louise at Compiègne, 28th March 1810

I am keeping very well indeed, I have been out riding so as to take full advantage of the last of these lovely autumn days, the weather has been superb and I've been to the Bois de Boulogne. Tomorrow I am to see an Italian play, they say there was an incredible crowd yesterday at Feydeau for the performance of two of Grétry's plays in which all the actors wore mourning because of his death, they say his funeral procession was a very fine sight too.

I have sent the P[rin]cesse de Neuchâtel[1] news of the P[rin]ce, she was very anxious about him, as she had heard nothing for several days.

Good-bye, my Darling, fondest greetings from

Your true and loving Louise

On 29th August Napoleon, playing the dutiful son-in-law, had written to the Austrian Emperor whom he had just 'trounced'. His father-in-law's reply contained a letter for Marie-Louise which she answered on 23rd September.

Owing to the activities of irregulars operating behind the Emperor's lines, the letters he wrote between 29th September and 5th October have disappeared. On 27th September he bade the Empress preside over a meeting of the Senate at which was to be presented a Senatus Consultum, authorising the conscription of fresh reservists—they were to be the gallant youngsters of the 'Marie-Louise' Regiment of 1814. On 7th October, with all due pomp and ceremony, the Empress proceeded from the Tuileries to the Luxembourg, where she delivered a speech, already prepared, which was handed to her by the Arch-Chancellor. Wearing her diadem and a white dress embroidered in silver, she made an excellent impression. 'She appeared', Talleyrand noted, 'neither bold nor timid, and conducted herself with dignity, to which were added considerable tact and charm.' Her success, nevertheless, remained little more than a drawing-room triumph.

[3]

Dresden, 5th October [1813] 2 *a.m.*

My Dearest, I enclose 2 letters from Vienna. I duly received your letter of 28th September. All your letters have reached me; I have lost none of them. The month of September has been a

[1] Wife of Marshal Berthier, before her marriage Princess of Bavaria.

very rainy one, October, therefore, seems unlikely, in my opinion, to be very fine. The Prince de Neufchâtel is very weak. He is recovering, however, but it will take him a few days longer. My health is very good. Give a kiss to my son. You speak of him in such glowing terms that I long to see him. Adio, mio bene. All my love.

Nap

The Empress-Regent

With Bernadotte hastening from the north, Bavaria and Württemberg deserting him in the west, Blücher coming up from the north-east and Schwarzenberg from the south, Napoleon found himself hemmed in on the plains of Leipzig. Between 5th and 25th October there is a break in the correspondence. During those twenty days, on 16th, 18th, and 19th October, was fought at Leipzig the 'Battle of the Nations', in which the Grand Empire foundered. On 4th November, Napoleon retreated with the tattered remnants of his army to Mainz, then hurrying on without a pause returned on 9th November to Saint-Cloud, where he met Marie-Louise again. On the 20th they were back once more in the Tuileries.

In a prodigious burst of activity, the Emperor endeavoured to forge himself a new army. He believed that three clear months lay before him for the task; in reality there was only one. He was still reluctant to face the fact that his marriage and its 'indissoluble bonds' counted for nothing, yet on 21st December, Schwarzenberg, marching through Switzerland, entered French territory, and Blücher crossed the Rhine and advanced into Lorraine.

Napoleon hastened to resume command and attempted to halt the enemy's advance. Against the 200,000 soldiers of a Europe united to thrust France back within her former frontiers, he could put in the field only the troops massed in Champagne. To Carnot, the man chiefly responsible for the annexation of Belgium, an act which England never forgave, the Emperor entrusted the defence of Antwerp. He delegated the Regency a second time to Marie-Louise, with all the rights she had exercised during the German campaign, and with Cambacérès continually at hand to guide her. Fearing the intrigues of his ministers and of his brother Louis, who had fled from Holland and was in hiding near Paris, he offset their influence by giving authority to Joseph, with whom, after the Spanish disasters, he had recently become reconciled. Installed in the Luxembourg, 'King Joseph' received the title of Lieutenant-General, with command of the National Guard, and communicated every day with the Emperor, from whom he was the first to hear news of military developments. Even whilst confiding in him, however, Napoleon mistrusted him, as witness his appointment of General Caffarelli to the office of Palace Governor to the Empress, with the duty of reporting to him daily. In addition, the Emperor received bulletins every day from Cambacérès and from the Minister of Police.

Marie-Louise was at her husband's side in the Throne Room when, on New Year's Day 1814, the members of the Senate, of the Council of State, and of the Legislature filed past the Emperor; it was the very day on which Blücher crossed the Rhine. She was present again with the little King on Sunday, 23rd January, when the officers of the recently revived National Guard took an oath of loyalty, and swore to defend both her and the King of Rome. So loud was the outburst of enthusiasm that it brought her near to fainting.

The eve of his departure was a sad one. On 24th January, after dinner, Marie-Louise, in tears, was in Napoleon's study when he burnt his most secret papers. The Emperor endeavoured to raise her drooping spirits: 'Have faith in me! Do you think I've forgotten my job?' As they said good-bye, she asked him when he would come back. 'That, my darling,' Napoleon answered her, 'is God's secret.' He kissed her once more, handed her over to the care of the Duchesse de Montebello, and at six o'clock in the morning leapt into his carriage. He was never to see either his wife or his son again.

On the evening of the 25th, full of sad forebodings, Marie-Louise took up her pen once more.

[4]

[*Paris*] 25*th January* 1813 [=1814]

My Darling, I don't know what to say to you to-day, I am sure I shall keep coming back to the same old subject, my heart has been so heavy since your departure that I can think of nothing else. I keep telling myself that you bade me be cheerful, but it's no use, I think it will be quite impossible, this parting has upset me even more than the previous ones. I have been depressed for such a long time that you really must forgive me. Besides, this is one of those things I shall never learn to get used to, even though it is always happening, because I love you too dearly to be happy and well until you come back, or at least until I hear from you. Do, please, write to me very regularly, and don't take risks as you so often have done before; remember that my happiness, that of your son and of a host of people who love me, depends utterly and entirely on your safety, for you can be quite sure that if anything happened to you I should die of grief.

I have been to see Madame, who is not at all well, and we've had a good cry together. The King of Spain and the Arch-Chancellor have been to see me, the former wants me to receive the National Guard tomorrow, the latter says it is quite out of the question, as the address won't have been signed yet, but I shall try and get it over tomorrow. That was the day you wanted, and that's enough for me to want it too. But I'm worried about the reply I shall have to make them; if I say a lot of silly things, you really will have only yourself to blame for not wanting to give it me today.

Your son sends you a kiss and says I am to tell you he loves you with all his heart. He is wonderfully well and very cheerful, he doesn't even mention you very often. What it is to be young and carefree! I sometimes wish *I* could worry as little about you, because people are really lucky when they have no feelings.

I want you to tell me whether now, in my new capacity of Regent, I ought to have four Ladies-in-Waiting instead of two. This evening I was asked to sign a decree appointing General Carnot Governor of Antwerp. Those Gentlemen have at last come to an agreement, they have decided that it will be the right thing for me to receive the National Guard tomorrow.

I am sending you this letter by the Duc de Bassano, so I shan't be writing by the courier this evening. I will try to be less miserable, but it will be difficult because every time I think of you I begin to cry.

Good-bye, my Darling, I kiss you and love you with all my heart

Louise

37

The day after his departure, Napoleon sent her his first note.

[5]

Châlons, 26th [January 1814] 9 *a.m.*

My Dear, I have reached Châlons. It is cold. I was 18 hours, instead of 12, on the way. I am in very good health. I am going on to Vitry, 6 leagues from here. Good-bye my dear. All my love.

Nap

The National Guard presented an address to the Regent in reply to the speech delivered by the Emperor before his departure. Cambacérès rejected the discourse planned by Méneval, and reduced Marie-Louise's reply to two comparatively insignificant sentences.

Jérôme Bonaparte, ex-King of Westphalia, and his wife Princess Cathérine of Württemberg, a royal couple deposed and in disgrace, now solicited the favours of the Empress.

[6]

[Paris] 26th January 1813 [=1814]

My Darling, I am very sad at not having heard from you, 36 hours have already gone by since you left. I am all impatience to know whether you have arrived safely, the roads are so bad that I fear you may have had an accident of some kind, and the thought of it makes me very miserable, so do write soon, my Darling, you know how much pleasure it gives me. I have spent a wretched, gloomy day, I miss you everywhere I go, I have never felt your absence so keenly as I do in our present situation, but I won't talk about it, I feel my distress might grieve you.

I received the National Guard this morning and read them a reply prepared for me by the Arch-Chancellor and of which I enclose a copy. I had made one of my own with the help of Mr Méneval, and between you and me I thought it better than the other, but I suddenly took fright lest you shouldn't like it, and turned it down for that reason.

I held a Council of Ministers at 9 o'clock, just a short one, there was some business about the victualling of Santona[1] which aroused a certain amount of controversy between the Minister of

---

[1] A town in Spain.

War and the Minister of Marine, the Arch-Chancellor will tell you all about it. He is going to send you the address from the National Guard as well.

I owe your son an abject apology, I did him wrong when I said he hardly ever mentioned you. The poor little lamb began to cry last night when I talked to him about you, and when I told him you wouldn't be back for some time it was quite a while before I could console him. He is fairly well, but has had a touch of diarrhoea this last day or two, so is going to have a dose of chicory syrup for the next three days.

The Queen of Westphalia has written to me saying that you had given them permission to come and settle in Paris; I want you to tell me if I can see them, and whether I can invite them to the family dinner-party.

My health is fairly good, as good as it can be when I am fretting so much. Mr Corvisart agrees that doctor's stuff is no use at all. He begs me to present his respects to you. I am just off to bed as sad as can be at not having heard from you.

Good-bye, my dearest, fondest love from your Darling

Louise

On the 26th, Napoleon set out for Vitry-le-François which he left on the 27th for Saint-Dizier, where he overthrew the enemy.

[7]

[Paris] 27th *January* 1813 [=1814] *in the evening*
My Darling, This morning I at last received your dear letter of 26th January, I am so happy to know that you have arrived safely at Châlons. Your letter has restored my spirits a little, for I assure you I have completely lost heart; everyone agrees that I am excessively sad and they can't blame me, for we really have had a great deal to worry us during the past three years. I am very vexed to see that you are leaving Châlons, because it will mean a break in our correspondence. If you could just see how peevish and fretful I am when I am left one single day without news of you, you would take pity on me. I am afraid this bitter weather might give you a chill, it is extremely cold here and seems likely to continue so, I hope you are wrapping up warmly and not letting yourself get wet.

I saw the Arch-Chancellor and King Joseph this morning, they said there was nothing new. The Queen of Spain came to see me too, she is still very poorly.

Your son was sweet this morning. When I told him I'd heard from you, he shouted, 'King very glad', and dragged at my hand saying, 'Let's go and see Papa', he thought you were actually here; when we explained to him that it was a letter, he began to cry; fortunately sad impressions fade quickly at his age, and by evening he was as merry as a cricket.

My health is fairly good, but I have to apply leeches on Monday or Tuesday, which scares me quite a lot as I've never done it before and I feel sure it will weaken me very much.

Write to me very regularly, my Darling, and fondest greetings from your Darling

Louise

Napoleon's letter of the morning of 27th January 1814 *is missing.*

On 28th January, Marie-Louise received another deposed brother-in-law, King Louis of Holland, now a semi-invalid. 'This prince is No Good', declared the Empress in a letter to Vienna.

[8]

[*Paris*] 28th *January* 1813 [=1814]

My Darling, This morning just as I woke up I received your letter of the 27th, thank you for writing so quickly my Darling. It helps to make me less miserable. I hope I shall hear from you regularly now, I still remember what I went through during the last campaign when I was sometimes left as long as eleven days without news of you, so I'm hoping and praying that communications won't be interrupted this time. It is very sweet to me to know that in the midst of all your vast enterprises you sometimes think of me, but I deserve it, for I think of nothing else but you. The Arch-Chancellor has just brought me this morning's telegraphed despatch, I am so glad you have gained a small advantage over your enemies and recaptured a good position from them; it will give great pleasure in Paris, where people are inclined to be nervous.

There is nothing new here, this morning I signed a decree

for the appointment of a large number of officers in the National Guard. King Louis and King Joseph came to see me afterwards, they asked me all your news. Madame has had a dreadful cold; if she is still indisposed tomorrow I shall go and see her; Corvisart says there is nothing to worry about and that she will soon be quite well again.

Your son sends you a kiss and is very fit; he hasn't had his chicory syrup yet, I don't think he is going to need it at all as he is eating and sleeping well. He is full of life and said I was to be sure to tell you that he had learnt his lessons beautifully, actually he is learning a fable by heart, it is 'The Grasshopper and the Ant', he already knows a dozen lines of it.

My health is fairly good. General d'Harville[1] has written asking me to receive him—shall I say yes or no? I hope you will give me details of the Saint-Didier affair tomorrow, meanwhile I beg you to spare an occasional thought for the one who loves you very tenderly

Your Darling Louise

Setting out again from Saint-Didier on the 28th, Napoleon next day at Brienne fell upon Blücher, who was marching to join Schwarzenberg, but it was an empty victory.

Napoleon's letter of the evening of 27th January 1814 is missing.

[9]

[*Paris*] 29*th January* 1813 [=1814]

My Darling, Thank you so much for the news you give me in your letter of the evening of the 27th; you are very good to write to me so punctually, I assure you it gives me intense pleasure, I need to know how you are faring if I am to keep calm and happy. I have been in rather better spirits for the last few days and am no longer afraid of these Gentlemen paying a visit to Paris now that you are away; I'm convinced they are so frightened that they haven't the least desire to advance. If only you will come back soon and bring us peace again, I shall be filled with happiness because then you'll stay with me for always.

[1] Governor of the Tuileries.

There is nothing new here, I've signed a tremendous number of things today and seen the Arch-Chancellor and King Joseph; the latter told me the organisation of the National Guard was going well.

I beg you to let me have a definite answer one of these days about the King and Queen of Westphalia, they ask every day if they can come and see me, and as I don't know what to tell them, it puts me in a very difficult position. Tomorrow I am to receive Mr de Lacépède[1] and the two Secretaries of the Senate who are coming about the letters patent for the Regency which the Arch-Chancellor submitted to them at the last session.

Your son sends you a kiss, he is extremely well and tomorrow will be wearing his National Guard uniform for the first time, he's very delighted about it. Mme de Montesquiou wondered whether she might take him to King Joseph's, since she was to take him to see King Louis, I didn't think you would raise any objection, so I told her to do so.

I went to see Madame this morning, she is still very poorly, with violent pains in her stomach, perhaps the wild weather has something to do with it, there's a howling gale just now. I must finish my letter because I have such a headache that I can't see properly. Good-bye until tomorrow, my Dearest,

Your ever-loving Louise

On 31st January was performed a one-act opera, *The Oriflamme*, with music by Méhul and others. The piece provoked conflicting demonstrations—was the Oriflamme the tricolour or the fleur-de-lis?

[10]

[*Paris*] 30th January 1813 [=1814]

My Darling, I've been waiting all day to hear from you, but in vain, I'm afraid my hopes are going to be disappointed. I only hope something comes tomorrow, if it doesn't I shall be afraid you are indisposed, otherwise I feel certain you would write to me. One of these days I am expecting to get a letter in which you tell me some really good news; meanwhile people have been very frightened in Paris ever since the barriers were erected for defence, everyone imagines the Cossacks are here already,

---

[1] President of the Senate.

and crowds of women and children are leaving; it's ridiculous to be so scared, I am growing so brave that I'm astonished at myself, I think it must be because I know you are at the head of your armies that I feel so safe, because before, I was just as terrified as all the rest.

Next Tuesday at the Opéra they are giving a topical piece called *The Oriflamme*. The Minister of Police wanted me to go, I told him I would do whatever the Arch-Chancellor thought best, because I confess that for my part I had no desire to go, I didn't think this was a suitable time to go gallivanting to the theatre. Fortunately the Arch-Chancellor agreed with me, he said it would be better to have you scold me for not going than for having been, so I'm waiting for you to say I did the right thing.

Your son sends you a kiss, he's wonderfully well; today he wore his National Guard uniform for the first time, he got such pleasure out of it, and so did the officers of the National Guard too; there were crowds of people at Mass.

Afterwards I went to enquire about Queen Hortense who has had a wen removed from her eye, she showed me a letter from the Viceroy which touched my heart because in it he spoke of his affection for you.

I am keeping well. Dinner has just been announced and as it is the family dinner-party I don't want to keep the Princesses waiting, so I will leave you for today, but my thoughts will go with you.

Your Darling Louise

[11]

[Paris] 31st January 1813 [=1814]

My Darling, I am almost tempted to pick a quarrel with you because you haven't written to me for two whole days, it really is too bad of you, and if I didn't know you were so busy, I shouldn't forgive you for it. Let me hear from you regularly, I do implore you, just a little note to say you are well, and I shall be satisfied. Today I need news of you more than ever, this is one of those days when I see the gloomy side of everything; since you went away all my days have been like this. I wish I need not see anyone, my heart is so heavy that I'm in no state to

43

appear in public, only when you come back shall I be more settled in mind.

The Arch-Chancellor will be telling you about a piece of news which, from what he says, will have a very bad effect in Paris, they are going to have to suspend payments from the Mont-de-Piété; they should be paying out twelve hundred thousand francs tomorrow and the Minister of Finance can't find the money; this evening King Joseph has had to call together the Ministers of Police, of the Interior and of Finance to discuss this matter.

Tomorrow there is to be a parade in the Courtyard of the Tuileries, there will be 6000 men. They are beginning to put up palisades at the barriers, they have cut wood from the Bois de Boulogne and Vincennes; they say that Le Raincy especially has been quite spoilt. These Gentlemen think at the moment that I ought to attend a performance of *The Oriflamme*, I have said I wanted to have your opinion about it, so do please write and tell me what to do, I shan't go before you have said I may, unless there is a resounding victory before then, which is what I most fervently long for.

Your son is wonderfully well, he went out for a drive this morning, he's growing into a really sweet child and very intelligent; if I were to try and tell you all the clever things he says and does I should need to write volumes.

I am fairly well but am much troubled with stomach-ache this evening. I beg you to let me hear from you soon and to spare an occasional thought for the one who loves you with all her heart.

Your Darling Louise

Napoleon's letter of 30th January 1814 is missing.

Defeated and narrowly escaping capture, Blücher summoned Schwarzenberg to the rescue. Napoleon saw him hastening up: at La Rothière his small army was almost surrounded and on 1st February escaped only after four hours' hard fighting. The Emperor with difficulty began to fall back on Troyes. These events explain the absence of any letters between 26th and 30th January; the letters of 30th January and 1st February actually reached Marie-Louise, but they too are missing.

[12]

[Paris] 1*st February* 1813 [=1814]

My Darling, I am delighted with the news I received from you today, I had a lovely surprise when I woke up and found your letter of the 30th, but at the same time I was distressed to learn that you have been weary; do try and look after yourself, my Darling, and not get overtired, you know that worries me as much as the knowledge that you are in danger, and God knows you must have been these last two days. The very idea of such a thing always ruins all the pleasure such brilliant engagements would otherwise give me.

It is a week now since you went away and there have already been two successes, no one but you can do things so quickly and so well. At the moment I want nothing but peace, I am so wretched and so miserably far away from you that all my prayers are confined to this one single plea, I believe there are very many people who share it with me; so I was very happy when the Arch-Chancellor told me that Mr de la Bernardière was leaving, it gives me good grounds for hope.

The King has held a fine parade today, there were 2000 men; the Arch-Chancellor told me there was nothing fresh. The Minister of the Interior has taken it upon himself not to allow payments from the Mont-de-Piété. The King has been obliged to hold a Council to discuss the defence of Paris, it seems they are proposing to withdraw the command of the Engineers from General Chasseloup-Laubat and to give it to General Dejean alone, they say the former is very bad-tempered and that they can't get on together.

The article sent me by the Duc de Bassano could not be inserted in the *Moniteur*, as it only arrived at 4 o'clock in the morning, so it will be included tomorrow.

Your son sends you a kiss, he was delighted with today's parade, but he realised it was not you who had inspected the review and said he wished it was time for you to come back, and that meanwhile he would like to learn to read properly so as to please you.

I am in fairly good health, I went for a drive in the Bois de Boulogne and met a lot of Spanish prisoners on carts. Very few people came to my reception, everyone was at the play awaiting

45

my arrival. The rumour is spreading here that you have taken
15,000 prisoners and captured 25 pieces of cannon, I wish it
were true, each victory will be one more step towards the
moment of your return to her who loves you tenderly and
devotedly.

Your Darling Louise

Napoleon's letter of 1st February 1814 is missing.

At Brienne the Emperor passed his old college. Even at such a time
as that, Napoleon dreamed of turning it into an imperial residence or
founding a military high school there.

[13]

[*Paris*] *2nd February* 1813 [=1814]

My Darling, I have heard from King Joseph that you were quite
well on the 31st and were pleased with the way your affairs were
going; the news delighted me, I was afraid you might be tired
and that the rain would have given you a cold, which would
have made me very anxious indeed; I really love you far too
much not to be perpetually uneasy about a hundred thousand
things to which anyone else would pay no attention whatever,
and so your absences make me deeply unhappy.

I held a Council of Ministers this morning, it lasted rather a
long time, they complain that there's no more money, and
eagerly want peace for that reason. King Joseph went to inspect
the barriers today; he said they were beginning to palisade
them, he has also had to dispatch some wooden poles to the
army. People are still very frightened here, judging by what the
Arch-Chancellor has told me. They are burying their money,
and a lot of women are leaving for Normandy, I myself am
growing very brave since your latest successes, and I hope I
don't deserve to be called a Child any longer—that's what you
used to like to call me before you went away—but I hope you
don't call it childishness to worry about you, and I warn
you that it's a form of childishness I could discard only if I ceased
to love you, and you know I can't possibly do that.

Your son talks a great deal about following you to the wars,
he declares he wants to sleep in the mud and the snow and says

46

he'll eat dog's crusts if only he can be with you, so that shows you he isn't forgetting you; he had a touch of colic last night, and I'm afraid I brought it on myself by giving him a big bunch of grapes; he's quite well this morning and sends you a kiss.

I am fairly well, I think I'm going to have sciatica in my right leg, as it is very painful, and then I've hurt my knee; I should never have mentioned it except that I know other people write and tell you everything and I was afraid they would scare you about this tiny little bump which is really nothing at all.

Please, Darling, let me hear from you soon, in the meantime fondest greetings from

Your true and loving Louise

P.S. I have just received your letter of 1st February, thank you so much for letting me know you are well, I needed some such assurance because I was very worried about your health, my Darling; your kind thoughtfulness has made me feel much better.

On 2nd February, at 4 a.m., Napoleon halted at Piney.

[14]

Piney, 2nd Feb[ruary 1814]

My Darling, You ask me whether you should go to the Opéra to hear *The Oriflamme*. You have gauged my opinion correctly, you must not do so. So long as the territory of the Empire is overrun by enemies, you should go to no performance; the only one that would be worthy of you would be to go to Ste Geneviève to pray. You ask me whether you should receive the King of Naples [=Westphalia] and the Queen; no, because I have not received them. I shall be at Troyes tomorrow. My health is very good, though the weather today is most unpleasant.

Good-bye, my darling. All my love.

Nap

On 30th January, forty-hour prayers were started in Notre-Dame. Recalling the processions and litanies addressed in times of danger to the guardians of her native city, Marie-Louise thought of going in pilgrimage to Sainte-Geneviève.

The news now coming in of the defection of Murat, 'the Bernadotte of Italy', was more than a little disturbing; it was a certain Neipperg who conducted the negotiations between the King of Naples and the Austrians.

[15]

[Paris] 3rd February 1813 [=1814]

My Darling, I have heard that you were engaged in battle all day on the 1st, and were still at Brienne on the evening of the 1st, you must have been exceedingly weary after those three long days. I can hardly wait for a line from you reassuring me about the dangers to which you may have been exposed, I do want you to keep your promise not to run risks, all those who are fond of you wish the same and I hope you will pay some regard to our entreaties.

The Arch-Chancellor has told me there is nothing new, he has given me a report to read about the conduct of the King of Naples, it must be so distressing for you, when you have such a generous heart and have shown so much kindness both to him and to so many others. You meet with nothing but ingratitude from people, truly an ill reward for your kind offices, and I can assure you it fills me with indignation; I only hope *my* heart is made differently from that of a lot of people, and is a heart capable of gratitude, and devoted to those I love.

King Joseph has been to see me, he said the King and Queen of Westphalia had commissioned him to tell me that they very much wanted to see me. I told him I had not had an answer from you; he advised me to receive them as you saw the King, in my private apartments, and not to see them at the family dinner-party nor anywhere else, until there was an answer from you. I shall ask the Arch-Chancellor for his opinion too, and if he thinks the same, I shall see them tomorrow, and if you don't approve, just blame these two Gentlemen, or else yourself, for never giving me an answer to the things I ask.

I have just this moment received your letter of the 2nd, I am so glad you approve of my not going to the performance; nothing is sweeter than to find that my ideas coincide with your wishes. If you think it a good idea for me to go to Ste Geneviève, I ask nothing better than to go, I only beg you to tell me in what manner you would like me to go, in full ceremony or simply with my personal attendants. If you will only be good enough to

The marriage of Marie-Louise and Napoleon in the Chapel
of the Louvre in 1810

by G. Rouget

Napoleon presenting the King of Rome to the leading dignitaries of the Empire
by G. Rouget

answer straight away, I can go at the beginning of next week to pray God for the success of your plans; but you will be victorious so as to give us a sound peace which will never separate me from you again, meanwhile I am very unhappy at being parted from you. I will tell King Joseph that you don't wish me to receive the King and Queen of Westphalia, and he will tell them, then they won't be able to grumble at me for not receiving them.

Your son has had a dose of syrup today, it hasn't prevented him from being very lively and well; he has had several naughty little fits of temper, but we put them all down to the syrup.

I am keeping tolerably well, I have twinges of rheumatism which are fairly painful, but they wouldn't matter at all if my spirits were not so cast down by the grief I feel at your absence and our present situation. However I am trying to be of good cheer. Good-bye my Darling, I send you a kiss.

Your true and loving Louise

Reaching Troyes on 3rd February, Napoleon remained there on 4th and 5th February. Those same days witnessed the opening, at Châtillon-sur-Seine, of a 'Congress' which laid down 'bases' for armistice negotiations.

[16]

[*Troyes, 3rd February* 1814]

My Darling, I have received your letter of 1st February. You did very well indeed not to go to the Opéra; it was not at all fitting. I have reached Troyes in good shape although it is rather cold at the moment. The Congress has met today 3rd February at Châtillon-sur-Seine. The Austrians are represented by Satadion [=Stadion], the English by their Foreign Secretary and 3 or 4 negotiators, the Russians by Rasum[ows]ki. Good-bye, my Darling. All my love.

Nap

At Châtillon the Allies no longer kept to the proposals, deliberately obscure, put forward at Frankfurt in 1813. For Metternich, the chief aim was to gain time in which to foment discontent in Paris: he would willingly agree to a Regency, with Marie-Louise at its head, replacing

D

Napoleon. The Tsar, for his part, urged on by Pozzo di Borgo, wished to march straight on the capital.

At Brienne, defeat was threatening, and in Paris there was a situation approaching panic.

[17]

[Paris] 4*th February* 1813 [=1814]

My Darling, I have just received your letter of 3rd February telling me of your safe arrival at Troyes; this news has given me immense pleasure, and I do thank you for writing so quickly. It is very good news about the Congress, only I am vexed to see who its members are to be. They are persons very partial to the English, and that makes me think the prospects of peace are not very hopeful. The thought of it depresses me, since it will perhaps keep you away from me for a long time.

You cannot imagine what alarm there has been in Paris ever since yesterday. The news they had printed in the news-sheets announcing your capture of fifteen thousand prisoners had a terribly bad effect when it was denied, I can't conceive how they ever came to do such a silly thing. Yesterday everyone, even the Ministers, went about my drawing-room with such long faces that they almost sent me crazy, I got it into my head that there was some bad news they wanted to keep from me, with the result that I had the greatest difficulty in the world not to look as gloomy as they did. King Joseph is the only one who is calm and unruffled, I find him very like you in a lot of things.

Your son sends you a kiss, he is quite well, his syrup has given him a touch of diarrhoea today. When he woke up he told us he had been dreaming that he had been to see you at Châlons and had said to you, 'Me tell dear Papa come back very quickly', and that you had come back with him; you see how he goes on thinking about you even in his sleep, his fondness for you is one more reason why I love him so.

I am not very well, I don't know what ails me, I think it must be all the worry and trouble which is making me like this, ah, if only you could return with peace, I am certain I should make a marvellous recovery on the spot. All my fondest greetings.

Your true and loving Louise

[18]

[*4th February* 1814]

My Darling, I have received your letter; it has been very cold today. my health is good. Kiss the little King for me.

Your Nap

Caulaincourt, Minister of Foreign Relations, dispatched from Austria to Châtillon, found that the peace conditions had been made considerably harsher: they demanded the restoration of the 'ancient' frontiers of France, and the handing over of the strongholds in the east. But was it possible for Napoleon to sacrifice the conquests of the Republic without sacrificing also his own position?

[19]

[*Paris*] 6th February 1813 [=1814. *Morning*]

My Darling, Just an hour ago I received your letter which I suspect was written on the 4th (for you are not dating them any longer). I am delighted to see that you are still in good health, it is so satisfying to have such recent news, it makes me feel much calmer; I would rather you were at Troyes than at Brienne, you must be better accommodated there too.

I am eagerly awaiting news of the Congress; I wish I were two months older, then at least our uncertainty would be at an end, nothing is worse than the state of anguished suspense in which we are living at the moment. The King and the Arch-Chancellor will have written to tell you how alarmed people still are in Paris, they are longing for peace, and in my secret heart I am longing for it too, though I don't say so out loud, because I don't know whether you would like it. They are also terrified of my leaving; yesterday someone, I don't know who, had started the rumour that I was going, which so alarmed Mr de Lacépède and the Minister of Police that they rushed off to the Arch-Chancellor, one to know if it was true, the other to find out what the Senate should do if I really was leaving.

Tomorrow the King is to review a division just arrived from Spain, they say it is superb, and that the men are magnificent.

Your son sends you a kiss, he is wonderfully well, but has a slight cold affecting his eyes, which are very bloodshot; the Doctors said no treatment was needed and it would soon pass off; he begs me to tell you he is learning his lessons very nicely, he really has an astonishing memory for his age, he already knows 'The Grasshopper and the Ant' and half the fable of the 'Crow and the Fox', he is really comical when he's repeating them, he talks a kind of gibberish which is quite incomprehensible.

I am keeping fairly well, but am having pains in the small of my back which make it hard for me to stand for any length of time; I fear they may keep me from attending Mass tomorrow, as it means a lot of standing about receiving people, but I shall do my very best to go, or else they won't fail to say there is bad news, or that I've gone away. I have given your son a kiss for you, he and I both kiss you with all our hearts.

Your true and loving Louise

The battles at Brienne and La Rothière upset the plan of campaign. Napoleon, however, hid his reverses from the Empress; it was essential to 'keep her cheerful'.

[20]

6th [February 1814] 4 a.m.

My Darling, I have just received your letter of 4th February. I am sorry to hear you are worrying. Cheer up and be gay. My health is perfect, my affairs, while none too easy, are not in bad shape; they have improved this last week, and I hope, with the help of God, to bring them to a successful issue.

Adio, mio bene. All my love.

Nap

The Emperor's affairs were indeed in a critical state. Beating a retreat, his troops became demoralised, and meanwhile no reinforcements were forthcoming from the Minister of War; he believed that Blücher and Schwarzenberg had joined forces for a march on Paris, and hesitated to confront them.

The news reaching the Tuileries was bad.

[21]

[Paris] 6th February 1813 [=1814. In the evening]

My Darling, No news from you yet today, and I'm waiting for it with an impatience beyond all words, I see so many long faces all around me here that I shall very soon go crazy. I can't tell you how harassed I am, and how upset at not being able to be with you, nothing would reassure me so much as that, for when I am near you I am brim-full of courage. I feel then that nothing can possibly happen.

Everyone here is in great consternation. Just as I was on my way to Mass the Arch-Chancellor buttonholed me between the double doors to ask whether I had received orders to leave, and the King too had a face as long as a fiddle; I wish to goodness we could put an end to this state of anxiety. Meanwhile the only thing in the world I long for is to hear from you regularly. I do hope you are keeping well, your health is so precious to us just now, as indeed it is at all times.

Very few people were with me at Mass; even though I feel very poorly and was feverish, I got up specially to go, I would rather have made myself worse than give rise to the idea that there was bad news. I am not at all well. My rheumatism is bothering me, and I don't want to follow the Doctor's advice; when you are worried, drugs must do much more harm than good.

Your son sends you a kiss, he is wonderfully well, he behaved beautifully at the reception, and asked the Arch-Chancellor if he had heard from you. They are just arriving for the family dinner-party, so I'll leave you and assure you that I love you very dearly.

Your true and loving Louise

[22]

[*Paris*] *7th February* 1813 [=1814]

My Darling, I received your letter of the 6th at 1 o'clock this morning, I long so much for news of you that I have told them to wake me up whenever any comes in. What you tell me about the state of your affairs makes me feel much more settled in mind. If everything depended on the prayers we offer here for you daily, you would indeed be fortunate, your happiness would be complete, and mine too, because then you would never leave me again.

You have no idea what ridiculous stories are circulating in Paris. King Louis has just called on me to ask about the good news which had just come in, he said that one of Madame's

Chamberlains had just seen with his own eyes two couriers hurrying through the streets on their way to the Tuileries shouting, 'Good news!', and waving their arms in the air; several people have seen them. I simply can't imagine who can perpetrate such things. King Joseph has given me news of you written on the 6th at 6 p.m.; he said you had left Troyes and moved on towards Nogent-sur-Seine. I wish you were already back here with us, I tell myself what a baby I am, but it's no use, I worry in the most absurd way. Every single thing that concerns *you* makes me nervous, but for the rest I'm braver than lots of other people.

Your son sends you a kiss, he is wonderfully well; I am very much in his good books today, he positively insisted that I and no one else should tie his shoe-lace, and he wouldn't stop kissing me, he really is the sweetest child, I only wish peace could be concluded so that you could enjoy him at your leisure, you've seen so little of him since he was born.

I am keeping fairly well, I found Mass yesterday less tiring than I should have expected, but my rheumatism is still troubling me. We are having dreadful weather which will be very bad for your manoeuvres, I am so upset because I fear it may give you a cold. Good-bye, all my fondest greetings.

Your true and loving Louise

On 7th February Napoleon reached Nogent-sur-Seine, only to be inundated with bad news: the government in Paris was in a state of anarchy, the armistice conditions were unacceptable, even dishonourable, and Murat's treachery was final and complete. The Emperor was aroused from this nightmare by a dispatch announcing that Blücher, separated at last from Schwarzenberg, was marching on Paris.

[23]

Nogent, 7th [February 1814] at noon.

My Darling, I have arrived at Nogent and beaten the army which was marching on Paris from Châlons and Vitry. I have succeeded in pushing back the main enemy force 3 marches.

My health is good, I am full of hope. Good-bye my darling.

Nap

The prayers at Sainte-Geneviève in which the Empress wished to join irritated Napoleon. He advised her to consult the Archbishop, the Master of Ceremonies, the Comte d'Aix, and the Arch-Chancellor.

[24]

Nogent-sur-Seine, 7th [Feburary 1814] 5 p.m.

My dearest Louise, I realise you must be anxious. But I do beg you not to worry too much. I hope to beat the enemy soon. Several fine divisions have just reached me. My health is very good and I hope that in a few days time all will be cleared up. Give a kiss to the little King for me. See the Archbishop and Cambacérès about the ceremony at Sainte-Geneviève. It must come from you; my opinion is that you should not fail to go there as a matter of faith, but without ostentation; it would be necessary, however, to inform the clergy beforehand, and it would become known. Moreover I am not sufficiently familiar with such matters; you must ask Méneval about it. All my love.

Nap

[25]

7th [February 1814] 7 p.m.

My Darling, I have just received the courier of the 6th. Your letter grieves me deeply; it tells me you are discouraged; those who are with you have lost their heads. I am quite well and I hope my affairs will take a turn for the better, but I do beg you to cheer up and take care of yourself. If I were to hear you did not know how to keep well, it would distress and hurt me. You know how I love you. Good-bye my dearest Louise, have courage for those about you. A kiss to the little King. All my love.

Nap

With Blücher and Schwarzenberg separated, Napoleon, certain of victory, was already, in theory, planning his battle of the Marne and reassured his wife as best he could. Now began the amazing recovery of February 1814.

[26]

8th [February 1814] 3 a.m.

My Darling, I wrote to you three times yesterday, for I am sorry to know you are anxious; I will tell you, as between ourselves, that peace will probably be signed within 4 days; besides, the enemy is pushed back from Paris in every direction. They are far too frightened in Paris. All my love.

Nap

On the very day on which he penned these optimistic confidences, Napoleon ordered Joseph to move his wife and son out of harm's way if the enemy should reach Paris. 'The fate of Astyanax as a prisoner of the Greeks has always seemed to me the saddest in all history. I would rather see my son murdered and thrown into the Seine than see him handed over to the Austrians to be led to Vienna.' In this long and vivid letter, of which the original is amongst Joseph's papers in the Bernadotte Archives, the Emperor shows himself well acquainted with the system of hostages.

[27]

[Paris] 8th February 1813 [=1814]

My Darling, I want to thank you most warmly for your kind thoughtfulness in writing to me three times in one day. All the loving things you say move me very deeply. They made me cry. Indeed, Darling, I *will* try not to be too much distressed, and to be more cheerful, I will keep thinking to myself that you would wish it so, and that the thought of it pleases you, and I am sure my attempts will succeed, because I've always had a certain amount of courage, and I assure you that if it has momentarily deserted me somewhat, it's not my fault but that of the Gentlemen I see about me. The King is the only one who remains calm, the Minister of Police has completely lost heart, much more so than the Arch-Chancellor, who is much less discouraged today than I have seen him recently. I too will try to keep up, though it will be rather difficult, not that worry will make me ill, but my health has been badly undermined this last fortnight, and I think even if my mind were at ease I should still be ill, besides, the grief caused by your absences doesn't help to make me feel any better, but I promise you once again to be cheerful. I find that, on the whole, we women have more courage this year than the Gentlemen in Paris.

I saw Mr de Ségur this morning, he has returned from his mission; he is very anxious to go to headquarters to give you an account of it, he is very disconsolate at not having been more successful. He asked to come with me if I was leaving; I assured him that I was not, that there was no question of it yet.

I told the Archbishop of Aix and the Arch-Chancellor that I should like to know just what happened in the olden days when the Queens used to go and pray to Ste Geneviève; the first said he would let me have a note about it, the second said I should be well advised to go. I myself (and this will really amaze you) take the liberty of giving a different opinion, which is that if I go when such fear prevails in Paris, they will, I firmly believe, assume that all is lost, I told the King what I thought and he agreed. I am not sure whether you know that in the Chapel [of the Tuileries] after Mass the other day they had prayers, I thought it was you who had ordered us to say them.

I went to see Madame this morning, she is frightened to death; I reassured her as much as ever I could, and told her the enemy was still a long way from Paris. I saw the Queen of Spain too; she is very ill but has much more courage.

Your son sends you a kiss, he said he wanted to be a courier and go and see you. He thinks about you all the time, he is so sweet, I've given him a National Guardsman's sword and he said he would use it to defend Papa against enemy attacks. He is keeping fairly well, he had a raging toothache this morning and was in great pain for more than three-quarters of an hour; he already has two bad teeth, I am really upset about it.

I am feeling rather better today, I have taken some pills which have done me good and am going to have leeches applied one of these days as I'm too full-blooded. Good-bye Darling, I love you with all my heart.

Your true and loving Louise

A letter which the Emperor had addressed to the bishops had, in fact, been read in all the churches on 6th February. After the reassuring news she had just received, Marie-Louise hesitated to carry out her projected pilgrimage—a decision which Napoleon was to approve.

[28]

[Paris] 8th February [1814] 8 *p.m.*

My Darling, This evening I have received the letter you wrote
this morning; it is so good of you to tell me of your hopes that
peace will be signed in four days' time, I promise to keep the
secret well, it makes me wonderfully, wonderfully happy, I am
so lighthearted this evening that the King, who dropped in to
give me news of you, was simply amazed. He asked me what
was the matter with me, I told him I had heard from you, which
always filled me with delight, but I took good care not to tell
him the truth. I hope this will hasten your return, how happy I
should be if it did! Meanwhile I promise you to keep calm and
to take care of myself.

Your son and I are both well. I have written to you by the
courier King Joseph sent, so you will have more recent news
and get it more quickly. Your son says I am to tell you that he
loves you with all his heart and thinks about you a great deal.
He is romping here beside me like a little mad thing, he's turning into a real little demon. Do let me hear from you regularly
and believe me when I say I love you devotedly.

Your true and loving Louise

[29]

Nogent, 9th [February 1814] 3 *a.m.*

My Darling, I have received your letter of the 8th. I am glad to
hear you are easier in your mind. I do beg you to be cheerful
and not to worry, it would harm you and my happiness depends
upon knowing you are in good health. Give a kiss to the little
King for me and believe me ever your

Napol[eon]

'Put a stop to these forty-hour prayers and these "Misereres"',
thundered the Emperor in a letter to King Joseph. 'If they started up
all these monkey tricks, we should every one of us be afraid of death. As
the old saying goes, it's priests and doctors who make death dreadful!'

[30]

9th [February 1814]

My Darling, I agree with you that there is no need for you to
go to Ste Geneviève; it would have been a good thing a year

58

ago. My health is very good; do take care of yourself and be brave. The weather is still bad, and the army has many sick in consequence. Good-bye, dearest Louise. All my love. A kiss to your son.

Nap

Everywhere in Paris, alarm was making itself felt. At private receptions in the evenings, people were questioning each other, and asking for news with bated breath; their ignorance of what was happening added poignancy to their anxiety about the future. The very Ministers had already sent their families away to the southern provinces.

[31]

[Paris] 9th February [1814] 8 p.m.

My Darling, No news of you today; I hope I shall hear this evening, I am eagerly longing for it. I was spoilt yesterday, you wrote me 4 letters in 24 hours, the last one alone was worth its weight in gold because of the good news you gave me in it. The King confirmed it this morning, so I see it is quite true, I hope you will soon be coming yourself to bring us news of peace. How happy and contented I should be then! Meantime I am keeping more cheerful and am in good heart.

I held a Council of Ministers this morning. The King must have let fall a few reassuring words after I left—goodness knows they needed them—the Minister of Marine is terrified, they don't know what to do with their wives and children and many of them have already sent their families to Vendôme.

Your son sends you a kiss, he's wonderfully well and is getting very greedy; he appeared when I was having lunch this morning and wanted to sample everything he set eyes on; the last few days there have been crowds in front of his windows, trying to see whether he has gone away or not.

I am keeping very well, I still have stomach-ache, but it's nothing much, my health has been so bad for some time now that I never get through a day without aches and pains of some kind.

I have this very moment received your letter written this morning; it's delightful to get news of you so quickly, I am very glad to see that my courage pleases you, I hope it always will; I promised you, just to please you, that I wouldn't worry and would look after myself, and I shall do my best to keep my word. Good-bye my Darling, give a thought sometimes to her who vows she will be all her life

Your true and loving Louise

[32]

[*Paris*] 10*th February* 1813 [=1814]

My Darling, This morning at five o'clock I got your letter written some time during the 9th. I am truly delighted with what you tell me about the way your affairs are prospering. I pray they may continue to do so, meanwhile I am trying to be brave and cheerful; being brave I can manage, but cheerfulness is really very difficult, I can keep is up for a few minutes then I relapse into sadness, deep sadness, once again. I grieve so at your absence. But on the whole you have reason to be pleased with me, because it's not affecting my health. I am keeping fairly well, and I shall feel a little better every day; hearing from you is a great help, when you write to me twice a day it does me a world of good. I calm down at once.

This morning I saw the Queen of Spain and Madame, they asked to be remembered to you. Madame is very frightened, she has asked me to let her know beforehand if I am leaving, because she wants to leave too; I hope it won't come to that, it would cause such distress in Paris. The Arch-Chancellor is quite confident again but is not at all well. The P^{cesse} de la Moskowa is leaving with her children this evening, she asked my permission to do so, and as she is only an extra Lady-in-Waiting, I didn't think you would mind very much. Mme Brignole begged leave, through the Duchess, to go with me if I left; I was very touched, particularly since she, of all my Palace Ladies, is the one whose manners most endear her to me.

Your son sends you a kiss, he is wonderfully well, very gay and as fresh as a rose, he plays a great deal and is applying himself to his lessons so as to know them properly when 'dear Papa' comes back home, at least so he tells me; I didn't see much of him this morning, as I went out riding. It did me good, but nothing will do me as much good as seeing you again and

60

being able to tell you with my own lips that I love you very dearly.

Your true and loving Louise

Having evolved a plan to cut off Blücher's army by a sudden flank attack, Napoleon left Nogent on the 9th, hurried to Sézanne, and at dawn on the 10th left Sézanne for Champaubert, where Olsufjew's corps was literally hacked to pieces. Napoleon was 'drunk with joy'. Cut off from Blücher, General Osten-Sacken fled towards Montmirail in an attempt to rejoin Yorck.

[33]
Champaubert, 10th [February 1814] 7 *p.m.*

My dearest Louise, *Victory!* I have destroyed 12 Russian regiments, taken 6000 priso[ners], 40 guns, 200 ammunition wagons, captured the Commander-in-Chief [Olsufjew] all his Gen[erals] and several Colonels, I have not lost 200 men. Have a salute fired at the Invalides and the news published at every place of entertainment. I am following up Sacken, who is at La Ferté-sous-Jouarre. I expect to reach *Montmirail* at midnight, hard on his heels.

Nap

News of the victory at Champaubert reached Paris just as King Joseph was reviewing the grenadiers of the National Guard in the courtyard of the Tuileries.

[34]
[Paris] 11*th February* 1813 [=1814]

My Darling, This morning in the Bois de Boulogne I received your welcome letter of the evening of the 10th, in which you tell me you have utterly defeated the enemy and are in a magnificent position; it's marvellous that you have lost so few men, no one but you could have got out of such a dangerous situation so skilfully. I spoke with the courier, who told me you were well and that he had seen you yesterday evening—that was another great relief to me; I must tell you that yesterday I had a premonition there would be a battle, I was incredibly miserable and anxious all day, then at last towards evening I calmed down, I shall certainly believe in premonitions after this.

Thank you so much for thinking of sending me the Commander-in-Chief's sword, it was such a very charming idea, I have been deeply touched to know that even in the midst of battles you still think of your dear one, it gives me fresh heart and strength.

I have carried out your orders. A salute was fired at the Invalides and King Joseph drew up an announcement which is to be read at all entertainments, and as you told him to make the news widely known, it will be printed in the *Moniteur* as well. He has held a really splendid review of the National Guard, the troops are very well turned-out and of excellent bearing, there were about 6000 men; they say when the King announced the good news they went wild with enthusiasm and shouted for joy; the King made them a very good speech, people say, I am so vexed at not having stayed indoors, if only I had known the courier was going to come with your good news, I should certainly never have gone out; now I want to hear what happened about your encounter with General Sacken. God grant it may be just as successful, and above all that you are not running into danger, but you promised me you wouldn't, so I'm not worrying. I have told them to wake me if news comes in. Do take the greatest care of your health, it is so precious to us.

Your son is very well, he enjoyed himself enormously at the parade and completely captivated all the National Guard. He wore his uniform and his three-cornered hat, you'll love to see him in it, he saluted really gracefully and had such an exciting time that he slept badly and couldn't eat a thing this evening.

I am very well indeed, the good news has swept away all my aches and pains, and then the weather is so very fair and mild, you must be pleased about it, I hope all your enemies are left stuck in the mud, that's what they deserve; really, I fly into such a rage whenever anyone wishes you ill; anyhow I'll end this letter by congratulating you once again on this splendid victory.

Your true and loving Louise

Whilst praising Marie-Louise's economy in everyday life, Napoleon was sometimes uneasy at her 'stinginess'.

[35]

[Champaubert, 11th February 1814]

My Darling, I hope you gave 3000 *livres* to the courier who brought you the Russian general's sword. You must be generous. When couriers bring you good news you must give them money, when they are officers, diamonds.

I am leaving for Montmirail; I hope to send you some good news today. My health is good. All my love.

Your darling Nap

A kiss to my son.

[36]

[Paris] 11*th February* 1813 [=1814]

My Darling, The Archbishop of Aix has been this evening to ask whether we should say prayers again in Chapel this Sunday as we did last. The Arch-Chancellor begged me to ask you about it, he was reluctant to put forward his own opinion, so do, please, tell me what to say. You have been given a wrong account of last Sunday's prayers, the Miserere was not sung, only a few prayers were said, followed by the benediction. I had crowds of people at my reception, everyone is delighted at the victory. Good-bye, Darling, my fondest love.

Your true and loving Louise

Attacked from the rear, von Sacken turned about. Napoleon overwhelmed him, and barely one third of his corps was able to join Yorck. This was the battle of Montmirail.

[37]

11*th [February* 1814] 8 *p.m.*

My Darling, To-day, the 11th, I attacked the large Russian and Prussian enemy forces one league in front of Montmirail. I beat them, put them to flight, took the whole of their artillery, captured more than 7000 pr[isoner]s, and more than 40 guns. Not a man of this routed army will escape. I am dying of weariness. All my love. Give a kiss to my son.

Nap

[In the handwriting of a secretary:]
From the farm of L'Epine-sous-Bois, between Montmirail and Vieux-Maisons. Have a salute of 60 guns fired and the news given

out at every place of entertainment. General Sacken has been killed.

In the courtyard of the Tuileries, parades and reviews went on without ceasing—to the vast delight of the little King.

In the theatres, which were putting on a host of patriotic and topical plays, the Empress received repeated ovations.

[38]

Paris, 12th February 1814

My Darling, Today I must congratulate you all over again on the glorious victory you have just won over the Russians, the news of it has made me very happy, especially as I was worrying all last night about the outcome of the engagement you were expecting yesterday. Thank you so much for sending Mr de Montesquiou to tell me, it was quite delightful to see someone who had left you only the previous day, and I bombarded him with questions as to how you were and whether you looked well, he reassured me on every point, and apart from this great victory, that was the only thing that mattered to me; now it needs only peace and your return to make my happiness complete. There is general satisfaction here, almost every anxiety is laid to rest, and for the past two days there has been great enthusiasm, and they say a lot of those who were planning to leave are now staying on.

There has been a superb review of more than 19,000 men; the King, who had just received the Prince de Neufchâtel's letter, announced the news to the officers, there was tremendous enthusiasm and shouts of 'Long live the Emperor!', I was very touched. When people show their love for you like that, it gives me immense pleasure, I want everyone to think as I do on this particular subject. I sent the news to the Princesses and told the Arch-Chancellor to have a salute fired as you had commanded. Mr Alfred[1] said they fired 300 guns, the Arch-Chancellor said it couldn't possibly be as many as that, so I don't know how they settled it in the end.

Your son sends you a kiss, he is well, but has been a thoroughly naughty boy all day; whenever there is a parade, there's no deal-

[1] One of the King of Rome's servants?

64

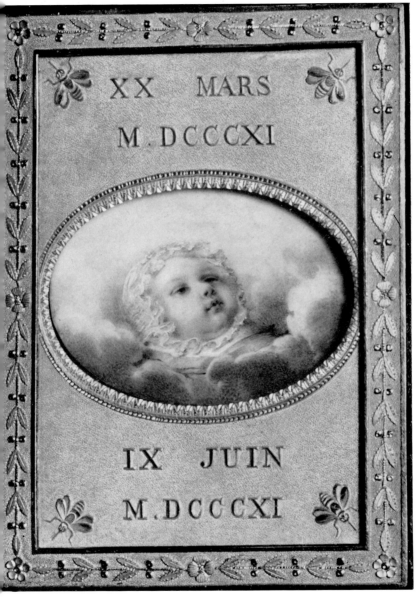

The King of Rome

From a miniature painted by Isabey on the occasion of the royal christening, 9th June 1811
(Royal Palace, Stockholm)

Marie-Louise

From a miniature painted by Isabey on the occasion of the christening of the King of Rome. (Royal Palace, Stockholm)

ing with him, he goes to bed later than usual, then growls and grumbles all the rest of the day and punches everybody. I told him I should tell you, but he simply said, 'Don't care if you do', so you see he looks like growing up to be a very model of obedience!

I am quite well except for such a splitting headache that I shall have to stop writing now, I think it was brought on by the warm weather we've been having today. Good-bye, Darling, all my fondest love.

Your true and loving Louise

[39]

[Paris] 12th February 1814 [evening]

My Darling, Just an hour ago I received your news of this morning's success: it's so marvellous, really my head's in a whirl —how delighted you must be, I enter whole-heartedly into your happiness, and hope you will believe that no one shares it as sincerely as I do, so I couldn't go to bed without writing you a few lines. Good-bye, my Darling, congratulations once again.

Your Darling Louise

[40]

The outskirts of Château-Thierry
12th February 1814 [evening]

I have been in the saddle all day, my dearest Louise. I have had the whole of the enemy rear-guard captured, 4 Russian and 3 Prussian battalions strong, and 2 guns. Everything was taken, even the general in command; he is a Russian major-general. The enemy lost the whole of his artillery, all his baggage and 2/3 of his army, and was compelled to take flight and cross the Marne at Château-Thierry, on his way to Soissons. All his field-hospitals and his lines of communication with Châlons and Vitry were captured.

My health is very good. Now that communications have been opened up with La Ferté-sous-Jouarre, I shall be hearing from you within a few hours' time. Good-bye, darling, be cheerful and happy.

Nap

E   *65*

Have all the news I give you published as an article in the Paris column.

[41]

[Paris] 13*th February* 1814, 10 *a.m.*

My Darling, At 2 o'clock in the morning I received your letter written on the evening of the 11th, and on waking this morning the one you wrote at 8 p.m. yesterday, so I haven't been able to carry out your orders about the newspapers, or to announce the news at public entertainments. Consequently the news I received to-day will be published in the Paris column tomorrow. How weary you must be, Darling, with all these long, hard days, I hear you have been continually in the saddle; I am reassured and delighted by what you tell me about your health. I needed some such comforting news to keep me happy and in good spirits. I hope you really believe, now, that all my anxieties have vanished except those which spring from your absence, and they will end only with your return. I hear you were wretchedly housed at Château-Thierry, in a castle which had been pillaged, you see I collect every scrap of news about you.

I am perfectly well, my headache disappeared during the night, I haven't seen your son yet this morning, because I wanted to write to you and it's out of the question when he's in the room, he gets up to all kinds of tricks. I know he is well and has eaten a hearty lunch. I must stop now to go and dress for Mass, but will write again this evening. I expect you will be glad to have news of us twice in one day. Good-bye, all my warmest love.

Your darling Louise

After crossing the Marne, General Yorck blew up the bridge. Mortier, Duc de Trévise, was commissioned to pursue the Prussians towards Soissons and Rheims.

[42]

Château-Thier[ry], 13*th* *[February* 1814*]* 5 *p.m.*

My Dearest, I am very glad to hear you feel reassured and are easier in your mind. I have spent the day here having the bridge restored. The Duc de Trévise has just passed through and is following up the enemy, who is fleeing in disorder towards Rheims, making for the Ardennes.

My health is good.

Nap

[43]

[Paris] 13*th February* 1814, 7 *p.m.*

My Darling, I have already written once this morning and here I am again at my desk to give you news of your son; I find it really wonderful to be able to write to you so regularly; I am only afraid my constant notes will end by boring you; I have had no letters from you so far today, I hope that's a pleasure in store for this evening.

King Joseph has composed a short article for the *Moniteur*, following on what you wrote to me yesterday, I hope you will like it; he is also going to put one in the news-sheets. Crowds of people were with me at Mass, and were thrilled with the good news I had had; everyone looked extremely happy and gay.

Your son has been watching all the officers of the National Guard coming to take the oath to King Joseph, there were more than 300 of them. They tell me he was rather taken aback at their shouting 'Long live the King!' and began to cry, but Mme de Montesquiou soon calmed him down; apart from that he has been very sweet and has told me to tell you that he's eaten up all his spinach—there's a staggering piece of news for you!—but it means a great deal to him because he had to overcome one of his pet aversions.

I am keeping fairly well on the whole, but am rather out of sorts tonight with one of those indispositions which will last a day or two. I went out for a walk today, the weather is really spring-like. Good-bye, my Dearest, all my fond love.

Your Darling Louise

From one day to the next, Marie-Louise alternated between hope and fear. On 13th February she heard the triumphant order of the day read out at the guard-house of the Tuileries; two hours later, the Minister of Police announced that the enemy had entered Fontainebleau.

Napoleon's letter of the morning of 14*th February* 1814 *is missing.*

[44]

[*Paris*] 14*th February* 1814

My Darling, I was just going to answer your yesterday's letter when I got the one you wrote this morning; I can hardly wait for the news you hope to let me have this evening, and have asked to be wakened in the night if it comes; I hope today will bring you all the success you expected.

I have seen Mr Gourgault[1] who gave me the latest news of you. He said you were quite happy and cheerful, which I was delighted to hear; you know I promised you to try not to worry at all, well, ever since you've been having these wonderful successes, I've managed it fairly well. At 5 o'clock one of the Duc de Reggio's[2] aides-de-camp arrived and went to see the King, I don't know what he has brought, I'm so afraid it may be bad news, because no one has told me a thing about it.

I will carry out your orders about the courier; when he handed me the sword I was on horseback; I told the Prince[3] to give him 20 napoleons, but he hadn't the money on him. I enquired whether he had paid them, but I don't think he has, so I have told them to give the man 3000 francs. I have also told the Grand Chamberlain to let me have presents for the officers you send.

I found the Arch-Chancellor thoroughly depressed this morning, and it seems I made the same impression on him, because he came to tell King Joseph that I looked very downcast, whereas I was really feeling very cheerful.

Your son is wonderfully well, in high spirits and as good as gold; he talks very clearly now. After the family dinner yesterday evening he had a lovely time, the King made him the Great Pyramid of Egypt out of cards and he was delighted with it.

I am keeping fairly well; I had a bad stomach-ache this morning, it's better now, but I stayed in my room. Good-bye, my Dearest, give a thought sometimes to the one who loves you so very dearly.

Your Darling Louise

Turning back towards Blücher on the 12th, Napoleon was at Montmirail on the 14th, and launched an attack on Kleist who was

[1] General Gourgaud.　　　[2] Oudinot.　　　[3] Joseph.

in command of the last Prussian corps to remain intact. Grouchy's charge turned the battle into a Prussian rout—the result was the victory of Vauchamp.

Napoleon made ready to pursue as far as Châlons the remnants of the army led by Blücher, who was planning to retreat in the direction of Nancy. The news reaching the Emperor from the Bohemian army stopped him.

[45]

Montmirail, 14th [February 1814] 9 p.m.

My dearest Louise, I have some good news to give you. I have beaten General Kleis[t] who had 36 battalions with him. I took 8000 prisoners and killed 4000 of his troops; I took 10 flags and 3 guns without having more than 200 or 300 dead and wounded. The cavalry of my Guard covered themselves with glory. Have 30 guns fired and an article inserted in the *Moniteur*.

All my love
Nap

[46]

[Paris] 15th February 1814, 7 p.m.

My Darling, At 1 o'clock I got your letter telling me that you have won a victory over General Kleist and taken 8000 prisoners, it really is wonderful to be gaining so much ground every day, I am so glad, you really are getting us quite used to successes— not that we shall ever get bored with them; there is one in particular that I'm still longing for, I mean the one you simply must win over Pᶜᵉ Schwarzenberg. I am very vexed that you have been unable to pass through Paris on your way to meet him, I should have been overjoyed to hold you in my arms, and I venture to flatter myself that you too would have been just the least bit pleased to see me again.

I will have the bulletins you sent me inserted in the *Moniteur* tomorrow, the King has written an article about yesterday's affair. I had a thirty-gun salute fired, everyone thought it was Prince Schwarzenberg you had defeated, his army is held in great fear here. I went to see the Queen of Spain this morning, she is still very ill. I found Madame and Queen Hortense with her, so I saw the whole family, King Louis called on me afterwards.

Your son is wonderfully well; I won't write any more now as I started such a violent headache when I was out walking that I shall just have to go to bed. I will write at greater length tomorrow, meanwhile I send you a kiss and love you very dearly.

Your Darling Louise

[47]

[*15th February* 1814]

My Darling, I have had no letters from you today, and no newspapers either. I am moving towards Brie-Contre-Aubert.[1] I am in very good health. I hope soon to be rid of all our enemies, at least to push them many a day's march away from Paris. All my love. Your faithful

Nap

Give my son a kiss.

The Empress's reply seems to indicate that the previous letter was written on 15th February, not 16th, as Madelin presumed. Leaving Nogent, Napoleon left Oudinot and Victor in the Seine valley to hold off Schwarzenberg. Driven back, they summoned the Emperor who, at Guignes, was about to embark on a fresh manœuvre.

[48]

[*Paris*] 16th February [1814] 8 [*a.m.*]

My Darling, I have sent you one letter by the orderly and another by one of King Joseph's couriers, and this, which Mr Gourgault is taking, is the third I have written, so you can't accuse me of laziness; I only wish *you* could contrive to send me news as often, it would take a courier every hour to keep my mind at rest, I am so terribly eager to hear from you.

I am sending you a portrait of the little King painted on my comfit-box, I heard you wanted one like it; I do hope it will please you and that sometimes when you look at it you will think just a little about the one who gave him to you. Your son and I are both very well. I envy Mr Gourgault his good luck in seeing you face to face, but until such good fortune comes my way, I remain my whole life long

Your Darling Louise

1 For Brie-Comte-Robert.

[49]

[Paris] 16th *February* [1814] 10.30 *a.m.*

My Darling, At 2 o'clock in the morning I received your undated letter, written yesterday I imagine, I can hardly believe you are not hearing from me regularly; I write twice a day and always put the time at which I send my letters off.

I had the article printed in the *Moniteur* yesterday, you will probably get them all today. I do wish that what you say would come true, and that your enemies might soon be miles away from here, this time I hate them more than ever before.

Your son sends you a kiss, he is very well indeed and is making such a din in my dressing-room that I hardly know what I'm writing about, he is turning all my things upside down and he says he loves you with all his heart.

I am keeping very well, my headache has absolutely vanished. I will write at length this evening, meantime I send you an imaginary hug.

Your Darling Louise

Good news arrived from Montereau.

[50]

Guignes, 16th [*February* 1814] 6 *p.m.*

My Darling, I received your letter this morning at 10. I was glad to find you were in good health and pleased with your son. Give him a kiss from me. I hope to send you some good news tomorrow.

My health is very good.

Good-bye, my dearest Louise. All my love.

Nap

The news coming in from Italy depressed the Empress: the Viceroy of Italy was putting up a stout defence on the Adige against the Austrians, who, however, were counting on speedy reinforcements from the King of Naples. Consequently Eugène was to find himself prevented from marching to join Augereau in an attempt to cut the Austrian lines of communication to eastern France. Marie-Louise continued to plead the Viceroy's cause.

[51]

Paris, 16th February 1814, *6 p.m.*

My Darling, I have already written once this morning by the orderly, and am going to write again by one of the King's couriers, who I hope will get my letter to you more speedily; the orderlies have been taking ages to bring letters for quite a time now, and I'm going to try and see whether you hear from me more quickly this way.

I held a Council of Ministers this morning, only a very short one, they never last long when you are not there, the Arch-Chancellor doesn't like them any more than I do. I talked a lot about you to the King this morning, you know it's my pet subject of conversation, in fact talking about you and thinking about you are my sole occupations at the moment. I am immensely pleased to hear about the handsome victory the Viceroy has won over Mr de Bellegarde,[1] the news of which must have been brought you by Mr Tascher.[2] Queen Hortense has told me that the Viceroy is in a most cruel dilemma because of the Vicereine, she is so ill that she can't be moved, so he is afraid he may have to leave her in the power of either the Austrians or the King of Naples—how desperately worried that poor woman must be, I think I should die if I were in her place.

I am very well indeed this morning, your excellent news is doing me a world of good, but don't immediately jump to the conclusion that it was lack of courage that was making me ill, the King can vouch for it that I've had plenty all the time.

Your son sends you a kiss, he is wonderfully well and has been galloping up and down the terrace, which has done him a lot of good because the weather's marvellous, though rather chilly.

Good-bye, Darling, all my fondest love.

Your true and loving Louise

On 17th February, Napoleon marched towards Nangis. At Mormant, he came in contact with Wittgenstein's Russian Corps, and compelled him to retreat beneath a rain of cannon-balls. The Allies hastened towards Montereau where they hoped to recross the Seine.

[1] Austrian field-marshal.
[2] Marshal Berthier's aide-de-camp.

[52]

Nangis, 17th [*February* 1814] 4 *p.m.*

My dearest Louise, I had two letters written to you on the battle-field to give you some good news. I have taken 6000 Russian prisoners, and defeated Wit[t]genstein's Corps, taking 15 of his guns and 50 artillery wagons. Several generals have been cap-tured; my troops are following up the enemy in the direction of Mont[e]reau, Provins and Bray. By tonight the whole of the big enemy army will have retreated across the Seine in great disorder.

Good-bye, my dearest. A kiss to my son. I have given the necessary instructions to enable you to have 30 guns fired.

Nap

Marie-Louise considered it her duty to appear in public, on the ter-race of the Tuileries overlooking the banks of the Seine: it could not then be said that she and the little King had left.

[53]

[*Paris*] 17th *February* [1814] 4 *p.m.*

My Darling, At 3 o'clock this morning I received your letter from Guignes dated 6 p.m. yesterday, I do thank you for writing so promptly, I hope you were pleased that I had done the same. I wrote to you three times yesterday. I am waiting most impa-tiently for the good news you are expecting to send me; I hope after that we shall be rid of all the enemy armies which have entered France.

I begged Mr Gourgault to tell you he had found me quite calm and unafraid, I fear the Arch-Chancellor, who was thoroughly frightened himself, thought I was in the same state, and I should have been very upset if you had thought I really was.

Your son sends you a kiss, he is wonderfully well, very gay and in fine form; he was so naughty when he was in here with me that there was absolutely no dealing with him; he came to my luncheon and threw the water-jug down, and the glass after it, which made everybody laugh.

I am very well indeed and have been for a walk on the terrace to keep people from saying I have left. There is a certain amount of uneasiness in Paris over the corps which has been moving on Soissons and Sens, and a lot of people still seem to be leaving. They say crowds flocked around Mme Anatole de Montesquiou's carriage at Châteaudun because they thought it was your son escaping. Today the Place Vendôme is packed with people to watch the prisoners passing through.

I have just this moment received the news sent me by the Duc de Bassano for the *Moniteur*; it will be inserted tomorrow. I'll write again this evening, so will leave you now, but my thoughts will be ever near you.

Your Darling Louise

[54a]

[Paris] 17th *February* [1814], 10 *p.m.*

My Darling, For a week now you have been receiving nothing but letters of congratulation from me and only three hours ago I heard of your victory over General Pahlen. Thank you so much for the sabre you have sent me. Since then I have also had the Grand Marshal's[1] letter telling me you are following up your successes, so I'm fully expecting to be wakened up again in the middle of the night; the most welcome feature of all this is the assurance that you are not running into danger; I need to hear it over and over again, because I always have a suspicion that on this particular subject you may not be telling me the truth. I had money given to the couriers as you told me to. You will almost certainly sleep at Nangis tonight, I hope you'll be rather more comfortable there than you have been for the past few nights, I'm always so afraid you are overtiring yourself, I do beg you most earnestly to have a care for your health.

I have just this moment received your letter written at 4 o'clock this afternoon, it is sweet of you to write to me so promptly, and I'm very happy to know you are keeping well and that the army has crossed to the other side of the Seine.

Your son sends you a kiss and is wonderfully well this evening. I am very well too, no one could be anything else with all this good news. Everyone is very pleased indeed. They say the prisoners have been very well treated and have been given food and money.

[1] Bertrand.

Good-bye, my Dearest, I hope I shall be wakened up again tonight with good news from you.

Your Darling Louise

I have had the guns fired as you ordered.

Even before fighting could begin, Schwarzenberg had requested a cease-fire, which Napoleon was now unwilling to grant unless the Allies had 'purged his territory of their presence'. He would consent to an armistice only if its terms formed the preliminaries of a peace based on the Frankfurt proposals, namely: natural frontiers and complete independence. As a result, the Emperor was to find himself in conflict with public opinion in Paris.

[54b]

Nangis, 18th [*February* 1814], 7 a.m.

My Dearest, My affairs are going so well that Schwarzenberg asked me for an armistice last night. I have given him no answer. I hope we shall have peace in a few days' time, a lasting peace, worthy of me and worthy of France. Give a kiss to my son and all my love. Good-bye, dearest Louise.

Nap

[55]

[*Paris*] 18th *February* 1814, 10 p.m.

My Darling, I received your morning letter two hours ago, thank you so much for writing so promptly and especially for giving me such good news. I am delighted to think you may have peace in a few days' time, and above all a lasting peace, because if you had made a bad one, I feel sure you wouldn't have kept it long. How cowardly of P^ce Schwarzenberg to ask for an armistice just at this moment! It gives one a deplorable impression of his character and of that of the Allies too, they must have a wholesome fear of you and your victories, I hope they have precious few of their own. I am expecting you to tell me of a fresh victory over P^ce Schwarzenberg tomorrow or the day after. They are already discussing it in Paris, they say a courier has arrived at the Exchange with the news that you have taken 20,000 prisoners. I hope that will really happen tomorrow or the next day, meanwhile I implore you not to run into danger and to take care of yourself, you know it's the only sure way of keeping me calm and cheerful.

On the way back from the Bois de Boulogne, where I went for a drive, I met the last prisoners of the column which marched through today, they looked very wretched and were covered with rags, I was told they were Prussians. The Arch-Chancellor told me there was no fresh news, and I've seen the King, who brought me news of you as soon as it reached him, he realises I simply must hear several times a day how you are getting on.

Your son is well, he sends you a kiss and is full of life, I've given him a drum which has charmed him so much that he could scarcely eat any dinner, so I've vowed never again to give him a new toy at that time of day.

I am feeling perfectly well and have never been better than during the last few days. Crowds of people have been to my receptions, but I have said nothing about the good news in your letter, as I was not at all sure whether it could be made public. All my fond love.

Your true and loving Louise

Moving on towards the Surville plateau, above Montereau, Napoleon, who himself directed the firing, swept it clear of Bianchi's Austrian corps and a joint force of Russian and Württemberg troops. Desperately hard-pressed, the Württembergers and Austrians had no time to blow up the bridge at Montereau.

[56]

Mont[e]reau, 18th February 1814, 6 p.m.

My dearest Louise, I am feeling tired. I have had a splendid day; I defeated Bianchi's corps 2 divisions strong, and the Württembergers. I captured 4000 of them, killed 2000, took 6 guns and large numbers of wagons; best of all I carried the bridge at Monte[reau] before they could cut it. I am closing in on the enemy, I have captured 2 Austrian colours, one general and several colonels.

Good-bye, my darling. All my love.

Nap

[57]

[*Paris*] 19*th February* [1814] 11 *a.m.*

My Darling, I am sending this note by a courier who is sup-
posed to be leaving at once, I have had no news of you today,
I do hope I shall hear in the course of the day. The King has
sent to tell me that you won a victory over the Bavarians yesterday. I am so delighted.

Your son is well. I am feeling marvellous myself. Good-bye,
my Dearest, I'll write a longer letter this evening. All my fond
love.

Your true and loving Louise

[58]

19*th* [*February* 1814], *noon*

My Dearest, I was so tired last night that I slept 8 hours on end.
Have 30 guns fired in honour of the fight at Montereau. It is
necessary, when I write to you to have guns fired, that you
should write a letter to the Minister of War, signed by you, and
that you should tell him of any advantage I write to you about,
until peace is signed, for the Minister of War should always be
informed of military developments direct.

Good-bye, my dearest Louise. All my love.

Nap

On the 14th, however, the Allies drew so near to Fontainebleau
that three regiments of Austrian cavalry appeared at Essonne, a
development which terrified Marie-Louise and which accounts for the
following strictures on her former compatriots.

[59]

[*Paris*] 19*th February* [1814], 10 *p.m.*

My Darling, This evening at five o'clock I received the letter you
wrote at eight yesterday evening. It has taken an endless time to
come. It is so unsatisfactory not to be able to get news of you
more quickly. I have already written once this morning to congratulate you on your latest successes, they really are splendid,
it's the Austrians who are catching it now! I hope they'll be
beaten like the others and that you'll soon compel them to make
a good peace, they richly deserve to be punished. The most wel-

come part of your letters is always the news that you are keeping well and thank goodness it recurs in all of them. There is great rejoicing in Paris at the good news you have sent us; everyone is looking much more cheerful, and even those who were really scared have grown quite brave.

The Arch-Chancellor has told me nothing fresh, except that in Calais they refused to believe the good news, it seems that the man who is acting as temporary mayor was responsible for the whole thing.

Your son is very well and is growing most inquisitive, when anyone whispers in my ear he immediately wants to know what it's all about and gets terribly annoyed when we don't tell him, but you'll be even more surprised to learn that he's got a sweetheart; it's Mme de Montesquiou's grand-daughter; whenever she comes to see him, he keeps taking her away into corners to kiss her and hides so that no one will see him, yesterday evening he kept calling her 'my dear love' the whole time.

I am very well indeed except for a heavy cold in my head, I can't think where I caught it. I only hope it won't keep me from attending Mass tomorrow, although now the news is so good it wouldn't really be very inconvenient.

I have just got your morning letter. I am truly delighted to hear you are taking care of yourself and that at long last you have had a whole night's sound sleep.

I intend writing this very evening to the Minister of War about firing the guns, I don't know whether he will fire them tomorrow morning or tonight, it's late now, ten o'clock in fact. Everyone has been bombarding me with questions about you, I merely say you are well and nothing more, otherwise they would lure me into talking too much.

Goodbye, Dearest, all my fond love.

Your Darling Louise

On 20th February, Napoleon wrote thanking his wife for the comfit-box she had sent him. The portrait of the little King painted on the gift gave him a useful idea for propaganda.

The Emperor broke the news to Marie-Louise that the Allied sovereigns had advanced as far as the château of Pont-sur-Seine, which belonged to Madame, his mother.

[60]

Montereau, 20th [February 1814], 9 *a.m.*
My Dearest, You have sent me a very beautiful comfit-box with
the portrait of the King of Rome at prayer. I want you to have
it engraved with the caption: '*I pray God to save my father and
France.*' This little picture is so interesting that it will please
everybody. I am sending you Mortemart[1] with 10 flags captured
from the Russians, the Prussians and the Austrians. My health is
good. The Emperors of Russia and Austria, and the King of
Prussia were at Pont, at Madame's; they went from there to
Bray, and their headquarters were to have been at Fontainebleau on the 18th. They are now making post-haste for Troyes.
My troops have entered Nogent and Sens. Give my son a kiss,
keep well, and never doubt all my love.

Nap

[61]

[Paris] 20th February 1813 [=1814]
My Darling, I have already written to you once this morning and
will write again tonight, so am only sending this little note by
M. de St. Aignan[2] because I don't want to miss a single opportunity of telling you that I love you with all my heart and am
terribly sad when you are away.

I am quite well. My cold . . . [illegible]. Your son is wonderfully fit, both of us send you a kiss.

Your Darling Louise

[62]

[Paris] 20th February [1814], *after dinner at* 4.30
My Darling, I have not heard from you yet today, though the
King has told me there is a note for the *Moniteur*, I can't imagine
why there are days when your letters take so long to get here;
all the time I'm waiting for them to come, I keep thinking hard
about you and praying for your speedy return. You must be
dreadfully cold just now, the temperature here has been more
than five degrees below freezing-point. It must be very, very
hard for you when you are marching with your army.

I had such a violent cold last night and all today that I

---

[1] An orderly officer.
[2] Brother-in-law of Caulaincourt.

couldn't possibly go to Mass, all the same I did want to try and get dressed, but Corvisart forbade it, he makes out that I was feverish last night. In spite of that however, I asked the Arch-Chancellor what he thought before I decided what to do. He said that since the news was good I really need not go, and I took his advice. The King was not anxious to go either, he said he didn't know whether you would approve, but he would rather keep in the background than push himself forward too much. He also advised me not to have the family dinner-party as I had cancelled my reception and was not well, so I did as he suggested.

There is nothing new to report here, I hear there were crowds of people at Mass. Your son sends you a kiss, he's wonderfully well and is wearing his National Guard uniform today, it suits him beautifully. He was very merry this morning, and told me all kinds of stories about the games he'd been playing yesterday.

All the Princesses are ill, it seems that Madame has a sick-headache. I have already written to you once this morning by M. de St. Aignan who has left for headquarters. I may perhaps write another little note this evening. I shall have to close this one as the orderly is ready to go. Good-bye then, Dearest, I love you and hug you with all my heart.

Your Darling Louise

After the victory of Montereau, Napoleon passed through Bray and reached Nogent on 20th February. Half an hour after his arrival he scribbled a note to Marie-Louise.

[63]

Nogent-sur-Seine, 20th February [1814], *6 p.m.*
My Darling, I have arrived here. The weather is terribly cold today, which inflicts suffering upon us and has been very useful to the enemy, because all the crossings are very good in this sort of weather, so that he has been able to evacuate everything in the direction of Troyes without trouble and without our being able to take half of all he has. My health is good. The Emperor of Austria has not got beyond Troyes, the Emperor of Russia was at Bray and wanted to sleep at Fontainebleau.

[Napoleon]

*Je père Dieu pour mon Père
et pour la France.*

The King of Rome

An engraving by L. Bouillon (see Letters 66 and 68)

Je prie Dieu pour mon Père et pour la France

The King of Rome

An engraving by L. Bouillon (see Letters 66 and 68)

[64]

[*Paris*] 20*th February* [1814], 10 *p.m.*

My Dear, I am writing only a short note this evening to tell you I have received the letter brought by M. de Mortemart. I have such a dreadful cold tonight that I can't keep my eyes open any longer. I questioned him closely about your health and all the details he gave me were quite satisfactory, I'm really delighted that you are keeping well.

I will have your son's portrait engraved with the motto you wrote, I think it will give general pleasure, but it will take at least two months to complete. I am *so* glad you liked it, it makes me very happy when I find something that can give you pleasure, because I love you so much, my Darling, and I do want you to believe that.

Thank you for the flags you sent me. The little King is inclined to be feverish this evening, I think he has caught my cold, but don't worry, it's not going to be anything much. Good-bye, my Darling, I'm off to bed now, my last thought will be of you.

Your true and loving Louise

[65]

[*Paris*] 21*st February* 1814

My Darling, I received your last night's letter at breakfast this morning. I am so angry that the cold weather has upset your plans, but hope the thaw will soon come so that you won't be prevented any longer from taking full advantage of your victories. I am deeply touched by the things you repeatedly say about your feelings for me, you know I thoroughly deserve them, because I love you most devotedly and long to see you again, for every day feels like a hundred years.

They got me to hold a Council this morning about requisitioning the 2000 horses you ordered from the Minister of War, it was agreed to leave it to the individuals concerned to give a horse, or the equivalent in money, and the Prefect of Paris will make every attempt to get the 2000 horses as quickly as possible. The Council lasted a long time, as they were also discussing whether the slaughter-houses should be turned into hospitals. The King has settled with the Minister of War to hold the Presentation of Flags on Sunday, he thinks it better to wait until

F

then, seeing that most of the National Guard are workmen and would lose a day if they were to be called up during the week.

Your son is in good form today, the feverish chill he had yesterday has not developed any further; I sent Corvisart to see him this morning, he found him well and said there was no need to do anything for it, it was just an ordinary cold. He still feels a little discomfort this evening, but is full of fun, he didn't want any dinner; he is having a lovely time with a set of pictures of Russian and French soldiers, the kind you buy on the embankment, and which I've given him as a present; he has handed the enemies over to Albert and kept the others for himself.

I still have a heavy cold, I went out of doors for a little while in spite of the pronouncements of the medical faculty, which I never listen to, and as it was bitterly cold I feel very much the worse for it, I have such a raging headache tonight that I'm just about at the end of my tether and I think I shall have to go to bed instead of holding my reception. It's terribly cold, about [6?] or 7 degrees.

I spent the morning re-reading all your letters, it was a most moving experience, all the loving things you say in them stir my heart so deeply and bring back memories of the past two years spent apart from you, and for me so full of sadness, but I hope you'll come back very soon. In the meantime, whilst I'm waiting for you, fondest love from

Your Darling Louise

On that same day, Napoleon ordered the Director of Museums, Vivant-Denon, to engrave the little King's portrait 'immediately'; Denon at once entrusted the task to the artist Bouillon, but with the suggestion that the motto be altered to 'May God guard my father and France', since the word 'save' might possibly 'cause a sensation'.

[66]

Nogent, 21st [February 1814], 4 p.m.

My Darling, I have just received your letter of the 20th at 10 o'clock at night. The portrait of the little King with the caption *God save my father and France* should be engraved in 36 hours' time. A well-finished copy can be made in 2 minutes. Give orders for it to be done and on sale in Paris within 48 hours. Good-bye, my darling, tell me your cold has left you and that you are well again.

Nap

Meanwhile Augereau, Duc de Castiglione, was driving Napoleon to despair by his inactivity. Given the task of falling on Schwarzenberg's rear with the Army of Lyons, he made no move of any kind. For this reason the Emperor resorted to a most unusual method of forcing him to march.

[67]

Nogent, 22nd [February 1814*], 9 a.m.*

My Darling, Have the Duchesse de Castiglione sent for. Tell her to write and tell her husband that he must be asleep, that he ought already to have freed Mont-Blanc, and the Aisne Department and dislodged the enemy. Let her write to him to that effect and urge him to fight well. My health is good, the weather is very fine, but rather cool. Good-bye, my sweet. All my love. A kiss to the little King.

Nap

[68]

[Paris] 22nd February 1814*, 10 p.m.*

My Darling, On waking this morning I got your letter written at 4 p.m. on the 21st. I loved it, because you say you are thinking about me, and that is a very great comfort. It is just 4 weeks today since you left and they have seemed like so many centuries to me, I love you far too much to bear your absence patiently.

I will attempt the impossible and try to have the engraving of the little King completed within 36 hours, but I don't think it can be done. M. Denon, to whom I have spoken about it, says it will take at least until Thursday evening, and will be very rough and unfinished at that. The engraver will hurry on with it as fast as ever he can. Would you not prefer to have him dressed as a National Guardsman rather than as a Polish lancer, I think it would please people in Paris?

This morning the King read me a letter you had written him about the letters I am to write to various cities, the Duc de Cadore has drawn up two rough drafts which the King has almost certainly sent you, he thought several of the expressions had better be toned down, as he said they would sound too vigorous coming from me. You are certainly going to give me plenty of hard work writing all these letters, but when it is in your interests, nothing is too much trouble, and even if it meant sitting up night after night, I would do it gladly.

Your son is very well, he still has a heavy cold but the feverishness has quite gone. Corvisart told me this morning that if he were not a King, no one would pay the least attention to this little indisposition of his, so that will show you it's nothing much, besides, he's as merry as a lark and thrilled at having a Madras handkerchief round his head, because it gives him a chance to inform everybody he sees that he's a Colonel in the Lancers, wounded in the head by a bullet in the last battle.

My cold is taking its course, I'm going out in spite of it, you know I never fuss about colds, so mine last rather longer than other people's; I am coughing a good deal, but apart from that am really very well.

I went out just for a little while this morning, it was intensely cold. Madame called in to see me after I got back, she is fairly well. The Queen of Spain is ill, she has such wretched health, it's a whole week now since she had even a spoonful of soup, so naturally she is extremely weak.

I hope I shall hear from you this evening, I am so used to your writing regularly that I don't expect to be left one single day without a letter, but it's a sweet habit you have, and one which is exceedingly good for

Your Darling Louise

The wish expressed by Marie-Louise about the little King's engraving was granted: on 28th February, the Duc de Cadore commanded, by order of the Emperor, that he be depicted also in the uniform of the National Guard.

[69]

[Paris] 23rd February 1814

My Darling, At 1 o'clock in the night I got your letter of 9 a.m. yesterday, and although I intend writing to you this evening, I am taking advantage of the mid-day courier to send you a few lines in reply. The article for the *Moniteur* came in rather late, it was four o'clock, I sent it straight away to the Duc de Cadore, who sent word back that it would have to be inserted tomorrow, as the *Moniteur* had already been printed.

I will do as you ask about the Duchesse de Castiglione, I don't know yet which of us will be the more embarrassed, for you know how exceedingly timid I am by nature, but when it's a question of doing you a service, my courage increases.

Your son is still coughing a little this morning and is very full of cold, but he's very lively, and just at this moment is busy playing with all his might and main.

I am keeping very well, my cold is still taking its course. M. Corvisart was scolding me just now for not taking the medicines he prescribes, but I'm just a little sceptical on the subject; he begs me to present his respects to you. The Duchesse de Castiglione is just being announced, so I must stop now and will give you an account of the visit a little later on. Good-bye, my Dearest, I love you and send you a fond kiss.

Your true and loving Louise

[70]

[Paris] 23rd February 1814, 10 p.m.

My Darling, I have already written to you once today, this morning before the Council, but I don't want to go to bed without writing just a line. It's a sweet habit I've grown into and one I simply can't break, because so long as you are away, it's the only pleasure left to me. The Council this morning was a very short one, I don't think it lasted twenty minutes in all, there was nothing of interest, and the Minister of Marine, who usually talks at far greater length than anyone else, had nothing of importance to say.

Before that I saw the Duchesse de Castiglione, the poor woman came in thoroughly frightened and in floods of tears, convinced that either her Husband or her brother was dead and that you had asked me to break the news to her. I told her what you had said to me and she replied that she was quite sure it was not her Husband's fault that he was so late advancing, he had been compelled to wait for the troops coming from Catalonia, but nevertheless she would write to him and was certain he wished for nothing better than a chance of proving his complete devotion to you.

My son is quite well, and more comfortable than he was last night, though he still has a very bad cold, but he's playing about this evening and listening most intently to the tale of Tom Thumb which Mme de Montesquiou is telling him.

I am very well in spite of my cold which still persists. I have been to see the Queen of Spain who is really quite ill. Do, please, believe that I love you very fondly.

Your Darling Louise

With a view to encouraging Marie-Louise to win back her father's support, Napoleon made out that he had been the dupe of his Allies and that he himself was kindly disposed towards the Austrians.

The Emperor's entry into Troyes on the 24th was a triumph.

[71]
Tr[oyes] 24th [*February* 1814], 8 *p.m.*

My Dearest, The weather is very cold. I am rather tired. I have pushed on south of the Marne as far as Bar-sur-Seine and intend to continue. 'Papa François' was at Troyes, very sad and worried, and seeing but little of the Russians. They are not very fond of each other. The French like the Austrians better than the rest of them. My health is good. I give you a kiss. Good-bye, my darling.

Nap

[72]
[*Paris*] 24th *February* 1814, 10 *p.m.*

My Darling, I am desperately anxious at not hearing from you for 36 hours, I do hope news comes tonight, or else I shall be most upset. I shall be afraid something has happened to you. You have got me into the adorable habit of receiving letters once or twice every day.

The bulletin printed in this morning's *Moniteur* has caused much alarm, because it seems to hint that peace may not be expected after all. The King foresaw what would happen when I gave it him to read, but daren't cut out that sentence without your permission, they say people are even more seriously alarmed in Paris. I may turn out to be one of the calmest of the lot, I have such complete confidence in your success that I am not in the least afraid; not that I'm light-hearted for how can I be when you are far away? I shall hold an extraordinary Council of Ministers tomorrow to deal with the two matters you have referred to the Arch-Chancellor.

Your son is still a little out of sorts in the evenings, not exactly feverish, but terribly tired, as a result of the heavy cold he's had and which has settled on his chest. They are going to give him some ipecacuanha syrup tomorrow, not to make him sick but to cut the phlegm. I feel happier about him tonight than I did yesterday. He is coughing less and is more ready to play.

I am keeping fairly well, I have cured my cold by taking it out for a walk in spite of what the doctors advised, I have been out again today as far as Bagatelle in 10 degrees of cold. I do so pity your poor troops, they must be suffering dreadfully, but my chief worry is to know whether you yourself have caught cold or got overtired.

M. Corvisart has begged me to recommend a friend of his called M. de Leval, a collector of taxes; he wants you to be kind enough to appoint him to the post of Receiver-General of the Drôme Department which has just fallen vacant, I have asked him to let me have a formal petition so that I can send it you.

I have just seen your son who is sleeping very peacefully, I don't think he'll be feverish again tonight. Good-bye, my Darling, warmest love from

Your Darling Louise

Now, to the Emperor's great satisfaction, there began from the Vosges to the Aisne the general uprising, the revolt of the 'blue shirts', which filled the Allies with alarm. The account of his father-in-law given here by Napoleon is a complete fabrication.

[73]

Troye[s,] 25th [February 1814], 2 p.m.
My dearest Louise, The cold weather here is most painful for poor soldiers who are obliged to be in the saddle night and day. Your father was at Troyes, very downcast and rather ill, he did not see much of the Russians—they do not like each other. You

had better write to him complaining that he does not let you hear from him, that he has forgotten you, and that, while serving the interests of his monarchy, he might help us; that he should be reasonable and have a will of his own, and not be the instrument of England and Russia. In short, write him a strong letter commending to him your interests and those of your son. Tell him at the same time that we are determined to die rather than agree to a shameful and unfair peace, which, moreover, would be a bad policy, for it would not last. Good-bye, my darling. All my love.

Nap

My troops have entered Bar-sur-Seine and Vendeuvre. I am very pleased with my people; they are filled with enthusiasm and keenness. They kill a great many of their enemies piecemeal. The Cossacks are committing horrors. The Emperor Alexander is much hated here. Your father is esteemed and better liked, but he kept on declaring he could do nothing. He spent the day walking about in his garden, went out rarely and saw but few people.

The Special Commissioners who, since the beginning of the year, had been dispatched into the provinces to speed up the carrying out of defence measures, had a task fraught with difficulty.

[74]

[Paris] 25th February [1814], 10 *p.m.*

My Darling, I spent a really wretched night until I got M. Fain's letter telling me about your successful cavalry engagement on the 23rd, I badly needed some such news, I was terribly anxious, I don't know why, but I often feel like that when you are away. I am always afraid something is happening to you. I can hardly wait to hear the details, and most of all I long for a little note from you telling me you are well, because I haven't had a single letter from you for forty-eight hours.

I have had the thirty guns fired as you ordered, I wrote to the Minister of War about it. I have held a special Council today to deal with those two reports from the Minister of the Treasury that you referred to the Arch-Chancellor. It seems these Gentlemen were in favour of letting the Special Commissioners stay on in the provinces, nothing was settled about the second matter.

Your son is quite well, his cold is getting better and he is hardly coughing at all now, this morning he took the ipecacuanha syrup which has had no effect so far; he has had a really raging toothache this evening and has been in great pain, but nothing can be done about it, it comes from a decayed tooth. Dubois[1] is talking of pulling it, but we shall never get him to agree to such an operation, for if anyone so much as mentions putting a piece of cotton in the tooth, he screams his head off. He is very dejected because his little playmate has a chill.

I am fairly well, I still have occasional bouts of coughing, but that will pass.

I have just this moment received your yesterday evening's letter which has completely set my mind at rest about your safety and has given me great pleasure, because I see you are thinking of me continually, in spite of all the important things you have to do. I wish my father would get so sick of the Russians that he would throw in his lot with you, for really the Russians are such horrible people, just to read in the newspapers about all the outrages they have committed makes one shudder. I have seen the Arch-Chancellor and Queen Hortense, it was lovely to be able to tell them I'd heard from you.

Good-bye, Dearest, I love you and kiss you with all my heart.

Your Darling Louise

At Lassigny, General Flahaut conferred with the representatives of the Allied generals, with a view to concluding an armistice still based on the Frankfurt proposals, as Napoleon had instructed. The suggested frontier, passing from Antwerp—a port vital to the Imperial fleet— through Mainz to Chambéry was, however, considered unacceptable.

[75]

Troye[s], 26th [February 1814], 3 p.m.

My dearest Louise, The weather is still very cold today, though I was hoping it would become milder. My health is very good; I hope to hear from you that the little King is well and that he has got rid of his cold. My troops are at *Bar-sur-Aube* and at

---

[1] A surgeon.

Châtillon-sur-Seine. It appears that your father does not like the Russians, he sees the Emperor Alexander but very rarely. They are negotiating a truce; I do not know whether they will be successful. Good-bye, my dearest Louise. All my love.

Keep well, a kiss to the little King.

Nap

At Troyes there was another victory—but 'only a victory'. The dust on the courier's shoes, as Parisians did not fail to observe, was too recent to allay their fears.

[76]

[Paris] 26th February 1814, 11 *p.m.*

My Darling, Just as I was sitting down to write to you I got your letter dated the 25th at two o'clock in the afternoon. Thank you so much for writing so promptly, it makes me feel much better, and I'm far more cheerful when I've had a letter from headquarters. I will set about writing to my father in the way you suggest, and will send you the letter this evening if I can possibly get it done by then, if not I will send it by the orderly tomorrow morning, together with the copy in French. I am most anxious for my letter to produce a good effect—and the exact effect you want; there was one really dreadful sentence in your letter, about your being resolved to die rather than make a dishonourable peace. I do hope the threat will have its effect, but I beg you for pity's sake not to entertain such an idea, it's too frightful, you know that if the least little thing were to happen to you it would be the death of me, and I should never have a moment's peace if I thought you meant this seriously, so I beg and beseech of you, for pity's sake my Darling, not to think of such a thing. I am really angry with my father for his unwillingness to come to terms with you, he would be acting in his own best interests if he did, I'm sure no good will come of his present policy, but he is deluded and led astray by Metternich.

Your description of the enthusiasm in the district you have liberated doesn't surprise me in the least, for how could it be otherwise, you are so kind, so worthy of being loved, certainly if everybody could know and appreciate your good qualities as I do, no one would ever wish you ill.

90

I enclose a letter from the Queen of Naples which I received only today, I should be so glad if you would tell me whether I can give her a different answer, or send her news of you, I am so sorry for the poor Queen, she is dying of grief.

The Arch-Chancellor has written me a short reply to the speech the Minister of War is to make me tomorrow. I hope you will like it, I should have been far too stupid to compose one myself, besides I was afraid you would scold me if I did.

Your son sends you a kiss, his cold is gradually clearing up, he is in excellent spirits and has been playing ever since this morning, he has had a fairly good dinner and is running about a little, a proof that he has almost completely recovered, but they are going to give him ipecacuanha syrup for another two days to break the rest of his phlegm.

I am keeping well in spite of the bitter cold, which must be dreadful for the poor wounded. Instead of doing embroidery, I am making lint, my red ladies are doing the same, and in the past week we have already made more than four pounds; I am glad to think my efforts are helping to relieve the sufferings of some poor fellow who is fighting for your cause.

I have just received your letter and the enclosed bulletin, it will be inserted in the *Moniteur* tomorrow. I will send you the letter for my father tomorrow as well, I have no time to copy it out before the orderly leaves. Good-bye, my Darling, all my warmest love.

Your Darling Louise

The Allies, closing their ranks, resumed the negotiations begun at Châtillon, with a fixed determination to abide by their previous demands, to which, as they well knew, Napoleon would not submit after his recent victories.

Augereau was now on the march, but collided with the Prince of Hesse-Hombourg, who blocked his advance. The Marshal retreated as far as Valence.

[77]

Troye[s], 26th [*February* 1814], 6 *p.m.*

My Dearest, I am master of Châtillon-sur-Seine. So the Congress the Allies intended to hold in my country is now under my control. It was out of sheer vainglory that they determined to hold the Congress in Burgundy.

My troops are at Bar-sur-Aube, at Châtillon, at Auxerre. Marshal Auger[eau] is marching on Dijon. No armistice has yet been signed; we are not agreed as to the line of demarcation. The disposition of the inhabitants and peasantry could not possibly be better. They are coming forward to a man.

The Russians tried to put forward the Bourbons. They were laughed at everywhere, and no one would support them. On this point the Austrians did not second them, and would not hear of the Bourbons.

Good-bye, my Darling. I give you a loving kiss.

Nap

On the following day, Marie-Louise received from the hands of the Minister of War, the Duc de Feltre, the flags which the Emperor had set aside for her. These flags, declared the Empress in the speech of which she sent Napoleon a copy, were, in her eyes, 'pledges of their country's safety. At sight of them, let all Frenchmen rise up in arms, and gather closely around their Monarch and their Father! Their courage, guided by his genius, would soon have brought about the liberation of their native land.'

[78]
[Paris] 27th February [1814], 4 *p.m.*
My Darling, This morning before going to Mass I received your dear letter of the 26th, I was very glad to get it, because it makes me so happy to hear from you. I do wish the armistice you mention could be settled, I don't know why, but I simply daren't let myself hope for it, you know I'm always rather inclined to look on the gloomy side. People in Paris are very frightened this morning, because of the corps which is advancing from the direction of Coulommiers. I saw all the Honourable Gentlemen with faces as long as fiddles, really I think the women have more courage than the men this year.

I am enclosing the copy of the letter to my father and the actual letter as well, I would prefer you to forward it. I have fastened it with a flying seal.

They presented me with the flags this morning, I was told my reply was quite good. All the same, I know my heart was thumping violently and I was extremely nervous, fortunately you make every allowance for me, because I don't believe I carried it off at all well. The parade was marvellous, the National Guard turned out in considerable force and looked very smart, and there were troops of the line and cavalry too.

Your son enjoyed the parade immensely, he had the little Princes with him and they loved it. But your son was very upset, they made him keep his bonnet on under his National Guard hat, and he kept on insisting, 'The little King doesn't want to look like a Baby'. He is very well this evening, he slept until six o'clock this morning and was still very querulous when he woke up, I put it down to his toothache which comes on fairly often, this cold has made him much thinner, his arms are quite puny, but he is definitely better, and I hope I shall soon be able to report that he is in his usual health and spirits.

I am quite well, I am still taking some pills which have almost cured me of those griping pains in my stomach, no one can say it's happiness that is curing me. I never have any when I'm parted from you. But there, I don't want to weary you with my complainings, it will make you sad. I saw Dubois this morning, and he told me he very much hoped to save the life of General Château,[1] I know you will be glad to hear that.

Do please tell me whether I can receive the Duchesse de Rovigo, I have an idea the Duke is angry because I won't do so, he has been looking very surly for some time now.

It still continues very cold, I forgot to tell you that as the hospitals had run out of old linen I sent two carriage-loads of it, one to the Guards and the other to troops of the line, and when the Honourable Gentlemen said it ought to be reported in the papers, I said no, I didn't think it would show a becoming modesty to go boasting like that about my own good deed. I would rather have you say I did the wrong thing in refusing than have you scold me for boasting about it. Good-bye, my Darling, I must stop now for the family dinner-party, I send you a loving kiss.

Your true and loving Louise

---

[1] Huguet-Châtaux, fatally wounded at Montereau.

Copy of the letter written to my father.

[Paris, 26th February 1814]

I am very sad at not having heard from you for six weeks, I am afraid, dear Papa, that you have completely forgotten me. The very thought of such a thing grieves me to the heart, and is perhaps more calculated than anything else to add to my distress at a time when you are fighting against us, instead of coming to our aid, as you might well do, even in the interests of your own throne.

I am convinced that you would, in fact, do so, were you to turn a deaf ear to the insinuating words of Russia and England. Moreover it is not good policy on your part to offer us a shameful and dishonourable peace which could not possibly prove lasting. People here are resolved to die rather than accept such terms, and think, dear Papa, what would then be my situation, the blow would be so terrible that I should never survive it. I do earnestly beg you to consider the interests of my son and of myself, you know how devotedly I love you and how proud I have always been to enjoy your affection; I am hoping you will give me fresh proof of it in this matter which so closely coincides with the interest of your own throne.

I beg you to let me have news of your health, I have heard you are far from well and the news troubles me greatly.

I am in poor health myself, my son too has been indisposed for several days and I have been very worried about him; this anxiety, combined with the distress caused me by the Emperor's absence at such a time, cannot possibly contribute to my well-being, and consequently it rests with you to lighten at least some part of the burden of our cares. In this hope I kiss your hand, and am ever your most loving and respectful . . .

Napoleon's letter of 27th *February* 1814 *is missing.*

The Allies, meanwhile, were beginning to discuss a possible restoration of the Bourbons.

[79]

[Paris] 28th *February* 1814, 10 *a.m.*

My Darling, At one o'clock this morning I received your letter of the evening of the 26th, I was most agreeably surprised to hear

94

from you twice in one day. I hope the knowledge that you are making me very happy will lessen your aversion to writing. For the remainder of the night I had wonderfully pleasant dreams; I had been talking about you quite a lot in the course of the evening, and so was full of tender thoughts. I had been talking about the many proofs of affection you had so often given me —it's a subject on which I really love to let myself go.

I do congratulate you on having got your way about where the Congress is to be held, I only wish it could influence their attitude, they must be deeply mortified at not coming to Paris as they had so loudly proclaimed they would, and I hope too that they'll never go back to their own countries, no one wishes them ill as whole-heartedly as I do. They have conceived the crazy idea of putting the Bourbons forward, they have simply no idea how deeply the nation is devoted to you, I am so glad my father has not supported them in such a notion.

You must by now have received the little engraving of your son's portrait, I do hope you liked it. I am very well indeed, my cold has quite gone even though the weather continues bitterly cold.

Your son sends you a kiss, he is wonderfully well, he was still just a little upset yesterday evening, but it lasted only half an hour or so, and there was not even an increase in his pulse-rate, so the slight indisposition is all over now, I am so relieved, because I couldn't help being worried about it.

I will write again this evening, I do hope to hear from you in the course of the day. Good-bye, my Darling, I love you and send you a fond kiss.

Your Darling Louise

In Paris, the young Empress listened a little too readily to the gossip which her Lady-in-Waiting poured into her ear about the niece of her rival, the Comtesse de Montesquiou.

[80]

[Paris] 28th February 1814

My Darling, I received your letter of the 27th from Arcis-sur-Aube just an hour after mine had been sent off. I am delighted to see you are drawing a little nearer, and the news will give even greater pleasure in Paris, where the enemy's advance is causing great anxiety; I am not in the least anxious myself, for I have no fear when I know you are at the head of the army, but I do live in a constant state of nerves lest anything should happen to you, but I hope you will be good enough to remember the promise you have given me not to run into danger.

Please tell me whether you would like me to send a fresh letter to my father with the engraving of your son's portrait; I will wait for instructions from you before doing so.

Your son is wonderfully well this evening, and no longer feels any discomfort, he is really fit and is playing with his hobbyhorse. Mme de Montesquiou is in a terribly bad temper, as I have good cause to know, for she made a dreadful scene in front of me, I'll tell you all about it when I see you, as it would take too long to write, but it has rather lowered my opinion of her, especially since she started saying spiteful things about the Duchess, whom I like rather better in consequence. She even went so far as to tell me that it was the Duchess who had invented a story that has been going around for the last few days, and which the King of Spain told the Duchess and me—and that was the very first we'd heard about it—to the effect that Mme de Montesquiou's daughter-in-law and her niece were assaulted as they were leaving by the soldiers returning from Spain, I don't know whether it's true or not, but at any rate Mme de Montesquiou had no right to put the blame on two people who were perfectly innocent of the whole thing. I am sure I must be boring you with all this tittle-tattle, but I'm telling you about it because I'm afraid malicious people may give you a distorted version of the business. At any rate you would have approved of my conduct, as I met the anger and the insults Mme de Montesquiou poured out in front of me with the cold disdain she deserved. But I assure you, you wouldn't have recognised her, she was in such a rage, and that looks so horrid in a woman. I haven't told the Duchess about it, as there seemed no point in doing so and it would only upset her.

I am keeping very well, the weather is getting much milder, I am so glad for your sake. Good-bye, my Dearest, I love you and send you an adoring kiss.

Your true and faithful Louise

The King of Rome
by Isabey

The Imperial Family
by A. Menjaud

On 21st February Napoleon had addressed a somewhat truculent letter to the Emperor of Austria. He received only an evasive reply.

Napoleon attempted to hem Blücher in between the Marne and the Aisne by forcing him back against the Aisne. Leaving Troyes on the 27th, he arrived at the château of Esternay on the following day; Blücher again marched on Paris, but came up against Marmont and Mortier. Having crossed the Marne, the Emperor's one thought was to march straight towards the Aisne in order to entrap Blücher between his own forces, the marshals and the river. Late on 1st March, he reached Jouarre.

[81]

Jouarre, 1st March [1814], *6 p.m.*

My Dearest, I have received your letter of the 28th. I have sent you your father's letter. A worthy and upright man, he is so often led astray! All this will turn to his confusion, but meanwhile he is injuring us a great deal.

We have had the rain behind us all day today. I have captured some baggage, taken 3 or 400 prisoners and driven back the enemy to the right bank of the Marne. We will see what can be done tomorrow. Good-bye, my dearest Louise, keep well and give my son a kiss.

Nap

[82]

[Paris] 1st March 1814, 10 p.m.

My Dearest, No news from you today, and I'd almost decided to be cross about it, because they said you were in Meaux, but the King has told me that you are further away, so I won't scold you; I imagine you were in the saddle all day yesterday and had no opportunity of writing, but at least you will have been thinking about me a little and that's a great comfort.

People in Paris are still very frightened and a lot of them are convinced the Cossacks will get here tomorrow, but do believe me, Darling, when I say that I myself am not in the least worried, on the contrary I have never felt so brave and so well, and if I *am* sad and distressed, it is simply and solely because you are away.

Today I signed a whole mass of things connected with the Council of State. You must have been very amused at my

G

account of Mme de Montesquiou's angry outburst. Today, when she is somewhat calmer, she said someone had told her I had been poking fun at that story about her Nieces in front of quite a number of people, but really that was utterly untrue. Fortunately I found out who it was who had kindly put such words into my mouth, it was one of my Palace Ladies, the very one who said the Duchess had invented the story; I'm glad to have seen her in her true colours, but I won't tell you her name, that would be too hard on her. So now I am hoping to convince Mme de Montesquiou of our innocence, and I won't be angry with her any more; there really are times, my Love, when in my opinion, I'm *too* kind and good, you see, Darling, what wonderful compliments I'm paying myself, I expect they'll amuse you vastly!

Your son is very well, his indisposition has quite gone, he has been enjoying himself immensely this evening, having battles and making magnificent cavalry charges on his hobby-horse.

I am keeping very well, but my rheumatism is bothering me because it has been so damp today. Mme de Monteleone has asked me to pay her the pension you had promised her, it seems she has had no money at all for two months and is in extreme poverty, I have sent her word that I would write to you about it.

I hope I shall hear from you tonight, I can hardly wait for news and will write back straight away; meanwhile all my warmest love.

Your true and loving Louise

The wretched quarrels about which Marie-Louise had told him on 28th February and 1st March, moved Napoleon to address a long letter to the Minister of Police, charging him to spare the Empress all possible worry and distress. His reply to Marie-Louise was kindly and dignified.

Blücher, filled with alarm, began to retreat towards Soissons, which was held by the French.

[83]

Jouarre, 2nd March [1814], noon

My Dearest, I have just received your letter of 1st March. I was sorry to hear that Mme Montesquiou had made a scene that annoyed you; it was a piece of forgetfulness on her part. She is so good to the little King that you will forget it and continue to be kind to her. What has been said about Mme Anatole is very ill-natured; such talk is infamous, for nothing more is needed to bring into ridicule and contempt worthy and deserving people who are highly virtuous and quite blameless. The Duchess, who is such an upright woman, should be the first to disapprove of such ill-natured talk, which affects women's happiness so deeply. It would be better to stab such young women with a knife than to countenance such rumours, which dishonour them and make them ridiculous and repulsive.

It rained a great deal yesterday. I consider it unnecessary to give audience to Madame la Duchesse de Rovigo. Write to your father and urge him to be a little bit on our side and not to listen solely to the Russians and the English. The enemy is falling back on La Ferté-Milon. My health is good. Good-bye, my dearest.

Nap

The shortage of hospital supplies, mentioned by Marie-Louise in her letter of 27th February, inspired Napoleon to put her in touch with the Duc de Cadore, Comptroller of the Household, who was commanded to distribute to the hospitals any equipment and supplies not required at Fontainebleau, Compiègne and Rambouillet.

[84]

La Ferté-sous-Jouarre, 2nd [March 1814], 6 p.m.
My Darling, Send for the Duc de Cadore. Tell him to have a list drawn up of all the pallets, straw-mattresses, sheets, mattresses and blankets I have at Fontainebleau, Compiègne, Rambouillet, and in my several mansions, and that are not needed in my Household—there must be at least a thousand—and to hand them over to the military hospitals. My affairs are going well. I am expecting favourable results very soon. Good-bye, my dearest Louise.

Nap

[85]

[Paris] 2nd March [1814], 8.30 p.m. after dinner
My Darling, I hear a courier is leaving and can't wait a moment longer, so I have only just time to tell you I have received your

letter of the 1st, which was most welcome, I was extremely worried at not having heard from you.

Your son is still out of sorts, I am fairly well myself. I love you and send you an adoring kiss.

Your Darling Louise

[86]

[*Paris*] *2nd March* 1814, 10 *p.m.*

My Darling, I wrote to you this morning by a courier M. de la Valette sent off, this time I am using the orderly, but I really am depressed to find that my letters are not reaching you promptly. I hear you have still not had one written on the 28th, I do hope it isn't the one in which I enclosed the letter to my father, do please let me know whether it is, and if so I'll write it out again. I should also like you to tell me whether I may answer the one I received today, in which he tells me nothing at all except that he is well, that he wants to hear from me, and that he is forwarding some old letters from my step-mother and my sisters. He doesn't even say where he is writing from. I do so wish he would be sensible and come over to your side, I am sure he is surrounded by some very horrid people, because my father is much too kind-hearted to turn against his son-in-law like this, but unfortunately he is weak.

I am very much afraid the rain may have given you a cold; I am worried because you say not one single word about your health, I do hope it is good, and that you will be sending me good news of today. I am expecting you to defeat the enemy.

Your son was still out of sorts this morning, he's having a great deal of trouble with his teeth, he has dreadful pangs of toothache every few minutes, I'm afraid these bad teeth are going to mean a lot more pain in store for him yet. He is very merry tonight, is busy playing and has had a very good dinner, but he still has a cold.

I am keeping well, but have caught yet another bad cold, they seem to be really chronic this year.

I have just this moment received your letter of 2nd March, and am delighted to see that you are in good health. Your remarks about the rumour concerning Mme Anatole are very true, it is most disagreeable for her and very nasty of the people who invented it; however, I must give the Duchess her due, for whenever the subject crops up, she dismisses the whole story as a frightful calumny, and I do the same, but no one believes us, I only hope it will die a natural death like many another. I know quite well who is spreading it around, I wouldn't have believed any woman could be so horrid.

You may rest assured that I forgave Mme de Montesquiou long ago for making such a scene in front of me, I don't bear her the least grudge, because I owe her a debt of gratitude for the care she lavishes on my son; but those are not the first harsh words she has spoken to me recently, and I have borne them all without complaining, because I know you like her and want me to be kind to her, but as for real friendship, that's quite a different thing, as I've often told you.

If you forbid me to receive the Duchesse de Rovigo her husband will harbour a mighty grudge against me, and it will be all your fault. I will write to my father and will send you the letter, meanwhile all my warmest love.

Your true and loving Louise

It was Madame de Montmorency, one of the Empress's Ladies, who had been implicated in the quarrel.

Napoleon moved swiftly towards the Aisne with the intention of 'annihilating' Blücher; from La Ferté he drove straight on Fismes and Berry-au-Bac, where he planned to cut off the Prussians from the only bridge available to them. It was, however, essential that Soissons should hold firm.

[87]

La Ferté-sous-Jouarre, 3rd [*March* 1814], 8 *a.m.*
My dearest Louise, I have received your letter of the 2nd. I am sorry to see you pay attention to silly people. Never argue with anybody; it is unworthy of you. It was ill-mannered of Mme Montesquiou to lose her temper in your presence. If she had a quarrel with the Duchess, they should have had it out away from you; never argue with Mme Montmorency. It all smacks of small-minded women, and is unworthy of your nature. Never argue with anyone about all this, but hold the Minister of Police and all the Ministers at a distance. In this country, people are only

too ready to eat out of your hand. Above all, be cheerful, and look after your health. Mine is good. Good-bye, my darling. All my love.

Nap

On the same day, Napoleon received the proofs of the engraving of the little King, the motto having finally been altered to '*I pray God for my Father and for France*'. The Emperor sent this portrait by courier to Troyes, where the foreign rulers were assembled, hoping perhaps in that way to soften the heart of the King of Rome's maternal grandfather, and produce a favourable impression on the other European princes.

[88]

[Paris] 3rd March 1814, 3 *p.m.*

My Darling, Just as I woke up this morning I received your letter of 7 p.m. yesterday, it's really delightful to get news of you so quickly, it makes me so happy. I have been very depressed for the last two days, I don't know why, it's not anxiety, but a feeling of sadness that I simply can't fight down, and I don't think it will disappear completely until I see you again.

I asked the Duc de Cadore to come and see me to discuss what beds we might send, he insists there isn't a single one in any of the palaces which is not needed, and he even declares that when you are on your travels, beds have to be transported from one palace to another, so that there'll be enough to go round, so do please send me fresh instructions about this. I hear the Paris Hospitals have all they need at the moment, but that those in the towns and the surrounding countryside have absolutely nothing. The Parisians have shown up extremely well in this business, and even the poorest of them have contributed as much as they possibly could.

I have been to give Madame all the latest news about you, she is keeping well, and like me is deeply distressed at your absence; when *will* it end, and when will you come back to me for good?

Your son is very well, he slept soundly all night, and has been very merry all day long. I think his little indisposition has quite gone now, if only his wretched teeth will leave him in peace, they've been giving him a lot of pain for some time.

I am keeping very well, even though the bad weather is making it almost impossible to take any exercise, it keeps raining and is very cold, I'm very vexed about it for the sake of your poor troops, they must be suffering great hardship.

I will write just a few lines again tonight, but I can't end this letter without telling you all over again something you know quite well already—that I love you with all my heart and soul.

Your Darling Louise

[89]

[Paris] 3rd March [1814], 10 *p.m.*

My Darling, I have just this moment received your letter of this morning, I am delighted to hear from you so often. You can rest assured, my Darling, that I'm not worrying any more about the stupid gossip you mention, and am quite determined not to enter into any explanations on the subject, I don't think it would be at all seemly. I should never have mentioned it to you but for the fact that I was so angry and upset about it, and when I get all worked up I just have to unburden myself to someone, and since you are the person I love best in the world, you are fated to listen to my secrets, for you know I pour out all my thoughts to you.

I am so grateful for all the good advice you are giving me, you may be sure I keep the Ministers at a distance; to begin with, my shyness and my natural reserve are a great help in fending them off, and then I must confess I am bored to tears by all the long rigmaroles they are likely to tell me at any moment. Your letter has quite restored my spirits; this morning, I don't know why, I was terribly depressed, so to know that you are well, and pleased with the way things are going, gives me immense pleasure.

Your son sends you a kiss and is as fit as can be this evening, he's in the seventh heaven because I've just given him a cape like those worn by the guard of honour, it's the only plaything he has wanted for some time now.

I am still keeping well, whenever I hear from you I pick up for a little while. Queen Hortense has been ill this last day or two, she has taken an emetic, which has cleared away her fever.

You don't say whether I am to answer the letter from the

Queen of Naples. I have also been asked to say a word in favour of M. Ricaud, whom the minister intends proposing to you as candidate for the Prefecture of Corsica, he could then marry the daughter of one of the Ladies[1] in the little King's household. All my fondest greetings.

Your true and loving Louise

[90]

Bésut-Saint-Germain, 4th March [1814, *morning*]
My Darling, You ask me whether you should write to the Queen of Naples. My answer is *No*; she has behaved improperly towards me, who made a queen of a mere nobody. My health is good. I am pursuing Blücher, whose position is very exposed. Be contented and cheerful, my affairs are going pretty well. All my love.

Nap

[91]

[Paris] 4th March 1814, 5 p.m.

My Darling, I have just come from the Council you asked me to hold for the purpose of acquainting the Honourable Gentlemen with the documents relating to the negotiation.[2] It has been such a long meeting, more than two hours, and the outcome of it all is that most of these Gentlemen think we should have peace at any price, that it is absolutely essential, and that if we cannot get it on good terms, then we must accept those put forward in the peace treaty we read this morning. It will be a happy day for me when it is signed, since it will bring you back amongst us once again, and there can be no happiness for me so long as you are away and I am worrying all the time about your health. I haven't heard from you today, I hope there will be news, and good news, before the evening is out, you really ought to be happy, you who are so kind and good, you are so deserving of happiness that life can't possibly deny it you; at any rate, Darling, if my prayers were answered, you would have everything your heart could desire.

Your son sends you a kiss, he is quite well today but is in a fiendish temper; these black moods come over him at times, I

[1] Darnaud.   [2] At Châtillon.

honestly believe there are days when he feels he simply *must* cry.

I am feeling really well this evening, I was feverish all last night and had a heavy cold, but what can you expect when the weather is so vile, I am so vexed about it because of your military operations. I will write to you again this evening, but now I shall have to end this letter so that it can go by the 8 o'clock messenger; all my fond love.

Your true and loving Louise

[92]

[Paris] 4th March 1814, 10 p.m.

My Darling, I am just going to bed, and here comes your letter written this morning, I had a pleasant feeling—quite justified it seems—that I should hear from you again today. I had heard that the Queen of Naples had behaved very badly, but was reluctant to believe it, it's the most flagrant ingratitude on her part after you had showered so many favours on her; you may be sure I shan't write to her, I'm too prejudiced against people who treat you badly ever to answer her.

Your son is well, my cold is very much better. I must close now as I'm dying of sleep. I send you a loving kiss.

Your Darling Louise

[93]

Fismes, 5th [March 1814], 10 a.m.

My Darling, I am off to Berry-au-Bac, on the way from Laon to Rheims. I have relieved Rheims, taking 4000 prisoners and 600 baggage-wagons. Have a salvo of 30 guns fired. I will write to you this evening. Good-bye, my dearest Louise. All my love.

Nap

At the very moment when the Emperor, closing in on Berry-au-Bac, believed the destruction of Blücher complete, the capitulation of Soissons on 3rd March allowed the Russo-Prussian forces to escape encirclement. Napoleon at once conceived the plan of cutting off their road to Laon.

Having taken Prince Gagarin prisoner, General Nansouty advanced towards Corbeny and Bouconville.

[94]

Berry-au-Bac, 5*th* [*March* 1814], 7 *p.m.*

My dearest Louise, I have crossed the bridge over the Aisne here this afternoon. I routed those who attempted to oppose me, capturing 200 horse and Prince Gagarin, who was in command. I also took 2 guns. My vanguard is half-way to Laon. *Buchler* was wounded, they tell me. All my love.

Nap

[95]

[*Paris*] 5*th March* 1814, 9 *p.m.*

My Darling, No news from you yet today, I hope it will be as it was yesterday and that I shan't have to go to bed without hearing that you are well. We are having wretched weather, it must be causing great hardship both to you and to your poor troops. I have never hated the sight of rain as much as I do now, when I dread hearing that it has made you ill.

People in Paris are extremely agitated and very uneasy wondering what was discussed at the Council yesterday. The Arch-Chancellor told me they thought it was about conscripting 200,000 men, which has had the worst possible effect in Paris, they are longing for peace; as for me, I only want whatever *you* want, you too must be in very great need of rest.

Your son sends you a kiss, he is very well and is picking up again, but is still very pale and looks heavy about the eyes, but he's eating and sleeping well, and playing even better. He is in a much better temper than he was yesterday, we've had a few tears, but they were soon chased away, it's such a pity the bad weather is keeping him indoors.

I am quite well, my cold is just the same, but I'm not doing anything for it. However, to avoid having to cancel my reception tomorrow, I shall go to bed earlier than usual and shan't see anyone this evening. All my fondest love.

Your true and loving Louise

[96]

[*Paris*] 6*th March* 1814, 11.30 *a.m.*

My Darling, I am all eagerness to tell you that I received the letter you wrote yesterday at 10 o'clock this morning and immediately gave the order for 30 guns to be fired. I am delighted with your good news, and above all to hear that you are well; I am waiting with the utmost impatience for the news you have promised to send this evening, I can never have too many letters from you.

Your son sends you a kiss and is well, and so am I. I must stop now as the orderly is leaving. Good-bye, I love you and send you a fond kiss.

Your Darling Louise

[97]

[*Paris*] *6th March* 1814, 10 *p.m.*

My Darling, I have already written once this morning to tell you I had received your yesterday's letter, but I don't want to let a whole day go by without letting you hear from me again. There were very few people with me at Mass this morning, and very few Ladies in particular, I really think a great number have left, and besides, no one feels cheerful enough to put in an appearance; I am the only one who is reassured by your letters, I'm not at all anxious, but still not exactly cheerful. You couldn't honestly expect me to be at a time when I'm racked with anxiety because you are away, and people would take a poor view of me if I were.

I did not see the King this morning, he was indisposed, but he has let me have the brief note you sent him for the *Moniteur*. I have held a presentation, it was for Mme Daru's[1] sister-in-law, she has just come from Rome with her husband.

Your son is keeping well, he has been as stubborn as a mule all day long, but we haven't given in to him and in the end he was obliged to do as he was told, after he'd said a whole lot of silly things. He has promised to be a very good boy this evening, he really is a good-natured little fellow.

I am keeping well, but have had a touch of stomach-ache this evening, it's a bad habit I've developed just lately. I enclose a letter Queen Hortense has given me for you, it's from Mme de Mailly asking for a post for her husband, he has lost the one he had in Illyria. He would like a job in the stud. Not many have

---

[1] *Née* Froidefond du Chatenet.

been to the family dinner-party, the King and Queen of Spain were missing. I send you a kiss and love you dearly.

Your true and loving Louise

[98]

Paris, 7th March 1814, 11 *a.m.*

My Darling, At 4 a.m. I got your letter written from Berry-au-Bac on the evening of the 5th. I do thank you for writing so promptly, it helps to set my mind at rest and reassures all those who love you too, and there are a great many of them. I haven't seen a soul yet this morning, so have no idea whether there is any fresh news.

Your son sends you a kiss and is wonderfully well, he is being particularly good to make up for yesterday's naughtiness, he is beginning to pick up and looks exceptionally well.

I am keeping very well and am very delighted to see that the weather is taking up again, a rumour has been going around that you had a terrible cold, and I was dreadfully worried, I was afraid you were hiding the truth from me; at least I shall be less apprehensive now that I know you are marching and bivouacking in such fine weather. Good-bye, my Dearest, I love you dearly.

Your Darling Louise

[99]

[*Paris*] *7th March* 1814, 10 *p.m.*

My Darling, I have already written to you once this morning, I'm sure I must be boring you with my letters just now when you have so much to do, but writing to you is my greatest pleasure. The King has given me more recent news of you than that I had yesterday, I'm so afraid we shall be left several days without hearing anything, with all the travelling to and fro you must be doing; meanwhile there is great uneasiness in Paris, everyone who comes to the evening receptions has a long, doleful face. People feel they can't go on much longer in this present state of uncertainty, it is so very harrowing.

The King was ill with a fever yesterday and didn't come to the family dinner. Today in the Bois de Boulogne I met the King and Queen of Westphalia, they were walking and I was

108

riding, they turned their heads away so that I shouldn't see them, so I pretended not to recognise them.

Your son sends you a kiss, he is wonderfully well and very merry this evening, he talks of nothing else but the battles he's going to fight tonight, and in which he is going to capture lots of Cossacks and Baschkirs; that name has stuck in his mind because I told someone in front of him that you had taken some of them prisoner; King Louis dropped in to see him this morning, he thought he had grown considerably, but was much thinner too, which isn't surprising after the slight chill he has had.

I am keeping very well and have been out for a walk, which has done me a lot of good. I send you a kiss and love you very dearly.

Your Darling Louise

In order to keep a watch on Blücher's march, Napoleon took possession of the Craonne plateau, but came into conflict with a Russian division there. A battle ensued, the Emperor repelled the Russians and pursued them through the Chemin des Dames. Eight of Napoleon's generals were wounded.

[100]
Bray-sur-Aisne, 8th [*March* 1814], 7 *a.m.*

My dearest Louise, Yesterday I attacked and thoroughly defeated the Russian Army under Wintzingerode, Worontzow and Langeron, 30,000 strong. I pursued them for 5 hours, from Craonne to L'Ange-Gardien. I killed 3 or 4000 of their troops, capturing 2000 and several guns. I had 600 killed or wounded. The Duc de Bellune and General Grouchy were wounded. I am marching on Laon. I am in good health, though somewhat fatigued. The weather is very cold. Good-bye, my darling. All my love.

Nap

[101]
L'Ange-Gardien, 8th [*March* 1814], 11 *a.m.*

I wrote to you this morning from Bray, my dearest Louise, but I hope this letter will reach you first, for it is going by way of Soissons, from which I have driven out the enemy. Yester-

109

day I defeated the Russian Army under Wintzingerode, Langeron and Worontzow. I wrote to you to have 30 guns fired in consequence. My health is good, though the weather is very cold this morning. I am marching on Laon. Good-bye, my dearest, a kiss to the little King. All my love.

Nap

[102]

[Paris] 8th March [1814], 10 p.m.

My Darling, No news from you yet today, I fear the letters may have been intercepted, it makes me quite wretched, I'm terribly distressed at not hearing how you are, and another reason for my misery is the thought that I may have to wait a long time without hearing from you. It will really make me wild to think of the Cossacks reading my letters, it drives every single idea out of my head, the King is even more disturbed than I am, because he can't think how to word the matters he has to communicate to you. It is six weeks today since you left, the time has seemed so long—if only I might venture to hope you would be back, and bringing peace, in six weeks time, but I daren't flatter myself that any such thing will happen! For two years now we have been so beset with anxieties that I no longer dare to hope for such a happy turn of events.

Your son sends you a kiss, he is wonderfully well, no longer has the slightest trace of a cough, is delightfully gay and begs me to tell you he's been a very good boy and learnt his lessons nicely —I must say all this is quite true; this evening he intends playing his favourite game again—engaging the enemy in battle. He made us roar with laughter yesterday because he kept insisting that Mme de Montesquiou should get on to his hobby-horse, he was quite sure it would give her tremendous pleasure.

I am fairly well, though the weather is frightful, it is snowing and freezing hard—what terrible weather for the army!

I am enclosing the petition sent me today by P^{cesse} Génoise,[1] it looks as if she is greatly to be pitied. Good-bye, fondest greetings from

Your Darling Louise

---

[1] Either the Baronne Dalberg, née de Brignole, or her mother, née Fieri.

[103]

[Paris] 9th March 1814, 10.30 *a.m.*

My Darling, I have just received your note dated yesterday from
L'Ange-Gardien, I was delighted to see your handwriting, I
hadn't had a single word for forty-eight hours and was dreadfully
worried, I was afraid you were ill, you see I love you so much
that whenever you are away from me I excel myself in finding
little things to worry about. It was so good of you to write to
me twice in one day, you were right in saying I should receive
it before the first letter, which I'm still eagerly awaiting, as I'm
hoping it will give details of the brilliant engagement you have
just fought. I am always happy to hear you are well, it restores
my peace of mind just for a little while.

I will have thirty guns fired as you request. Your son sends
you a kiss, he is quite well. I, too, am very well indeed. I must
close now, as the orderly is leaving at 11 o'clock. I send you a
kiss and love you very dearly.

Your Darling Louise

[104]

[Paris] 9th March 1814, 11 *p.m.*

My Darling, An hour ago I got the letter you mentioned this
morning with details of the battle you have won. I am so upset
to hear that you are overtired, do look after your health which
is bound to suffer a great deal with all this travelling up and
down in the cold. This success has given great pleasure in Paris,
they are hoping it will bring us peace, but all the same there is a
certain uneasiness when the end never seems to be in sight. I do
so wish I could have you here beside me, it would put an end to
all my anxiety.

You will doubtless already have heard of the success the Viceroy had in Parma on the 2nd of this month, the Arch-Chancellor
gave me full details about it this morning; I'm delighted he has
done so well, I only wish you had a whole host of servants as loyal
and zealous as he is.

I have had a salute of 30 guns fired as you commanded, and
afterwards I held a Council of Ministers which didn't last very
long; there has been very little business for some time now.

Your son is keeping well, he sends you a kiss and has been

behaving like a model little boy all day long, and looking extremely fit. I am very well indeed, and have been out for a walk in spite of the cold, it has done me a world of good. I send you a kiss and love you very dearly.

Your true and loving Louise

Napoleon prepared an attack on Laon, where Blücher's army was entrenched, but it was unsuccessful.

At long last a reply was received from the Emperor Francis to the letter written by Marie-Louise on 26th February. Anxious to keep on the right side of the Empress, Napoleon made out that he had opened it 'by mistake'; he sent it on to her so that he might know just what it contained.

[105]

Chavignon, 10th [*March* 1814], 8 *a.m.*

My Dearest, I am forwarding to you a letter from your father. I opened it by mistake; tell me what is in it if it is likely to interest me. I am in good health, though rather fatigued. The enemy is posted in very strong positions at Laon, where he is hiding. Give a kiss to my son, and never doubt all my love.

Napoleon

In the strained atmosphere of Paris, the Empress's least gesture was closely watched. When, for instance, accompanied by the little King in his cart drawn by two sheep, she walked through the underground passage constructed during her pregnancy in 1811, and which led from the château to the terrace beside the Seine, it was generally believed that the Government feared for her safety. Had she followed her usual custom, she would have gone through the iron gate leading into the Tuileries gardens, which were open to the public.

On 27th February, the English began the siege of Bayonne; the blockade was not to be lifted until the armistice in April 1814.

[106]

[*Paris*] 10th *March* 1814, 10 *p.m.*

My Darling, This morning I had news of you from M. Fain; I am hoping I shall hear something this evening about your arrival in Laon, I simply must have news because I am consumed

112

64051

PROMENADE DE S.M.LE ROI DE ROME.

The King of Rome in his carriage on the terrace of the Tuileries

From an engraving, 1812

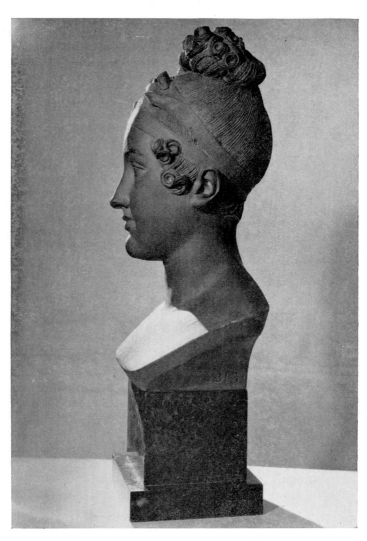

Marie-Louise
A terracotta bust by Delaistre, 1813

with anxiety for no reason I can think of; there are some days when your letters are even more vital to me than others, I can't ever be calm and sensible until you are back and I have no more fear of being parted from you. For the rest, yesterday's news has greatly reassured the Parisians, people are more cheerful today, the Arch-Chancellor and everyone else I've seen looked more confident.

I wish we could have equally good news from Bayonne, there are times when you ought to be able to be everywhere at once, because when you aren't on the spot your plans all go wrong, that's just the reason why I wish you could make peace, though of course it's an entirely selfish wish on my part too, because I'm a constant prey to anxiety when you are away.

I saw the King this morning, he advised me to tell you that people were most upset when they noticed me going through the underground passage to get to the terrace for my walk, and they said, 'That means they're afraid of us when they won't let her go through the gate' and they thought no one was wearing a hat for the same reason. He maintains it would be better for me to go by the way I always used to; I told him I didn't want to take the decision on myself so would consult you about it first.

Your son is quite well, he sends you a kiss, he's growing so sweet that I do wish you could see him, you would notice a great change in him and a great improvement too. I am fairly well, but have a bad head tonight, I think the cold weather has brought it on, we've never had such a Spring, this wretched weather makes me very angry because of your military operations. Good-bye, Darling, fondest greetings from

Your true and loving Louise

Once before, on 7th June 1813, Napoleon had semi-officially forbidden the Empress to receive the Arch-Chancellor when she was in bed. 'It is permissible only to women over 30.' The Emperor's attitude to his brother Joseph remained carping and suspicious.

[107]

Soissons, 11th March [1814], 5 *p.m.*

My Darling, I have received your letter. Do not be too familiar with the King. Keep him at a distance, never allow him to enter your private apartments; receive him ceremoniously, like Cambacérès, and in the drawing-room. Do not let him play the part of adviser as to your behaviour and mode of life, you manage better than he does. I approve of your going to the terrace by the underground passage. What the King says is nonsense and in any case it has nothing to do with the public. I hope you are not altering your mode of life in any way; it is perfect, marvellous, and has earned you the esteem of everybody. You have therefore only to go on as you have been doing. When the King attempts to give you advice, which it is not his business to do as I am not far away from you, you should break off the conversation and talk of something else, and be cold to him. Be very reserved in your manner to the King and keep him at a distance; no intimacy, and whenever you can do so, talk to him in the presence of the Duchess and by a window. This, however, is not absolutely necessary. But do not allow him to interfere too much in what is no concern of his and in your household affairs, which never are. Good-bye, my darling. The weather is very bad. All my love.

Nap

[108]

[Paris] 11th March 1814, 9 p.m.

My Darling, At noon today I got your letter written at 5 a.m. yesterday, it's incredible that it should have taken so long to come. I am happy to know you are well, but worried to hear you are face to face with the enemy's troops, I'm afraid there's going to be a battle one of these days, and the thought of it torments me long before it actually happens. I enclose the copy of my father's letter, it has made me lose all hope of being able to detach him from the Coalition. It is so wrong of him, I'm deeply vexed with him. I am sending you my reply to him, so that you can let him have it if you think it suitable.

The King has probably told you all about the Council he held this morning, it looks as if the Honourable Gentlemen are quite determined to make peace; I don't venture to put forward an opinion of my own on such a matter, but according to everything one hears, it does seem essential, and in Paris, where people have really lost heart, they are absolutely longing for it. I want to impress upon you that this prevailing depression has not affected *me,* I am full of confidence, but it saddens me very much to see you so exposed to attack on every side, it's a cruel and hurting thought and I don't want to talk about it any longer; I feel I might say things which would make you sad too.

Your son is quite well, he sends you a kiss and is very happy today because he's been allowed to play with Mme de Montesquiou's little girl, it's a very special treat, he looks really comical when he says to this little thing, 'Dear Aline, I adore you', then he takes her off into every available corner to kiss her, I really believe he's developed a passion for her.

I am very well, in spite of the dreadfully cold weather, there are at least two inches of snow today, it must hamper your operations considerably. I am sending this letter by a courier the King is dispatching this evening, so I shan't write by the orderly, I hope this time it will reach you more quickly. I shall write by the orderly tomorrow, meanwhile I'll think about you very, very often, Darling, that's the way I spend every moment of my time. I send you a kiss and love you very dearly.

Your Darling Louise

Copy of the letter from my father.

6th March 1814

My dear Louise, Your letter of 26th February reached me only yesterday. In the meantime you will have received a letter from me setting your mind at rest about my health.

If I have not written to you for some considerable time, it is because of political considerations, as I have explained in a recent letter to your Husband. No one is more alive to the present situation than I, and I take a most sincere interest in all that pertains to you and yours. That, after all, is only natural, and for that very reason I cannot but wish that your Husband would bring the war to a speedy conclusion. Any peace which, by bringing France within limits fixed with due regard to the strength of the other powers will secure for her that peace at sea of which she has so long been deprived, is honourable, practical and acceptable. Peace at sea can be achieved only on the terms already offered, and without such a peace no happiness is possible either for Europe or, most particularly, for France. You have a greater stake than anyone else in the re-establishment of peace and order. With the restoration of trade, with a government based on a lasting peace, your Husband will receive the blessings of the fairest state in Europe. His memory will be cherished by his subjects, and his dynasty firmly secured. Those who are giving him different advice are his greatest enemies; no one desires his good more sincerely than I do, and I offer him daily proof of my sound intentions in this respect. Were I his only adversary, we could arrange matters more easily between ourselves, but a separate peace with Austria, far from being of benefit to him, would merely do him a great deal of harm. I shall never break with the Coalition, whose real and sole aim is the welfare of mankind, so that if the Emperor wishes for peace, he must do what is necessary to obtain it.

The greatest service you can render to your Husband, your son and your new country, is to urge the acceptance of my friendly, I may even say fatherly, advice and opinions. I have been a reigning monarch for 22 years, and your Husband can honestly say of me that in all circumstances I have told him the plain truth as no one else has ever done. I hope your son and the Emperor will continue in good health. Believe me ever

Your affectionate father Francis

To this Marie-Louise replied:

[Paris, 11th March 1814]

My dear Papa, I have just this moment received your letter of 6th March, and I wish to lose no time in telling you how great a satisfaction it has given me. I got your last letter a week ago, together with those from Mamma and my sisters. I badly needed the reassurance it brought me, as I have been deeply worried about your health for some time now.

I have read with the closest attention all you have said about our present situation. I do assure you, dear Papa, that the Emperor is anxious for peace, but not for a dishonourable peace; *that* he could by no means accept, and neither I nor France would wish for it; in the meantime I am grieved and distressed to think that you are still determined to continue the struggle against us. You can well imagine my situation; believe me, I have never been so weighed down by cares as I am at this moment. You know how dearly I love the Emperor, you may then have some idea of my present anguish at seeing his health and person exposed to every kind of danger. I sincerely hope that you are giving some thought to my situation, and I repeat again that the Emperor is anxious for peace and would agree to it, if only they would put forward terms he could accept without loss of honour.

My son is well, but my own health is not at all good, it can hardly be otherwise in view of all this anxiety.

Let me hear from you soon, and believe me ever your . . .

Husband and wife were now, however, on the verge of a domestic crisis, brought about by the excessive trust which Marie-Louise was beginning to place in her brother-in-law King Joseph. The Empress, almost, it seems, out of spite, informed her husband of King Joseph's idea for drawing up a memorandum designed to force a peace settlement. Thus Napoleon was warned of what was going on. There were grounds for suspecting that this idea of a memorandum was instigated by Talleyrand.

[109]

[Paris] 12th March 1814, 10 *a.m.*

My Darling, I have just this moment received your letter from Soissons written at 2 p.m. on the 11th, I am delighted to have such recent news so quickly. I need to be told again and again that you are well. Your letter has given me great pleasure because you say you approve of my way of life and conduct; nothing in the world is sweeter to me than the knowledge that I am deserving of your approval, so you may be quite happy in mind, I shall never allow myself to be influenced by the King, and I'm very glad I didn't stop using the underground passage, as he absolutely insisted that I should. To let you see that I sometimes disregard your advice, I am going to tell you about something which happened to me yesterday. Whilst I was in the drawing-room with him, we received your letters of the 10th; he asked me if I had any news, I said you were well and had sent me a letter from my father which was fairly satisfactory; thereupon he started lecturing me about the importance of making peace and the necessity of sending someone to tell you in person a great number of things that couldn't be put into writing. He wished, come what may, to send off M. Molé, I pointed out that I didn't think we had any right to send Ministers to headquarters like that, that moreover you might be seriously displeased at such a step, and that I couldn't possibly take the responsibility upon myself, so then he wanted me to send M. Méneval; I said I should do no such thing without asking you, and that anyhow a courier would be just as certain to reach you and would get there much more quickly. I confess, Darling, that I would rather be scolded for not interfering in a whole lot of things than for taking too much upon myself. Last night I received the bulletin about the battle of Craon[ne], I had it put in this morning's *Moniteur*.

Your son sends you a kiss and is wonderfully well, I haven't seen him yet this morning, because he would have kept me from writing to you, and besides I've only just wakened up.

I am keeping very well, I'm so vexed about this wretched weather and afraid it will affect your health and hinder your military operations. I send you a kiss and love you very dearly.

Your true and loving Louise

Napoleon made no mention whatever of the letter of 4th March, in which Marie-Louise had given him the gist of the debates in Council when the members had expressed a desire for 'peace at any price'. The Empress's letters of 11th and 12th March increased his suspicions, for which, in fact, there were some grounds. Of the dignitaries and senators who had visited King Joseph to discuss a plan to force the Emperor to abdicate and to set up a Regency of which he, Joseph, would be head, his brother had said no word. Joseph, indeed, wished to send an address, signed by all the ministers, dignitaries, and senators, and even the National Guard, inviting Napoleon to make peace, whatever the cost—or to abdicate from power.

[110]

Sois[s]on[s], 12*th* [*March* 1814], 3 *p.m.*

My dearest Louise, I have received your last letter. I have forwarded your letter to your father through the out-posts. I am sorry you showed the King your father's letter and your reply. You trust this prince too much. Such communications should be made to no one but me. Everyone has betrayed me. Will it be

my fate to be betrayed also by the King? I should not be surprised if such were to be the case, nor would it break my forti-
tude. The only thing that could shake it would be if you had
any intercourse with the King behind my back and if you were
no longer the same to me as you have been. Mistrust the King;
he has an evil reputation with women and an ambition which
grew upon him whilst he was in Spain. If you wish to please me
and not make me unhappy, show the King none of my letters, or
your father's, or your own answers. Keep him at a distance.
They tell me the King has conceived the insensate and guilty
intention of having addresses sent me in favour of peace. Were
this to be done I should be very angry; it would lead to nothing
and would spoil all France's affairs. Why have you not told me
of all this? I tell you again, keep the King out of your confidence
and away from your person, if you care for my satisfaction and
happiness. All this depresses me rather; I need to be comforted
by the members of my family, but as a rule I get nothing but
vexation from that quarter. On your part, however, it would
be both unexpected and unbearable. Good-bye, my dearest. All
my love. Your

Nap

[111]
[Paris] 12th March 1814, 8 p.m.

My Darling, I have already written to you once this morning in
answer to your letter of yesterday morning, since then I have not
had a single word from you; you'll think me most exacting
when I say I just can't hear from you often enough. I am sending you a watch-chain made of my hair, the one you have was
getting rather worn before you left; I hope it will make you think
of me occasionally, and that you'll like it.

I have seen the Arch-Chancellor and the King, they have
given me no fresh news, the Arch-Chancellor was really very
poorly.

Your son sends you a kiss, he is very merry and extremely
well, he's growing sweeter every day, he often thinks about you
and talks to me about you, he keeps asking me when you are
coming back, I only wish it lay within my power to fix a date
for him, because then it would be very soon indeed.

I am fairly well, except for a headache, it looks as if I may be going to have an attack of migraine tomorrow, which would be very unpleasant in view of my reception and Mass. Fondest greetings from the one who loves you very dearly.

Your Darling Louise

If an address had, in fact, been presented, Napoleon, as he himself stated, would have ordered the arrest of Joseph, the Ministers and all the signatories. 'I will have no such thing as a tribune of the people; *I* am the grand tribune.'

[112]
Soisson[s], 13th March [1814], 3 *a.m.*

My dearest Louise, I have received your letter of 12th March, which gave me pleasure because I saw that you had no secrets from me and that you do not allow yourself to be led. You were right to refuse to send someone. I should have received him very badly. I do not need to have anyone professing to concern himself more than I do with the interests of the people. I know better than anybody what suits France, and if at all possible, I will make peace. My health is very good. Good-bye, my dearest. A kiss to my son and never doubt your

Nap

[113]
[Paris] 13th March 1814, 9 *a.m.*

My Darling, I received your letter of the 12th half an hour after midnight and should have answered straight away but for a violent chill accompanied by a raging headache; now I'm feeling better I hasten to write and tell you how very upset I was to think you could believe that I have more confidence in the King than in you, and that I would ever tell him things I kept back from you. I do so hope you don't believe any such thing, it would make me dreadfully unhappy. You can be absolutely certain that the truth is exactly the reverse—that I love you most devotedly and long to find some way of proving it to you. I am vexed with myself for mentioning my father's letter to the King, I merely translated a few sentences to him to re-assure him, because he had absolutely gone to pieces on that particular day, but you can be quite sure I didn't show him my answer, nor the letters you wrote me; if he says I did he's just boasting and is a liar into the bargain.

The King told me yesterday that but for the fear of displeasing you he would have a petition for peace drawn up and have it signed by all those Honourable Gentlemen, by the National Guard, the Council of State, and the Senate, and would then ask me to forward it to you; I told him I could never, never agree to such a course of action, that it was forcing the sovereign's hand, that I was far too devoted to you ever to do such a thing and that, besides, we ought to realise that no one knew better than you what was in the best interests of France, and what were her real needs, and that I thought the whole idea exceedingly wrong. The King retorted that I was talking like a baby, and stalked off in an extremely bad temper. I can tell you he is gradually falling in my estimation with every day that passes; just imagine it, the day before yesterday he did his very best to disparage the Viceroy and make me think ill of him; I couldn't resist telling him that I'd always found him the only member of the family who had never given you cause for complaint, I thought it was very mean of the King, and I can't think what he was driving at.

I tell you, I just wish I could arrange things so that I need not see him again, and could shut myself up in some remote little spot where I could live unknown until the moment of your return, or until such time as I could be of use to you and prove the measure of my love. It breaks my heart to think you may be angry with me, the very idea makes me utterly wretched. I should be so grateful, Darling, if the moment you get this letter you would just scribble a note straight away on a scrap of paper saying either that you are angry with me or that you aren't, I shan't have a moment's peace until I've been relieved of this dreadful anxiety.

You say nothing in your letter about your health, I hope it continues good and that you are not over-tiring yourself, it would be an added burden for me to know that you were ill.

Your son is well, he sends you a kiss, I haven't seen him yet this morning, but I'll tell you all the pretty things he's said and done when I write this evening. I feel rather better this morning,

121

but am still not myself again, I don't know whether my migraine will let me go to Mass or not, at any rate I'll do my best, but I want you to realise, Darling, that I'm making every possible effort to please you and to prove how dearly I love you. I am sending this letter by a special orderly, I very much want you to get it quickly, and above all I want you to tell me at once that you still love me a little. I send you a fond kiss.

Your true and loving Louise

On the same day, Marie-Louise again told him all the details of the King Joseph 'affair'. The Emperor's wrath was not yet wholly appeased.

[114]

[Paris] 13*th March* 1814, 2 *p.m.*

My Darling, I wrote to you this morning after receiving your letter, but I was so deeply affected by its contents that I'm afraid I didn't really explain all the details of that business I mentioned, so, Darling, you'll just *have* to submit to the tedium of hearing it all over again. On Friday the King came to see me about noon as usual; your letters were brought in whilst we were in the drawing-room, he asked me whether I had good news (he seemed particularly worried that day, I don't know why). I said you were well and I'd had a letter from my father which was fairly satisfactory and seemed reasonable to me, and I read out certain passages to him. Thereupon he asked me if I wrote to my father often and if I was obliged to send my letters through you; I told him I wouldn't think of doing anything else even if I could. He then said I ought to write and tell him you wanted peace on the conditions he was offering you. I told him I never interfered in political matters and besides I loved you far too much to want to do such a thing, and then I quickly changed the subject. Next he suggested I should send M. Molé to talk to you about the peace petition, to which I replied that not only did I consider it impossible for us to send off Ministers without your authority, but I thought the whole idea of the petition extremely unreasonable, that it would be forcing the sovereign's hand and that I had never heard of such a thing, and anyhow no one knew better than yourself what pertained to France's happiness. That put the King in a furious temper and he said I didn't know what I was talking about, because this was a most important moment. Then he suggested sending M. Méneval, but I dissuaded him from it as strongly as I could. However, as I met with no success, it was agreed that he should discuss it with M. Méneval in front of me. I saw M. Méneval, who was not at all in favour of going to headquarters. Then I went to see Queen Hortense. After that the King came back and saw M. Méneval in my presence, who told him almost exactly what I had done and in the end persuaded the King not to send him. Then by one of the King's couriers I sent off my letter to you with the letter to my father enclosed, I handed it sealed to the King so he didn't read either of them.

I hadn't mentioned the petition to you because I thought the plan had been abandoned, and I have to be extremely careful, as you should know better than anyone, not to involve you in quarrels with your family, but if a brother or sister of mine had said anything of the kind, I should have written to you about it at once.

I earnestly beg you to believe that I never receive the King in my private apartments, moreover all those around me can testify to the truth of this.

I have been so poorly that I couldn't possibly receive anyone and besides I couldn't make myself look sufficiently cheerful to put in an appearance, I am so miserable at having displeased you, and in all innocence having given you cause for mistrust, that I would just as soon die.

Meanwhile, all my fond love.

Your Darling Louise

[115]

[Paris] 13th March [1814], 7 p.m.

My Darling, I received your morning letter at 4 o'clock, it is as kind and generous as you yourself, I knew you wouldn't be angry with me for long, you are so kind that if my love for you could possibly increase, I should love you more with every day that passes. I am very, very happy tonight, I can tell you I spent a wretched morning, the thought of displeasing you made me most unhappy.

123

Your son sends you a kiss, he has had a raging toothache during the day, but is quite all right this evening and is full of fun. I am a little out of sorts and have a fairly high fever, but don't let it worry you, if I could start perspiring it would go; I have sent for Corvisart, it won't be anything much and by to-morrow I shan't even be giving it a thought, but in the meantime I haven't been able to have the family dinner-party, as I was in bed. Good-bye, Darling, I send you a fond kiss.

Your Darling Louise

[116]

Rheims, 14th [March 1814], noon

My Darling, I thank you for the beautiful and precious watch-chain you have sent me. I have received your two letters. The King is intriguing. He will be the first to suffer, he is a pygmy, swelling with his own importance. Without honour and a sense of duty a man can accomplish nothing. I recognised your beautiful soul in your letter and in the love you bear me. I cannot conceive how I can have distressed you, it upsets me very much, but I wanted to write to you plainly so as to avoid all unpleasantness. Good-bye, my dearest Louise. You know how I value your judgement and your character, and above all how deeply I love you. All my love. Your devoted husband

Nap

[On the reverse:]

I have defeated the Russian and Prussian Corps under St. Priest, capturing 25 guns, 5000 men; the Commander-in-Chief St. Priest was mortally wounded. Have a salute of 30 guns fired.

Thus put on his guard, Napoleon addressed blistering letters to Joseph and to the Minister of Police.

Hearing that St. Priest's Russo-Austrian Corps had driven General Corbineau out of Rheims, Napoleon hurled Marmont's division against the city. The enemy was defeated, and he rode in amidst tumultuous ovations. It was his last victory.

On 12th March, Wellington's army, advancing from the south, entered Bordeaux.

[117]

Rheims, 14th [March 1814], 3 p.m.

My dearest Louise, I have received your letter of the 13th. I was very sorry to hear you were grieved. I am sorry not to have spared you such a bad time, for you are so perfect and so good that one is always in the wrong. I have a very bad cold today. The weather is shocking, cold and damp, and it has a bad effect. I am hoping, however, that we shall at last have warmer weather. Pray be cheerful and contented and keep in good health. You know how necessary that is to my happiness. Good-bye, my darling. Give a kiss to the little King. All my love.

Nap

[118]

[Paris] 14th March 1814 [evening]

My Darling, I was just beginning to write to you when the King told me about the defeat of General St. Priest and the wonderful victory you have won over this division, I send you my warmest congratulations. You are getting us so accustomed to news of victories that we shall be really quite astonished when a day goes by without our hearing of one. Just now I am waiting for news of you with the greatest impatience, although I know you aren't angry with me any more, but my heart needs to be reassured all over again, as I am still terribly upset, and I long to know what I can do to make you pleased with me. The King told me this morning that he intends to come and see me less often; you can imagine how whole-heartedly I approved of this idea, in my heart of hearts I would rather he never came at all.

Your son is well and sends you a kiss, his toothache has completely gone. He is jumping up and down and is delightfully gay, the great game all this morning has been taking prisoners and bringing back booty, and he has also brought in General Sa[c]ken wounded and a prisoner. I have never seen a child so military-minded at such an early age. Really he's very like you in many ways, but I don't think he'll ever be as utterly perfect as you are.

I am feeling much better, I was rather feverish up to this morning, but have kept well all day and have even been able to go out for a drive; tonight I feel quite ill again, I've had another touch of fever, but will try to hold my reception so that people won't think there is bad news, but don't worry about my health, Darling, it won't be anything much. Do let me hear from you soon and all my warmest love.

Your true and loving Louise

Whilst, from Rheims, Napoleon was preparing a great wheeling movement towards the east, designed to bring him behind the Allied armies and compel them to turn about, Oudinot and MacDonald, convinced that Schwarzenberg was about to march on Paris at any moment, appealed for help. The Emperor decided to go to their aid. At Epernay and Châlons he made sure of holding the line of the Marne, whilst the Allies, forewarned, beat a hasty retreat in the direction of Chaumont and Langres.

[119]

Rheims, 15th [March 1814], 3 p.m.

My dearest Louise, I have received your letter of yesterday. I was glad to hear your health was better. I am very grieved to think you should have had any sorrow I might have spared you. My health is good. I am still here, which is a good thing for my Old Guard. It gives them a little rest. My troops will enter Châlons and Epernay this evening. Good-bye, sweetheart. A kiss to the little King. I long to see him exactly as you describe him to me, growing into a lovely, big boy. All my love.

Nap

[120]

[Paris] 15th March 1814, 10 p.m.

My Darling, Just as I came in from my walk, I received your letters of the 14th, one written at noon, the other at 3 p.m.; they have made me very happy, for they made it clear that you are no longer angry with me, and that you do not doubt the warmth of my devotion. I want you to understand, Darling, that I wasn't in the least put out by what you wrote; on the contrary I am grateful to you for giving me such sound advice. I very much want you to go on doing so, for you know quite well that I desire nothing better than to behave in a manner pleasing to you, and to prove to you that you are not squandering your affection on one who is ungrateful.

126

I am delighted to see that you liked my chain; I wish I could have sent it you earlier but it was ten days before it reached me. I am so grieved to see that you have caught cold; do look after your health if you don't want to add one more worry to all those occasioned by your absence: I hate to think of you on military operations in this cold, wet weather, I am sure your clothes must often be soaking wet when you can't possibly change them, and it makes me very worried and uneasy.

I have written to the Minister of War arranging for the salute of thirty guns. The bulletin sent me by the Duc de Bassano came at the same time as your letters, it will be in the *Moniteur* tomorrow. I didn't think you would mind my sending word to M. de Ségur that his son had been wounded, so that he could break the news to Mme de Ségur and Madame de Luçay, otherwise they might have a terrible shock when they read the *Moniteur*. I have seen the Arch-Chancellor, but not the King, today. The Arch-Chancellor told me he had received news that the English had entered Bordeaux.

Your son sends you a kiss, he is wonderfully well and still delightfully high-spirited, he is for ever capturing flags from the Russians, and prisoners, and has a special grudge against General Blücher, he just doesn't like him very much, and every day talks about killing him. He is learning his lessons very well indeed, he already knows three fables by heart, you'll be amazed at all the progress he has made.

I am feeling better today, I think the satisfaction of hearing good news from you is largely responsible. I send you a kiss and love you very dearly.

Your true and loving Louise

The Aisne campaign was a failure. On 16th March, in view of the critical situation, Napoleon repeated his orders for the evacuation of the capital if danger should threaten.

[121]
Rheims, 16th [March 1814], 3 p.m.

My dearest Louise, I received your letter of 15th March at 10 o'clock at night. I am glad to hear your health is better. Mine is good. My troops entered Châlons yesterday; these days of rest are doing me good. Give my son a little kiss. All you tell me about him leads me to hope that I shall find him much grown; he will soon be turned 3. All my love.

Nap

[122]

[*Paris*] 16*th March* 1814, 10 *p.m.*

My Darling, I received your welcome letter of yesterday only a moment before going to Council, so couldn't reply by the six o'clock messenger. I am deeply grieved to know that you were upset at the thought of having caused me pain, I am vexed that you are worrying about it; really Dearest, it is *I* who should be worrying about having upset *you*, because I'm always grateful when you give me good advice. I long so much to give you proof of my complete devotion, so beg you to believe that I am quite cheerful now, my only remaining worry is that you are far away and have a bad cold. It will soon be two months since you went away, and still no hope of your return, that's what is so sad. I wish I could convince myself of the truth of the rumour current in Paris that you will be returning on 20th March with news of peace, but unfortunately I can't bring myself to believe it.

In the Council today they discussed the proposed decree to conscript 12,000 men, the Minister of the Interior has probably sent it to you; the King raised a few difficulties, but nobody listened to them, he wanted all the National Guard in Paris to be exempt from the call-up; they pointed out to him the impossibility of such a course.

Your son sends you a kiss and is fairly well, he still has a touch of toothache. I assure you I'm not exaggerating when I tell you such charming things about him. He really is an unusual child for his age, without being *too* precocious.

I was not at all well again last night, I had a slight fever, but nothing much, I feel sure I shall be better again in two days' time at the most. The weather is beginning to turn a little finer and milder, I am so glad if only for the sake of your troops; never have I studied the weather with such interest as I do now; whenever it's wet I tremble for you, so I consult every barometer I can find. I had very few at my receptions today, those who came

asked me whether it was true that you had a heavy cold, I told
them you were very well indeed.

Good-bye, my Dearest, I love you and send you a fond kiss.

Your true and loving Louise

[123]

Rheims, 17*th* [*March* 1814], *noon*

My dearest Louise, I have received your letter. I hope the weather
in Paris is as fine as it is in Rheims. It will be very convenient for
your outings and will be good for your health. Give a kiss to
the King and never doubt the love I bear you. Your

Nap

I am going to Epernay this evening.

The weather cleared up, and Marie-Louise wished to move to the
Elysée-Napoléon Palace, with its spacious garden which she loved.

[124]

[*Paris*] 17*th March* 1814

My Darling, At 2 o'clock I got the letter you wrote at 3 p.m.
yesterday, at last they are coming rather more quickly, but
never quickly enough for me for I should like to hear from you
every minute of the day. I am delighted to hear the good news
about your health, my Darling, I was afraid your cold would
last much longer; the few days in Rheims have probably done
you good, you must have been sorely in need of rest after all the
tiring times you have gone through, I only wish I could have
shared them with you. At least I could have watched over your
health.

This morning M. de la Bouillerie[1] came to ask me for an advance of 600,000 francs he needs to pay the wages for the month
of March and the kitchen expenses; he said he had had a letter
from you saying that in cases of urgent need he could get me to
sign; I said that as you were so near at hand I would rather he
went direct to you, because an answer could come in a single day,
I hope you will say I did the right thing.

The Queen of Spain has been to see me, she begged to be remembered to you, she tried hard to draw me out about the letter

[1] The Crown Treasurer.

you wrote me about King Joseph, (I can't think how she knows I've had one) but I pretended not to understand what she was getting at; I am certain it was the King who put her up to it.

Your son sends you a kiss and is very well indeed, he says I am to tell you he has been a very good boy all day; he has been for a drive on the boulevards and has enjoyed it immensely.

My health is much improved, I slept better last night. M. Corvisart says he is going to make me take some herb-juices in a month's time, he says it pays to wait, because when a person is worried, they do more harm than good. The weather is wonderful, if it goes on like this, I shall be asking your permission in a day or two to move into the Elysée, which is much more comfortable than the Tuileries. Spare an occasional thought for her who loves you very dearly.

Your Darling Louise

On 17th March, Napoleon left Rheims, leaving Mortier and Marmont to keep a watch on Blücher in the north; he moved rapidly on Epernay.

[125]

Epernay, 18th [*March* 1814], 8 *a.m.*

My Darling, I received no letter from you yesterday. The weather has at last become very fine again. I am moving forward to strike at the enemy. My health is very good. Good-bye, my darling. All my love.

Nap

A kiss to the little King.

[126]

[*Paris*] 18th *March* 1814

My Darling, At 4 o'clock this morning I received your letter written yesterday morning, as I get them to wake me every time one arrives. I am too eager for news of you to wait until daybreak. I am so afraid the march you are going to undertake will prevent you from writing for several days. I'll try hard not to worry during that time, but I don't know whether I shall succeed. I fear all this continual travelling about will tire you and bring back your cold—don't stop taking care of it, will you?

I saw the King and the Arch-Chancellor this morning, they said there was no fresh news; they told me they would be meeting afterwards for the Council you had ordered them to hold. I don't know what was the matter with them, but they were both in a dreadfully bad temper. Madame has been to see me, she begged to be remembered to you, I found her greatly changed and particularly sad, but how can anyone be otherwise at a time like this, I wish I could make an effort to be cheerful but it's quite impossible.

Your son sends you a kiss, he is very well but has been complaining of toothache, we have discovered that he often complains when he has no real pain, but when I told him that walks and drives were very bad for any kind of inflammation and that he would have to give up such pleasures the pain vanished in a flash, and has never been mentioned this evening.

I am quite well; this lovely weather is doing me good and I am certainly going to ask you if I can move to the Elysée; do please write and tell me whether you have any objections, of course I shall wait for your instructions. I think it will do your son good too, as he will be able to trot around the gardens at all hours of the day. I send you a kiss and love you very dearly.

Your true and loving Louise

[127]

[Paris] 19th March 1814, 4 p.m., after dinner

My Darling, At 3.30 a.m. I received your letter written from Epernay yesterday morning. You make me very, very happy, Darling, by writing so regularly, you have no idea how it helps to calm me down, on the days when I get your letters I am much more cheerful and better in health. I can't imagine why you have been a whole day without hearing from me, as I've written once every single day and sometimes twice, I think it must be your march which has caused the delay. I think I rejoiced much too soon in the lovely weather, it's horribly foggy today, it must be very bad weather for your military operations and especially for your cold, so I wish all this was over and you were coming back never to leave us again.

I think you would be pleased with your son, he is making astonishing progress and is a very forward child for his age. He

131

has been pestering me ever since this morning to know what I'm
going to give him for a birthday present and he can be so very
coaxing when he wants to that I found myself compelled to hand
over some of the toys; you see I'm really just a little weak, but
I've made up my mind to spoil him for just a few more years, in
fact as long as ever I can. He says I am to kiss you, I won't say
anything about his health, which continues to be excellent.

Mine is very good too. I dropped in to see Queen Hortense
but found her out, which shows she is not ill any longer. I have
seen the Arch-Chancellor who told me there was nothing new.
Believe me when I say there isn't a single soul in the whole wide
world who loves you better than

Your Darling Louise

Setting out again from Epernay on the 18th, Napoleon reached
Fère-Champenoise, and on the 19th arrived at Plancy. Preparations
were now complete for an attack on Schwarzenberg's flank at Arcis.

The Allies, growing uneasy, retreated from Troyes towards Chaumont, but with the spearhead of the army falling back on the main
body of troops, Napoleon was to find, at Arcis, Schwarzenberg's whole
vast army concentrated in one spot, ready and waiting for him.

On 19th March, the conferences at Châtillon were broken off because of Napoleon's refusal to accept the 1791 frontiers.

[128]

Plancy, 20th March [1814], 1 *a.m.*

My Darling, I forcibly crossed the Aube and the Seine yesterday.
I gained possession of Méry, cut the road from Paris to Troyes
and took a fine pontoon equipment from the enemy, who has
evacuated Nogent, Vitry and the entire bank of the Aube. My
affairs [are going] well. My health is good, the weather is fine.

Write and tell your father that the idea of compelling us to
make peace by humiliating us and taking Antwerp from us is im-
practicable, that the nation has great energy, especially the
peasants, and that they will eventually be beaten, with the
Empire more powerful than ever. Entreat him not to sacrifice
the Empire to England's greed, and to take into consideration not
the passions of Stadion and the rest of them, but the interests of
his monarchy, the welfare of his family, the peace and quietness

of his life. Let him make peace on the basis of Frankfurt; it will be secure and is the only one consistent with the interests of his monarchy; tell him to beware lest he be compelled in a few months' time to make peace on unfavourable terms and to be quite sure that nothing will lead the Emperor to give up anything, for at Châtillon they would again declare it insufficient. All my love.

Nap

March 20th was the little King's birthday; Marie-Louise, deeply moved, called to mind once more the tenderness of her husband who, at the most critical moment of her confinement, agreed to sacrifice the child, so ardently desired, for the mother. That she could never forget.

[129]
[*Paris*] 20*th March* 1814, 10 *p.m.*

My Darling, This morning I received M. Fain's letter written from Fère-Champenoise in which he gave me news of your health. The sentence 'it has never been better' has restored my peace of mind, I needed to be reassured over and over again so that I shouldn't keep on worrying, I was very anxious indeed about your cold. It *is* kind of you to give someone a message for me when you can't write yourself, it helps to set my mind at rest.

I have been thinking about you so much today, it is three years since you gave me so moving a proof of your love that the tears come whenever I think of it, so it's an exceedingly precious day to me.

I am sure you will have been thinking a little about your son and me; he sends you a kiss and is fairly well, but is still having occasional bouts of toothache, it comes from several decayed teeth which will continue to bother him fairly often. He has been delightful all day today and has made a number of good resolutions, he said that now he was three he would be good all the time; everyone thought he was looking very robust and handsome. He is very happy because I've given him a lot of toys and books, and his uncles and aunts have given him a whole lot too; he has been playing with the little Princes this evening and they've

133

been shrieking with laughter and rushing about like mad things. He is at such a happy age, nothing upsets or worries him, I wish I could put myself in his place just now.

I am keeping fairly well, the reception tired me rather, there was quite a crowd and a fair number of Ladies at Mass. Afterwards I strolled on the terrace, the weather was lovely, as mild as the month of May; you really should give me an answer, Darling, about the Elysée and say whether or not you will let me stay there. I held the family dinner this evening, your son came and was very good. Good-bye, my Darling, let me hear from you soon; all my warmest love.

Your true and loving Louise

On that same day, Bary, official archivist of the Emperor's private papers, began to burn all the documents relating to the Bonaparte family, 'so that they might not fall into enemy hands'. Denon Director of Museums, requested permission to evacuate the contents of the museums.

[130]

[Paris, 21st March 1814]

My Darling, Last night I received your letter of 20th March from Plancy. I am delighted to see you are happy about the turn your affairs have taken. I hope now they will continue entirely to your satisfaction. At least that's what I'm praying for. I want you to be as fortunate as you deserve to be, Darling. The whole of Paris is buzzing with good news. It seems people have added a good deal to what the courier was able to tell them, so there is much talk of battles won, and above all of peace.

I have written to my father as you wished, but as it is getting rather late today, I'm afraid I can't make you a copy of the letter. You shall have it tomorrow, I'll send it by the 11 o'clock orderly. I long for my letters to have a good effect, but I don't think they will. My father hardly listens to me on matters of serious business. I found the Arch-Chancellor very brave today. He talked about his own courage in an astonishing way. I haven't seen the King. He scarcely ever comes to see me now in the mornings. I'm glad, because I think you will approve.

Your son sends you a kiss and is very well indeed. He slept

very badly last night and was very restless and cried a good deal in his sleep. We asked him what had been the matter. He told us that he'd been dreaming about his Dear Papa, but that he wouldn't say exactly how, and we have never succeeded in making him give us any further details.

I am keeping very well indeed. Spring suits me to perfection. For the past two years the cold weather hasn't agreed with me at all. It has been mild enough for me to go out riding. It has done me a lot of good, but it would do me even more good to see you again and to have no more worries. I love you and send you a fond kiss.

Your true and loving Louise

On 18th March, having engaged Schwarzenberg in battle so success-fully—though with an army vastly inferior in numbers—that the Austrian retreated from the field of battle, Napoleon, convinced that a renewed enemy offensive might prove fatal to him, concentrated on a secret withdrawal, made a pretence attack, and behind a screen of troops set out on the road to Vitry. His plan was to move eastwards in order to summon to his aid his ten besieged garrisons and the ever-increasing army of 'blue shirts'. Thus Schwarzenberg would be attacked from the rear and drawn away from Paris. It was, however, essential that Augereau should stand firm.

At one point, during the days of heavy fighting around Arcis, Napoleon almost certainly sought death on the battlefield.

[131]

[Saint-Dizier, 23rd March 1814]

My Darling, I have been in the saddle all the last few days. On the 20th I took Arcis-sur-Aube. The enemy attacked me there at 6 o'clock in the evening; I beat him on the same day, killing 400[0]. I took 2 of his guns, he took 2 of mine, which leaves us quits. On the 21st the enemy army formed up in battle array for the purpose of covering the advance of his convoys towards Brienne and Bar-sur-Aube. I decided to make for the Marne and his line of communications, in order to push him back further from Paris and draw nearer to my fortresses. I shall be at Saint-Dizier this evening. Good-bye, my darling. A kiss to my son.

Nap

Letter 131

This letter exerted a considerable influence on Napoleon's fate. Uhlans having captured the messenger from Arcis, Blücher at once sent a copy to Schwarzenberg, to whom the Emperor's intentions were thus clearly revealed at one single stroke. At the council of war at Pougy there was the greatest excitement. Schwarzenberg was in favour of falling back at least on Langres, but Tsar Alexander, strongly supported by Pozzo di Borgo, disagreed. It was decided to march on Châlons to give a helping hand to Blücher; they would then move towards Saint-Dizier in search of Napoleon.

In the meantime a second captured courier was brought in to the Allies, on his way from Paris with letters imploring the Emperor to return to the capital where 'influential persons' were awaiting the Allies. Impressed by this, the Tsar, on the 24th, initiated a conference which finally resolved to continue on the road to Paris.

Marie-Louise, naturally, was unaware that the courier from Paris had been captured.

[132]

[Paris] 24th March 1814, 10 *p.m.*

My Darling, I am exceedingly worried at not having heard from you for two days, you can't imagine how uneasy it makes me, I'm afraid you are ill and they are hiding it from me, and then I imagine that all the communications are being intercepted and that I shall be left for more than a fortnight without news of you, as I was last year. I asked the King if he had heard anything, he said not, I hope we shall have better luck tonight and get news of some great victory. Something of the kind is sorely needed in Paris, where there is great anxiety, a whole crowd of women flocked into Paris yesterday from Meaux, which alarmed everyone. I am glad I can be so brave in the midst of our present plight. But I don't think anyone just now is happier than your son, who sends you a kiss and is delightfully gay. I've been watching him all day—terribly busy imagining he was a courier bringing news of the armies and bringing us your letters. He asked me to tell you he thought you had been away a very long time.

I am keeping very well, I find I have been much better for some time now.

I have just heard that the orderly sent on the 22nd has been captured—what a sickening thing to happen! If you gave me any instructions in the letter you wrote, do please repeat them, I am so angry that those wretched Cossacks have cut the route, it takes away most of my pleasure in writing to you. Fondest greetings from

Your true and loving Louise

Blücher, the Blücher whom the little King 'just didn't like very much' and wanted to kill, was courteous enough, after copying and translating the letter of 23rd March, to have it sent on to the recipient.

[133]

[*Paris*] 25*th March* 1814

My Darling, I never thought I should be lucky enough to hear from you today, but this morning I got one of your letters which I think was written on the 22nd [=23rd March], but you forgot to put the date. It had been intercepted and opened, I got it this morning with a letter from General Blücher which I enclose; it was nice of him, in spite of his detestable character, to give a thought to the distress and anxiety I had been suffering through having no news of you, I really am grateful to him. I needed a letter just then to keep me from worrying, I was so afraid your health had taken a turn for the worse. I fear some of my letters may have been intercepted, including that particular one I was sending you, the one you had asked me to write; if so, it wouldn't be very pleasant. I beg you to let me know and I'll write another without delay.

Your son is wonderfully well and sends you a kiss, he has mentioned his toothache several times during the day, but as he was chuckling away all the time he was complaining, I didn't pay much attention, and it has turned out to be a loose [tooth], so that's some comfort [?].

I am keeping very well, even though the Arch-Chancellor assures me I am looking ill and says I should be well advised to follow a strict diet; fortunately M. Corvisart doesn't agree, or I should have been poisoned long since through taking physic; you see, my ideas on medicine are rather like yours.

I am hoping to hear from you again tomorrow or tonight, because even if the couriers are intercepted I have every hope that after his letter General Blücher will send me yours, and I should be delighted to get them. I had a great crowd at my receptions, but I didn't receive for long, as I was rather out of sorts. Fondest greetings from

Your true and loving Louise

[134]

[*Paris*] 26*th March* 1814

My Darling, No news from you since your letter of the 22nd [=23rd], I'm afraid they are being stopped; it vexes me extremely, as I am certain they are reading them all, it takes away all my pleasure in writing to you, I can't go on telling you all my thoughts, but nothing will stop me from telling you that I love you very dearly, and I flatter myself that you believe it, Darling. We think about you very often here, my son talks of you constantly and the poor little pet longs to have you back, he remembers the times you used to play with him, and asks me when they will return, I just wish I could fix an early date for him. He sends you a kiss and is wonderfully fit, he is already very excited about a grand parade of the National Guard which is due to take place tomorrow.

I am keeping fairly well, but am still having a good deal of stomach-ache, I think it's because I'm so worried at not hearing from you. I send you a kiss and love you very dearly.

Your Darling Louise

The tactics of Marmont and Mortier had, unfortunately, opened up the road to Paris for the Allies.

People were now leaving Paris in crowds. On 27th March, Marie-Louise herself advised the Duchesse de Montebello to send her children into the country: 'If Paris is lost, there will be the wildest disorder.'

[135]

Paris, 27*th March* 1814, 7 *p.m.*

My Darling, I am writing only a word or two because I feel sure my letter won't reach you, but even so I can't deny myself the pleasure of talking to you. I got news of you from a letter M. Fain wrote to M. Méneval; I am so grateful to you for thinking

139

of sending me news, I was badly in need of it, I am worried and miserable.

You will certainly have heard by now of that tiresome business about the Duc de Trévise and the Duc de Raguse, it is most unpleasant. I told M. Méneval to take advantage of an opportunity which unexpectedly cropped up to send you news of us; I didn't know whether you would approve of my seizing this chance, it would be so nice if you could let me have a line about this when you have a moment.

Your son sends you a kiss and is wonderfully well, he has been playing with some of his cousins and has had a lovely time at a grand parade we held today and which lasted more than three hours; the National Guard is magnificent.

I am fairly well, the weather is very fine and will be a great help to your operations. Never doubt for a moment the love and devotion of

Your true and loving Louise

'Tiresome business' was indeed brewing everywhere. In Paris people were still keeping up appearances: in the evenings Talleyrand still visited the Tuileries for his game of whist with the Empress, Queen Hortense and Molé, Minister of Justice. They joked about the prophecies that the capital would be occupied—it was an ideal opportunity for testing morale.

[136]

[Paris] 29th March 1814, 1 *a.m.*

My Darling, Tonight I am writing without knowing whether my letter will reach you, but I shall never be happy if I let a day go by without sending you news. We are in the depths of gloom here, the enemy is 40,000 strong at Claye and Meaux. The Arch-Chancellor and the King came to see me about 2 o'clock to say they thought it a matter of urgency that I leave Paris. The King read us an extract from a letter in which you told him not to let me be captured in Paris, whereupon the Honourable Gentlemen pointed out that we had no means of defending ourselves against so large a force, that there were very few troops here and that I should certainly not be exposed to the ignominy of having to wait for the Russian and Prussian armies. In an hour's time there is to be a Council at which all this is to be thrashed out; meanwhile we have made all our preparations for my departure, which is planned to take place sometime tomorrow, unless grave developments compel me to leave tonight, for they say the enemy is making rapid strides in the direction of Bondy. They are only one mile away from there.

[Later.] The Council has only just finished, it is half an hour past midnight; after long discussion they ended by declaring it was essential for me to leave, and by tomorrow morning at the latest; they also said the King should remain, with all the Ministers and high dignitaries except the Arch-Chancellor, the Duc de Cadore and King Louis, who would go with me; the treasure would be sent away too. I am to go tomorrow to Rambouillet, then further away to whatever place is selected. I tell you quite frankly that I am dead against this idea, I am sure it will have a terrible effect on the Parisians, it will rob them of all that courage they would otherwise have summoned up to defend themselves. The National Guard will do nothing any more, and when you arrive to liberate us, you will find the capital in the enemy's power. However, you told me I must follow the Arch-Chancellor's advice, and in this case I certainly shall, as I have no desire to expose my son to danger. Tomorrow I will send you the list of people I shall take with me.

Your son is well, I myself am just about as well as could be expected in circumstances such as these. I must stop now, or I fear my letter may not reach you, in the meantime I want you to believe that no one in the wide world is more truly devoted to you, or loves you more dearly than I,

Your Darling Louise

From 23rd to 29th March no letters were received from Napoleon —for this the Cossacks were responsible. Like a stag turning aside to draw off the dogs, he moved eastwards to divert the Allied armies from Paris. Passing between Doulevent-le-Château and Saint-Dizier, the Emperor returned to Doulevent on the 28th and was at Bar-sur-Aube on the 29th.

Informed, however, of the Allied march on Paris, Napoleon hastened with all possible speed towards the capital. Could it possibly hold out for a further five days?

[137]

Bar-sur-Aube, 28*th* [=29*th*] *M*[*arch* 1814]

My dearest Louise, I have been 5 or 6 days without news of you. Those wretched Cossacks are the cause of this. I am drawing nearer to you and I hope to hear from you tomorrow. I gave the enemy a good thrashing yesterday. I am anxious to have news of you. All my love.

Nap

At 8.30 on the evening of 28th March, as we have already seen, the Regency Council had met in the Emperor's study to decide on a course of action. Marie-Louise presided, and those present were King Joseph, the Arch-Chancellor, the President of the Senate Lacépède, the Ministers of War and Police, Talleyrand and Champagny.

Clarke, emphasising the indefensible position of Paris, proposed the immediate departure of the Empress and the King of Rome. The contrary opinion was hotly maintained by Savary and Champagny, who implored Marie-Louise to remain.

Boulay-de-la-Meurthe went so far as to beseech the Empress to betake herself to the Hôtel de Ville and call the Parisians to arms—a strange situation indeed for a Habsburg!

Talleyrand, contrary to the views he had previously expressed, took the side of Champagny and Savary. (Later, asked why he had given advice harmful to the cause he was already secretly supporting, he answered that his stock was so low that he had only to suggest a thing for them at once to do the exact opposite.)

A vote was taken—and the majority decided that the Empress and her son should not leave Paris. Then Joseph read out to the Council an extract from Napoleon's precise instructions for the present situation, instructions sent as long ago as 8th February (see note following Letter No. 26), and confirmed on 16th March. A second vote was taken; Marie-Louise, with the little King, was to leave at dawn for Rambouillet.

Marie-Louise accepted the verdict with resignation; the decision had been taken for her.

[Paris] 29th March 1814

My Darling, I am writing one more note before leaving. They insist on my going, only M. Boulay and the Duc de Cadore, with myself a third, are opposed to the idea. I should have been quite brave enough to stay, and I am very angry that they wouldn't let me, especially when the Parisians are showing such eager determination to defend themselves, but my opinion carries no weight at all in this matter, and the Arch-Chancellor told me it was absolutely essential for me to leave; if so, may God's will be done, but I'm certain you won't like it, it will undermine the courage of the National Guard and the enemy will be in Paris tomorrow. They say they have advanced no further during the night, but have sent out partisans in the direction of Rambouillet; it seems it would be better to be captured by the Cossacks than to stay quietly in Paris! But the whole lot of them have lost their heads, except me, and I hope in a day or two you will be telling me I was right in not wanting to evacuate the capital for a mere 15,000 cavalrymen who would never have got through the streets. I am really angry at having to go, it will have terrible disadvantages for you, but they pointed out to me that my son would be running into danger, and that was why I daren't contradict them once I had seen the letter you wrote to the King. So I am putting myself into the hands of Providence, quite sure it will turn out badly. I kiss you and love you with all my heart.

Your true and loving Louise

Nevertheless, indecision prevailed until the very last moment. Dressed in her travelling-clothes, Marie-Louise was obliged to receive the officers of the National Guard on duty at the Tuileries, who besought her to remain. With no word from King Joseph, the Empress lost her nerve; going back to her room, she angrily tossed her travelling-hat on to the bed, sank into an armchair and began to weep: 'Oh God! If only they would make up their minds and put an end to this anguish!' Modern research has proved that Marie-Louise was right in assuming that it would have been difficult to force an entry into the capital if only it had been defended: the narrow streets of Paris would have offered insurmountable obstacles to any such advance.

Flight and Abdication

On 29th March, ten green travelling-coaches bearing the imperial coat of arms, drawn up around the Coronation coach covered with tarpaulins, waited for Marie-Louise in the Place du Carrousel. Amidst an escort of Guards, the carriages passed the toll-gate of the Pont Royal and slowly traversed the well-known route along the *quais* and across the Place de la Concorde. Driving up the Champs-Elysées, the procession passed the Arc de Triomphe, which was little more than a wooden corridor, and took the road to Versailles. The Empress was accompanied by her Palace Ladies, her Equerry, Prince Aldobrandini, several Chamberlains, Cambacérès and La Bouillerie, Minister of the Treasury.

In the evening they halted at Rambouillet, where Marie-Louise received a letter from King Joseph in Paris advising her to continue her journey.

Disobeying the Emperor's express commands, most of the high dignitaries had remained in Paris instead of following the Empress. Putting forward a variety of pretexts, Talleyrand too slipped away there. Thus Paris was prevented from becoming a second Moscow, and the presence of these dignitaries was to assist the Allies in the formation of a provisional government with which they could negotiate.

[139]

[Rambouillet] 29th March 1814, 10 *p.m.*

My Darling, I wrote you a note this morning before leaving Paris, and since then I have received a letter from the Duc de Bassano dated the 27th, I desperately needed some reassurance about your health just now when we are so cruelly harassed. I am so wretched, Darling, and take the gloomiest possible view of everything, God knows how it will all end, I tremble for you and for all the consequences which will follow the surrender of the capital, no good will come of it, I only know that at this moment, more than ever before, I long to find some way of proving to you the full warmth of my love and the depth of my devotion; I have never rebelled so angrily at being a mere woman, because it means I shall be no use to you at all.

We have had such a melancholy journey. I set out at 10 o'clock; before leaving I saw the King of Westphalia and he entrusted to my care his Queen, whom he is sending with us; the Arch-Chancellor told me I had no choice but to see him at such a moment as this, he told me he would stay with King Joseph in Paris. Your son and I were in the same coach, and the poor little fellow was really touching, he was twice as demonstrative with me as he usually is; we had the greatest difficulty imaginable in making him leave Paris, he was determined not to come out of his room, he kept clinging to the doors and the chairs, and sobbing and screaming out, 'I don't want to go to Rambouillet, I want to stay at home.' He is quite well, and the journey hasn't tired him at all, he even ate ravenously on the way.

I am tolerably well, but very tired after a whole night without sleep. I saw the Queen of Westphalia and Madame just after they had arrived here, they are not at all well. This very moment I have received a letter from King Joseph advising me to leave here for fear of patrolling bands of cavalry, he says there are something like 60,000 men around Paris; so tomorrow I shall spend the night at Chartres, I can't undertake longer journeys because of the horses, as we are obliged to travel with ordinary stable horses. I think it will take several days to reach Tours if I have to go there.

I enclose a list of the people I have brought with me, I hope it will meet with your approval, most of them have asked to come with me. When can I hope to hear from you? Just at the moment I am afraid I'm going to be beset with a host of worries and anxieties—if only nothing happens to you and we can see each other again soon! That is the only wish of

Your true and loving Louise

The list referred to above is missing from the letter.

From Rambouillet they set out again for Chartres, the Coronation coach lagging in the rear, laden with equipment, military boots and sabretaches. During this stage of the journey, Marie-Louise took the little King into her own carriage since Russian scouts were ranging the countryside. The King of Holland joined her at Chartres, followed by Joseph, who left the capital after ordering Marmont and Mortier to surrender.

[140]

[Chartres] 30th March 1814, 8 *p.m.*

My Darling, I received your letter of the 28th on the way here, I am grieved to see you were left so long without news of me, I feel certain that the first news you do get will distress you very much, but it can't possibly make you as miserable as all this makes me. I do hope Paris was able to hold out until you could get there; I am very angry at being compelled to leave, all the more so as I fear you may not approve. I assure you I could quite well have stayed, if there had been no greater danger than that of failing in courage; I'm surprised myself that I have so much, and I'm really very pleased with myself.

Your son has stood the journey remarkably well, he sends you a kiss and is keeping well; he made as much fuss and noise about leaving Rambouillet as he did about leaving Paris; this evening he's full of fun and is playing as well as he can without any toys.

I am fairly well, but very tired and worried. King Louis came to join us this morning, he was so scared that he wanted us to move into a fortress; I stood out against the idea, he has lost his head so completely that he is becoming a great nuisance. This morning he wanted to make me give an order to Queen Hortense to send him his Children, which she refused to do and very rudely. However, I pointed out to him that I couldn't interfere in things like that, and I did no more than just write to the Queen, who had asked my advice, saying she would do well to come and join us and that, moreover, the King wanted his children. I hope you'll think I did the right thing.

I am waiting here for news; if it is good I shall stay in Chartres, if not, they want me to go on tomorrow to Châteaudun, from

there to Vendôme and then to Tours. This very moment I have
heard that Paris is still holding out, I long for it to do so until
you can get there; meanwhile I am still planning to leave for
Châteaudun tomorrow at 9 o'clock. I'm off to bed now, dead
tired. All my fondest greetings.

Your devoted Louise

Leaving Troyes on 30th March, Napoleon took an open carriage at
Sens and drove at high speed to Fontainebleau, which he reached at
11 o'clock in the evening. Setting out again immediately for Paris, he
stopped half an hour later to change horses at the posting-house at
La Cour de France. There he heard that Paris had surrendered. After
a last stand by Marshal Moncey at the Porte de Clichy, the armistice
had been signed in a café at the Batignolles.

[141]

La Cour de France, 31st March [1814], *3 a.m.*
My Darling, I came here to defend Paris, but it was too late. The
city had been surrendered in the evening. I am assembling my
army in the direction of Fontainebleau. My health is good. I suffer
at the thought of what you must be suffering.

Nap

Napoleon continued his journey to Fontainebleau, which he reached
at 6 a.m. on 31st March.

[142]

[*Chartres*] *31st March* 1814
My Darling, I am trying to send you news through a channel
which seems to me fairly safe. Your journey towards Paris is
causing me the cruellest anxiety, try to let me have news of you
as often as possible. It is absolutely essential that I should hear
from you, I am so worried and ill, I *must* know that you are well.
I am just going to get into my carriage to continue my journey.

Your son is well, he is in high spirits and very fit. I send a kiss
and love you dearly.

Your Darling Louise

[*On the back*: To His Majesty the Emperor and King—The
Empress.]

[143]

Fontainebleau, 31st March [1814]

My dearest Louise, I have had no letter from you. I fear you must be taking the fall of Paris too much to heart. I beg you to be brave and to take care of your health, which is so precious to me. Mine is good. Give a kiss to the little King, and love me always.

Your Nap

From Chartres, Marie-Louise went on to Châteaudun, where she was wretchedly housed in the Hôtel de la Poste. King Joseph's sister-in-law wrote to tell her husband that the Allied entry into Paris had been accomplished 'with a high degree of order', and that the Faubourg Saint-Germain had displayed the white cockade of the Bourbons. To Napoleon, however, the loss of the capital was by no means the end, and he waited for his marshals in order to inform them of a new plan of campaign. It would, he thought, be possible to move to the Loire, where he could rejoin the Empress and the ministers, then set out again with a remodelled army.

[144]

Châteaudun, 1st April 1814, 10 *a.m.*

My Darling, Just the briefest of notes today to thank you for your welcome letter of the 31st, which I received at 3 o'clock this morning, those few lines have done me a lot of good, I simply *had* to know that you were well and near at hand. However, I am still very uneasy, it makes my heart ache to think of you all alone there, and so few people with you, I'm terrified that something may happen to you. The very idea of such a thing makes me quite wretched. Let me hear from you as often as possible, I live in a constant state of anxiety, and when I am unhappy, I just *have* to know that you love me and are not forgetting me.

The King writes to say that you have sent him word I am to make for Orleans or Blois, so I'll go to Blois, I think we shall be safer there. The enemy has been very close to Orleans once already. I am going to spend tonight at Vendôme and tomorrow night at Blois, it is only a 16 league journey, but I am travelling with your horses, and we can't do more than 10 leagues in one day.

Last night we slept in a really horrible place, in the vilest of

148

inns, but luckily your son had a good room and that was all I cared about. He is wonderfully well, and just at this moment is crying because he wants some toys. Heaven only knows when I shall be able to get some for him!

I am not very well, but you know I'm not without courage, so don't be anxious. I can find strength to do all that will still be necessary to ensure our safety. God grant that you may soon give us news of yourself and news of peace at the same time. I want nothing else in this world, meanwhile, believe me as long as life shall last

Your true and loving Louise

On 1st April, in the evening, Marie-Louise reached Vendôme, where she stayed with the Marquise de Soisy.

[145]

[*Vendôme*] 1st *April* 1814, 9 *p.m.*

My Darling, This morning I sent you a courier with news of us; this evening, though very weary, I want to write you another note about something which seems to me fairly important. General Caffarelli[1] has just sought me out to explain what serious overcrowding would ensue in Blois if all the Kings and Princesses stayed there. The town is very small, and accommodation is exceedingly limited; if, by any chance, we had to leave in a hurry, there would be the most frightful congestion. The King and Queen of Westphalia have a dozen German officers with them, they may be quite decent men, but they may equally well be adventurers or spies, as no one knows who they are. Another thing, the Princes and Princesses insist that they and their households should be fed at your expense, which is going to be terribly costly just at the time when you ought rather to be exercising the greatest economy, and it is going to be a serious financial embarrassment to us. General Caffarelli has pointed all this out to me and asked me to decide that, with the exception of King Joseph, they should all go somewhere else. I said I could hardly do that, so that's why I am sending you a courier whom I have told to wait for your answer, I think a decision is urgent.

I have also learnt that King Joseph had ordered M. de la Bouil-

---

[1] Palace Governor to the Empress.

lerie to leave a wagon containing two and a half millions at Rambouillet, in case you needed money, so that the treasure is not all together in one place; I am writing to tell you because I don't know whether you have ordered this move or not. The King wanted to make me go to Tours, I said I wouldn't unless you told me to; terrible epidemics of prison fever are raging there and killing off 60 people a day, so you can imagine how dangerous it would be to go there; both your son and I might catch some disease.

Your son sends you a kiss, he is keeping very well. I too am fairly well, we have had quite a good journey, we reached Vendôme at 5 o'clock, and there we were housed rather more comfortably than at Châteaudun; we shall reach Blois tomorrow. They say all will be well with us there, and we shall be breathing good air. This evening the King ordered the English prisoners who are there to be evacuated, they are the ones who were at Verdun. I long to hear that you are back at Fontainebleau, I am so anxious about this. I beg you to let me have a speedy answer to this letter of mine. I send a kiss, and love you dearly.

Your Darling Louise

On that same day, Napoleon visited Marmont's division, which was still covering Fontainebleau. The Emperor had not the least suspicion that very soon Marmont was to go over to the enemy. He learnt that a Provisional Government had been set up in Paris at the instigation of Talleyrand. On 2nd April, Napoleon reviewed two divisions of Guards which had arrived from Troyes. On the same day, the Senate voted his deposition.

[146

Fontainebleau, 2nd April [1814]

My dearest Louise, I was very sorry indeed to hear from your letter that you were ill at ease and worrying. I beg you to compose yourself and to keep in good health. You know how vital it is to my happiness that I should know you are easy in your mind. I will arrange that we meet as soon as possible. My health is very good. Give a kiss to my son and never doubt your

Nap

On 2nd April, her wedding anniversary, Marie-Louise arrived at Blois, where she installed herself in the Préfecture. The following day was a Sunday, consequently there was the family dinner-party, a small reception and games. In spite of the gentlemen's boots and the ladies' travelling-costumes, Court life was taking shape again just as at Saint-Cloud in peace-time. There was to be a Council of Ministers, and the Empress was to receive the town officials.

[147]

[Blois] 2nd April 1814, 10 *p.m.*

My Darling, Tonight I have received the second of the letters you wrote on the 31st, it has given me so much pleasure, in fact the only joy I am capable of feeling at a time when we are so harassed. I am delighted to see that you are well in spite of all the hardships you have had to endure, I assure you I feel them as keenly as if I had actually shared them with you.

Since arriving here I have seen an auditor, M. de Pallavicini, who left you at four o'clock yesterday; I overwhelmed him with questions, all the details he gave me about your health were very reassuring, I need to hear the comforting news repeated over and over again. Believe me, Darling, when I say that I have plenty of courage; I feel we are going through a time when we need it more than ever, and I am fairly calm, but very sad at heart; I don't think anything but peace will restore my spirits, you really should give it to us soon.

King Joseph and the Arch-Chancellor showed me, this morning, a letter from the Duc de Bassano touching on several matters and prompted by my stay here; they are going to argue it out tomorrow morning; the Arch-Chancellor would like them to send you some intelligent person capable of giving you a verbal account of all the business transacted, they haven't yet decided who it shall be. Meanwhile I should much prefer us to stay here. We are much better accommodated than we could be in Orleans or Tours, there is no sickness here, and the air is excellent for your son. In any case we shall have to stay here all tomorrow, we have travelled over such frightful roads; the escort, which has just ridden 50 leagues in 5 days, is absolutely exhausted, and the horses which brought us need a day's rest too.

Your son sends you a kiss, he has stood up to the journey remarkably well, he is delightfully gay, and at such a happy age, I often envy him, he is a charming travelling-companion and not the least bit of trouble; he is such a sweet-natured, pleasant child that even people who hardly know him can't help taking to him.

I am fairly well, we have driven 10 leagues over shocking roads and in such mud that we could only go very slowly, so I am extremely tired. I am staying here at the Préfecture, where I am wonderfully comfortable, and so is your son, we have a splendid view over the Loire. Tomorrow morning I shall receive the town officials, I couldn't very well refuse as I'm making a stay here.

I have just this moment sent the billeting-officer to Orleans to investigate the lodging situation and find out whether there is any room; they say it already contains more than 10,000 people in excess of the normal population. He is coming to give me an answer tomorrow.

I shall also hold a Council of Ministers tomorrow. The Honourable Gentlemen think that in our present circumstances you should allow me to send you someone who could ask you a whole host of things which can't be put into writing, as for example to discuss which place I ought to withdraw to if I had to leave Orleans. If you really want us to send someone, I beg you to tell me who it is to be.

This very moment I have received your letter written this morning, I am delighted to have news of you so promptly, your remark about the possibility of our meeting soon has given me immense pleasure and is the only consolation left to me just now. Meanwhile I promise I will take care of my health. I am deeply touched by all you say about my being essential to your happiness, but my chief conviction is that no one loves you as tenderly, or longs to give you such manifold proofs of her devotion as

Your true and loving Louise

Without actually saying so, Napoleon was counting on the fact that Marie-Louise might intervene with the Emperor of Austria.

[148]

Fontainebleau, 3rd April [1814], *3 p.m.*

My dearest Louise, I have received your letters of April 1st and
2nd. I hope today's rest at Blois will have restored you and dis-
pelled your fatigue. I am very anxious about your health. You
take things so much to heart that I fear you may not be able to
bear up under it; that is one part of my worries. Do try and take
heart and keep well. Give a kiss to my son, and never doubt my
love.

Nap

The note written at 3 o'clock in the afternoon had scarcely been
dispatched when Pallavicini handed to Napoleon the Empress's letter
of 2nd April. Three hours later, the Emperor sent her fresh instructions. At 6 o'clock he conferred with his marshals, whose intention it
was to persuade him to abdicate. He dismissed them.

[149]

Font[ainebleau], 3rd April [1814], *6 p.m.*

My Darling, The auditor Pallavicini has just arrived and given
me news of you. You may: 1) remain at Blois; 2) send me whom
you please and take things upon yourself; 3) issue proclamations
and call meetings, as the Provisional Government of Paris does;
4) write a very strong letter to your father, commending yourself
and your son to his care. Send the Duc de Cadore to Vienna.
Make it clear to your father that the time has come for him to
help us. Good-bye, my darling, keep in good health. All my
love.

Nap

At the Council held at Blois on 3rd April, King Joseph, after hearing the news of the Emperor's downfall, was relieved of his duties as
Lieutenant-General. The Empress addressed to the nation a proclama-
tion intended to safeguard the rights of her son—but France left it
unread.

The minutes of the session were sent to the Emperor, and the following letter was the last written by Marie-Louise as Regent.

153

[Blois] *3rd April* 1814, 8 *p.m.*

My Darling, I have had no news from you since yesterday evening, it seems such a long, long time, I hope I shall be lucky enough to hear tonight and to know that you are still safe and sound at Fontainebleau.

Yesterday I held the Council of Ministers about which I wrote to you yesterday evening; all the Gentlemen were unanimous in advising me to remain in Blois until we have received an answer from you. They think there are many objections to staying in Orleans, and all these disadvantages are going to be set before you in the minutes of the meeting which are to be sent to you this evening. M. de la Bouillerie is also of the opinion that the treasure should not be sent there either, he is afraid it will be too near the main theatre of the war, and that in the event of unfortunate developments he would have no time to get it away. They have reached various decisions about all the other matters mentioned by the Duc de Bassano in his letter to the Arch-Chancellor; the Minister of Police is to be responsible for editing a newspaper in which the bulletins you send us will be printed. The Ministers ended by asserting that, in view of present conditions, peace is absolutely indispensable and must be concluded at all costs; the Honourable Gentlemen propose writing to you on the subject and setting out their various motives, I only pray it may be possible, because that would bring us together and put an end to so many of the troubles and anxieties we have endured for so long.

I saw M. de Nicolaï[1] after dinner this evening, he left poor Paris a quarter of an hour before the enemy entered it, but you probably have more recent news than that. Today at 5 o'clock I received the town officials, and as they had asked to see your son I took him with me; they thought he was the sweetest child one could possibly imagine, he had just wakened up and so had a marvellous colour. He is very well and has been out in the fresh air all day on the terrace near his room, it has done him a world of good.

I am keeping fairly well, I have been for a walk in the garden from which there is a wonderful view over the Loire; you can see the turrets of the château of Chambord in the distance.

[1] Chamberlain.

I have had the family to dinner and have just come back to finish off my letter. King Joseph told me you were sending us the Grand Marshal, I can hardly wait for him to arrive, I am hoping he will give me good news of you, at any rate it won't be for lack of questioning; I simply must have frequent news of you if I am to keep up my courage, which comes near to deserting me at times; our position, indeed, is far from favourable, and since I'm the person who loves you most, I worry endlessly on your behalf, but I won't go talking about such depressing subjects, I feel it may upset you, and you have quite enough troubles as it is. So I'll end by assuring you that there is no one in the whole, wide world who loves you as dearly as

Your true and loving Louise

Obeying Napoleon's request, Marie-Louise next day, through the Duc de Cadore, addressed to her father a letter which was just 'one long cry of distress, one string of reproaches from the daughter whose father had deceived her'. 'Paris', she wrote, 'would have been more stoutly defended if they had not believed it to be occupied with your consent.' She opened her heart to Napoleon.

[151]

[Blois] 4th April 1814

My Darling, This morning I sent you a note by King Joseph, but I don't want to let the orderly go without giving you further news of us. The Duc de Cadore left 2 hours ago, taking a copy of my letter in case one of them should be intercepted. I am hoping and longing for him to return soon with good news. Really you have been unhappy far too long, you who so richly deserve happiness, but I won't talk about that, I feel I shall be making you very sad if I tell you all that is in my heart.

We are going to take steps to lessen the congestion in Blois, and in order to achieve this we shall endeavour to divert elsewhere crowds of people who have arrived here since my departure. The Honourable Gentlemen have thought it expedient to give the Minister of Police power to open the Minister of War's dispatches in his absence. The Arch-Chancellor has also advised me to invest M. Re[g]naud de St. Jean d'Angély[1] with the

[1] President of the Home Affairs section of the Council of State.

155

powers of Secretary of State to the Regency until the Duc de
Cadore returns.

Your son sends you a kiss, he is very well indeed and has been
playing hard all day, the bad weather has kept him indoors, but
that hasn't prevented him from being extremely lively.

I am fairly well, I was so afraid you were worrying needlessly
about my health that I very nearly got M. Corvisart to make out
a bulletin so as to set your mind at rest, I hope in the meantime
you will believe me, on my word of honour. Fondest greetings
from

Your true and loving Louise

Before the Duc de Cadore could reach the neighbourhood of Dijon
where the Emperor Francis was staying, the irrevocable step had been
taken. On 4th April, the marshals compelled Napoleon to abdicate in
favour of the King of Rome. The Emperor sent them to the Allied
sovereigns to plead the cause of 'Napoleon II'. He wished to inform
Marie-Louise officially of this first abdication.

Already on 5th April, adopting the suggestion of the Tsar Alexander, the Allies had fixed on the isle of Elba as the place of exile. On
the 6th, the Tsar learnt of the defection of Marmont's corps, which
deprived Napoleon of his last means of resistance. Supported by
Talleyrand, Alexander then insisted on a definitive abdication. Informed of the exile awaiting him, Napoleon signed the fateful Act,
and sent it to Paris at dawn on 7th April.

[152]

Fontainebleau, 7th April [1814]

My dearest Louise, I have received your letter of 6th April. I am
glad to hear that your health is bearing up. I was very much
afraid that the disagreeable events now taking place might have
gravely impaired it. I am very much concerned about you and
my son, and but little about myself, as you may well suppose.
My own health is good. Give a kiss to my son and write to your
father every day, so that he may know where you are. Good-bye,
my dearest Louise; it grieves my heart to think of your trouble.
All my love.

Nap

At Blois, Marie-Louise spent the day in anguish of mind. The courage of which she had still boasted when she left the capital had now entirely deserted her. She felt herself lost in 'a whirlwind of intrigues and treachery'. Some advised her to join Napoleon at Fontainebleau, others—the Emperor's brothers and sisters—recommended her to take refuge with her father. Bred to passive obedience, Marie-Louise could neither act nor react.

[153]

[Blois] 7th April 1814

My Darling, Today I am sending my letter by a very safe means, by an aide-de-camp of the Prince de Neufchâtel,[1] so I can tell you everything I have done since this morning. I am very worried at not hearing from you more frequently just when you are miserable and exposed to such danger; the only thing in the world I want at this moment is to join you if I possibly can, I should be braver and calmer, knowing that I was sharing your fate; I will do everything in my power to comfort you for all the reverses you are suffering, and will try my utmost to be of some use to you. You know me well enough, Darling, and I promise that my presence shan't worry or distress you, so do, please, let me come.

I fear the Duc de Cadore cannot have reached my father, for rumour has it that the Russians are intercepting all letters which might tell him what is happening, so I have made up my mind to send him another messenger through Dijon; the Gentlemen have decided that M. Re[g]naud de St. Jean d'Angély would be the most efficient person. I have given him the same letter I gave to the Duc de Cadore, telling my father I knew of all the generous proposals you had made for the good of France, and that the enemy had refused to accept them. I have told him [St. Jean d'Angély] to take a route along which we can be quite sure of being intercepted by the Austrians.

The Guard here has been rather discontented at not receiving the pay which was in arrears, so acting on the King's advice, I have ordered 500,000 to be put at M. Mollien's disposal to clear off these expenses.

I believe the Princesses and the Kings are seriously thinking of going somewhere else. King Joseph has told me they are utterly

[1] Neuchâtel (Berthier).

and completely destitute, he said that, on leaving, you had told him you would put two millions at his disposal, so he was going to ask me to give one hundred thousand crowns to each of them, making nine hundred thousand francs in all. You really ought to give orders about what is to be done with the treasure, and where it is to be put; I am afraid it will attract the attention of the Cossacks.

Chartres is captured and the English have already appeared at Saintes, so that Tours is not very safe. That was one more reason for our decision to stay in Blois—*where are we to go next?* Our situation is dreadful, but yours is even more so, it really breaks my heart. You simply must send someone to tell me what I am to do, they have all lost their heads here, every single one of them.

Your son sends you a kiss and is very well, he is so happy, poor little fellow, and suspects nothing amiss—how very lucky he is!

My health is good; in serious crises it keeps up well enough to enable me to cope with any orders you care to give me; I shall be so happy when I am with you again. I am sending a courier who will wait for your reply, I beseech you not to leave us in this cruel uncertainty. Besides I want you to answer the questions I have asked in this letter. A kiss to you, and I love you dearly.

Your true and loving Louise

At Fontainebleau Napoleon learnt of the decision reached by the Allies. He directed Colonel Galbois to convey to Marie-Louise the news, skilfully veiled, of his final abdication, together with instructions about the redistribution of the money in her care at Blois. These instructions make it clear that the Emperor was thinking in terms of a lengthy separation.

[154]

[*Fontainebleau, 8th April* 1814]

My Darling, I have received your letter of the 7th. I was glad to see your health was better than was to be expected, considering the anxiety you must feel. A truce has been agreed upon, and one of the Russian Emperor's aides-de-camp was to join you for the purpose of escorting you to this place; but I sent word for you to stay in Orleans, as I myself was on the point of setting out, pending such time as Caulaincourt shall have settled affairs with the Allies. It was Russia's wish that I should be given sovereignty over the isle of Elba, and that I should remain there, and that you should have Tuscany for your son after you, which would have enabled you to be with me as long as it suited you, and to live in a pleasant country favourable to your health. However, Schwarzenberg objects to this in the name of your father. It appears that your father is our deadliest enemy. So I do not know what has been settled. I am sorry to have nothing left to offer you but a share in my evil fortunes. I would have put an end to my life if I had not thought that would but double your misfortunes, and make them heavier to bear. If Mme Montesquiou wishes to finish the King's education, she is free to do so, but she must not lay too great sacrifices upon herself. I suppose Mme Mesgrigny is returning to Paris. I do not know what the Duchess will wish to do, I fancy, however, that she will first wish to accompany you. You must have 1,000,000 given to King Joseph, and the same amount to King Louis, to [King] Jérôme, to Madame, to the Prin[cesses] Pauline and Elisa, which accounts for the 6,000,000. Issue a decree to that effect, and let the Princesses proceed to Marseilles and Nice via Limoges, which will lessen your difficulties. Your State Councillors and Ministers may return to Paris. Take 1,000,000 in gold with you in your coach. Have the same amount conveyed in the King's. Submit a scheme to me for reducing your Household to such as are kindly disposed and necessary to you. Two ladies are sufficient to have with you. It will make travelling easier. Beauharnais and Aldobrandini will follow later. Have wages paid to all up to 1st July, including those who are to follow you. We shall travel with the Court teams and the saddle-horses.

Good-bye, my dearest Louise. I pity you. Write to your father and ask to be given Tuscany for yourself. As for me, I want nothing but the isle of Elba.

Good-bye, my darling. Give my son a kiss.

[Napoleon]

When news of the abdication reached her, Marie-Louise was aghast. 'My father', she said, 'told me twenty times over when he placed me

on the throne of France that he would always stand by me, and my
father is a man of his word.' She kept her tears for the privacy of her
own room, and when she emerged, declared her wish to leave with
Galbois for Fontainebleau. She actually had a carriage prepared in
secret, but just as she was entering it, the Duchesse de Montebello
forced her to disclose her intentions, which she opposed with such
persuasive words that the Empress finally abandoned her project. She
went back indoors, whilst 'the dear Duchess' sent a secret warning to
the Austrians. Contrary to Savary's belief, she made no mention of the
possibility of assembling fifty thousand men to carry on the struggle
—on the contrary, in a fresh letter to her father, conveyed to him by
St. Jean d'Angély, Marie-Louise implored him to intervene.

The morning of Good Friday, 1814, marked, in fact, one of the
cruellest phases of the Empress's ordeal. Her retinue thought only of
abandoning her, her orders were no longer obeyed. Watching her, and
biding their time, were Joseph and Jérôme, hopeful of bringing off an
underhand deal. Marie-Louise was their ransom, whom they were
determined at all costs to keep, for she and her son were a most
valuable currency with which, one day, they might strike an excellent
bargain.

So the two brothers-in-law moved in to the attack. They declared
that Blois was no longer safe, and that she would be well advised to
give herself up to the Austrians, who alone could offer asylum, both
to her and to themselves. This she resolutely refused to do, whereupon
Joseph flew into a towering rage and Jérôme began to threaten.

[155]

[*Blois*] 8*th April* 1814

My Darling, I am sending a courier, an intelligent man, to implore you to give me your orders, and to beg you most earnestly
to let me come and join you, for they are upsetting me most
dreadfully here. There are 100 Cossacks at Châteaudun.

The King came this morning to persuade me to throw myself
into the arms of the first Austrian Corps I could find. He said
they would follow me, as that was their only hope of safety, and
the Emperor of Austria guaranteed their future; he said it was no
use telling you when there was not a moment to be lost and
when you might possibly disapprove of such a step.

I replied that I thought it would be treachery on my part,

that as long as there was breath left in my body I should continue to be loyal to you, that moreover I was not at all sure that
the Austrian Corps at Lyons had not been won over by the
Russians, and that I had no desire to throw myself on their
mercy. He told me those were feeble reasons, and the King of
Westphalia said they would positively compel me to leave by
force. Then I agreed to go to Rambouillet, but not a step further.
However, just as he was hoping to give orders for our departure,
the officers of the guard came into the courtyard and declared
they would never allow me to be forced into leaving, indeed
they had resolved to let themselves be hacked to pieces for you,
your son and me—they said they knew an attempt was being
made to force me to leave and go over to the Austrians, and
they would have no part in it unless you or I gave them a direct
order, and if your brothers were afraid they had only to get out;
they told all and sundry that they would rather be killed than
desert your son. We calmed them down and they went away
well-pleased. Then I told the King that I positively would not
go, that everyone agreed with me and that I wished to await
your orders, that made them furiously angry, but I don't care;
I'm above all that sort of thing.

So now I am waiting for orders from you, and I do beseech
you to let me come. I have made certain arrangements which I
will tell you about myself. One thing is quite certain—we can't
possibly go to Bourges, as we have heard extremely bad reports
of M. de Sémonville.[1]

Your son and I are both well. I send you a kiss, and love you
with all my heart.

Your true and loving Louise

P.S. I am enclosing a letter from the Minister of the Interior.

Foiled in their plan, Joseph and Jérôme withdrew. The former,
through the good offices of his sister-in-law Désirée, who was still in
Paris, sent a letter to the Tsar, who 'on several occasions' had 'shown
himself kindly disposed towards him'. By the 10th Joseph had left
Marie-Louise; later, both he and his wife were to beg the protection of
the Emperor of Austria.

Panic-stricken and with the additional fear of being captured by the

---

[1] Special Commissioner in Bourges.

Russians, Marie-Louise sent by the Comte de Saint-Aulaire a third letter to her father, begging him to grant her asylum in his territories. The arrival of the Tsar's aide-de-camp, Count Paul Schouvaloff, and the Baron de Saint-Aignan, the representative of the Provisional Government, reassured her. They informed her that they were about to accompany her as far as Orleans (which she regarded as being on the road to Fontainebleau). She had no idea that the Tsar had decided that husband and wife were never to meet again in any circumstances whatever, and that orders had been given to use force, if necessary, to prevent a reunion.

The two envoys confirmed that the Allies had offered Napoleon sovereignty over the isle of Elba. For Marie-Louise this was yet another disappointment; she would have preferred it to be Tuscany.

[156]

[Blois] 8th April 1814

My Darling, Just a note to tell you that I am leaving tomorrow morning for Orleans and that I shall be at Fontainebleau the day after tomorrow. I simply must see you and share your sorrows.

Your son is keeping well. I am really ill and have a high fever, I still hope to have strength enough to be able to drag myself as far as Fontainebleau, regardless of what may happen to my health afterwards. I love you and send you an adoring kiss.

Your true and loving Louise

In his reply, Napoleon gave no orders, as Marie-Louise would have liked him to do; he merely expressed the wish that the Empress should join him.

[157]

Fontainebleau, 9th [April 1814], 5 *p.m.*

My Darling, I have just received your letter of the 8th, delivered by a courier who had set out on the 8th at 2 o'clock in the afternoon. Saint-Aignan and the Emperor of Russia's aide-de-camp had arrived, so this courier said, an hour before he set out. You will therefore have been in Orleans this morning; you may stop there if you are travelling with your horses. If you have post-horses, and if you wish to come on to this place, you may do so, but I am writing to you this evening by the courier you sent me. How I sympathise with all your troubles, and fear lest it should impair your health! A kiss to your son. All my love.

Nap

Still under the impression that Schouvaloff and Saint-Aignan would accompany her as far as Fontainebleau, Marie-Louise left Blois on 9th April, protected by a detachment of the Guard. Her departure was the signal for a general dispersal. She distributed gifts to those of her Court who were going back to Paris. Only a few remained with her now. To this phase belongs the incident, reported by several historians, of the Empress being deprived of her jewels by an envoy of the Provisional Government.

Talleyrand, so the story runs, contrived the release from prison of 'a certain Dudon', entrusting him with the mission of going to Orleans to take possession of the diamonds and jewels given to Marie-Louise by Napoleon. Dudon is even said to have demanded the pearl necklace she was wearing around her neck, whereupon she threw it in his face. Further outrageous acts are also alleged to have been committed. According to M. Jean Savant (see Appendix, 'Note on Baron Dudon', p. 243) this 'certain Dudon' was a Baron Dudon who, far from being released from prison in 1814, was an official of the régime, imprisoned in error for only two days in 1812, and who had not been near Orleans. The fact that Marie-Louise makes no mention of the episode may be taken as an almost conclusive argument in support of this theory.

The last coaches accompanying the Empress were, however, exposed to pillaging Cossacks, and Marie-Louise arrived at Orleans in a pitiable condition. Horrified at the looting, she addressed three letters to her father, again imploring his protection, telling him that she was 'dying of fright', and terrified that 'they' wanted to take her to Orleans against her will. She placed the blame on the Provisional Government and not, as has been asserted, on King Joseph. The following letter is a decisive one.

[158]

[Orleans] 10th April 1814, [morning]

My Darling, I have received the two letters you sent by M. Anatole Montesquiou, I am grieved to hear of all your troubles, my only desire is to be able to comfort you and to prove how

163

dearly I love you. I am convinced that I can powerfully influence my father's mind, I have just written to him begging to be allowed to go and see him, and I have made up my mind not to go away with you until I do. I am certain that I could work strongly upon him, and that in doing so I should be acting in the best interests of your son. If I cannot see him for several days, I will join you later, bringing, I am convinced, better news than anyone expects, for you can have no doubt of my loving devotion and of all the tender care with which I shall endeavour to comfort you.

I am not sending the list of people making the journey with me. Mme de Montesquiou and the Duchesse de Montebello have decided to come with us so far, and after that to go back to be with our [=their] children.

And now, Darling, I tell you once again that I am determined not to leave until after I have seen my father; I firmly believe it to be my duty, and in the interests of both you and my son. Besides, my physical and moral strength has been all too gravely undermined by the anxiety I have endured on your behalf, I am ill and in such a state that I am quite unfit to move from here, but what upsets me most of all is the sight of your misfortunes, my only wish is to share them with you, in the meantime I send you a kiss and love you with all my heart.

Your true and loving Louise

If you agree to let me go and see my father, I feel sure, almost positive, that I can get Tuscany.

In Orleans, the rout and confusion continued unabated.

[159]

[Orleans] 10th April 1814

My Darling, I wrote this morning to thank you for your two letters. I am most eagerly waiting for news of you, I need to hear from you frequently at a time when I know you are sad and so beset with cares. At least you must be feeling like that, judging from my own state of mind.

I am still clinging hopefully to the idea that I might see my father; he has a kind heart, he will be moved by my tears and so your fate will be less harsh, because although you will be going to stay on the isle of Elba, you will have sovereign rights also in the territories they will probably assign to us, and by that I mean Tuscany.

Everyone is asking permission to leave us, it makes me just disgusted with this world when I see so many ungrateful people in it. The Duchess and M. Corvisart have asked to accompany me as far as Leghorn, M. Méneval too. Prince Aldobrandini declared he would do no such thing. Two of my first ladies are coming, and 3 of my second, and since all my son's Household, even, I believe Mme de Montesquiou, are deserting him, we might put one of them to be with him.

I have had money given to various people I am leaving here, I thought you would approve of my doing so, I asked M. de la Bouillerie to give me 900,000 for that purpose.

I have said nothing about the dreadful state of my health, which is growing more and more disordered every day. At this very moment of writing I have a high fever and am spitting blood. My only wish is to have strength to bear all these shocks, but it is ebbing away and I feel as if I need to rest and be cared for. Rest I shall find only when I know and see for myself that you are happy and contented, and resigned to your sad lot. That is the only happiness I want, next to that of always being loved by you. However, I am expecting great things from the overture I have made to my father, so I shall wait here most impatiently for news that I am to be allowed to see you. I love you and kiss you with all my heart.

Your true and loving Louise

P.S. This evening I saw M. Anatole Montesquiou, he made me long more than ever to be with you, I hope you will be more fortunate than fate seems to promise.

List of the persons who wish to accompany me.

The Duchesse de Montebello
Madame Brignole
General Caffarelli
M. Corvisart
M. Méneval
Mme Kastener [Katzener, a red lady]

Mme Rabusson [Lectress]
Mme Durand [a red lady]
If I can bring only 2, I should prefer to have the first two.

Ladies of the Wardrobe

Mme Eduard [a black lady]
Mme Geoffroy
Mme Barbier [a black lady] is not at all certain that her
husband will let her stay on the island, but Mme. Aubert,
who would like to come and is in Paris, would take her
place if necessary
A wardrobe maid

The Treaty of Fontainebleau, which confirmed Napoleon in possession of the isle of Elba, secured also to Marie-Louise the Duchies of
Parma, Piacenza and Guastalla.

The Emperor Francis, who disapproved of Schouvaloff's interven-
tion at Blois—for Marie-Louise, once separated from Napoleon, was
his responsibility alone—fell into line, and Metternich was equally
accommodating in not happening to be in Paris when the Allies
declared their resolve not to treat further with Napoleon, or with any
members of his family. He arrived only on 15th April.

Fully aware that Marie-Louise was hesitant and uncertain, Napoleon
asked his secretary Méneval to 'find out what the Empress really intended to do'; would she rather follow him to Elba, or retire with her
son either to Parma or to her father? The Emperor finally induced her
to make the voyage to Elba with him. Since Fontainebleau was so
near the enemy outposts, a meeting was arranged at Briare, and the
Emperor Francis could easily be seen 'on the way'.

[160]

Fontainebleau, 11th [April 1814], 9 a.m.
My Sweetheart, I have received your letter. Your troubles are all
graven on my heart; they are the only ones I cannot bear. Do try
and live down adversity. This evening I will send you the
arrangement that has been made. I am given the Island of Elba;
you and your son Parma, Piacenza and Guastalla. This means
400,000 souls and an income of 3 or 4 millions. You are to have
at least one mansion and a beautiful country to live in when you

tire of my Island of Elba, and I begin to bore you, as I can but do when I am older and you still young. Metternich is in Paris; I do not know where your father is. You should contrive to see him on your way. If you cannot have Tuscany and your fate is settled, ask him to give you the Principality of Lucca, Massa, Carrara and the Enclaves, and ask furthermore for your Principality to have an outlet on the sea. I am sending Fouler to see about all the terms. As soon as all is done with, I shall go to Briare, where you will join me and we will proceed via Moulin and Chambéry to Parma, and then embark at La Spezzia. Aldobrandini will accompany you during the journey. I approve of all the arrangements you are making for the little King; if Mme Boubers will come, she would be a suitable person to bring him up. My health is good, my courage unimpaired, especially if you will be content with my ill fortune, and if you think you can still be happy in sharing it. Good-bye, my darling; I am thinking of you, and your troubles weigh heavily upon me. All my love.

Nap

On that same day, 'Madame Mère' and Cardinal Fesch left Marie-Louise in order to seek the safety of Rome.

[161]

[Orleans] 11th April 1814, [evening]
My Darling, I am very worried at not having heard from you, I badly need news just now when so many problems are crowding in upon me. I simply must know that you are happy, and until I do, I can have neither rest nor peace of mind. I am waiting with the utmost impatience to hear from you, and from my father too I hope, granting me permission to go and see him. I am hoping that the sight of me will move him deeply, so that he will listen when I plead your son's interests, and consequently yours too. I hope to get something out of him, and will try to see him for that reason, even though it might cause me great pain and distress, for I am still quite ill and very weary; I assure you that if it were not for remaining alive to comfort you, I should be perfectly content to die, but I want to live so as to try to bring you some consolation and to be of some use to you.

167

Your son is well. Madame asks me to send you her letter, she has just left me to go to Rome with the Cardinal. She is very dejected, and told me she wanted nothing better than to share your fate and to join you. M. de la Bouillerie is leaving today, so the treasure is being left quite unguarded, consequently I have told them to put four millions, instead of 3, into our coaches, it will always make a little more money for you. You really should remember poor M. Méneval, he is determined to follow me to the ends of the earth and to settle wherever I make my home, but he is in dire straits for money and his debts amount to 200,000 francs, according to what I have heard; you really ought to give him a lump sum of 150,000 francs to pay off a part of them. He richly deserves it for his devotion to you. I am waiting to hear from you about this.

I have had 500,000 francs given to Mme de Montesquiou to share out amongst my son's servants, and I shall give something to mine too. Your generous heart will, I know, approve of this. Do try, Darling, to keep well, the certainty that nothing ails you is essential to bolster up my own wretched health, which will soon have no more resistance left after all the shocks it has undergone during the last two years. I am taking good care of myself whilst waiting for my father to send word that I can go and see him. Spare an occasional thought for her who has never loved you as devotedly as she does at this moment.

Your true and loving Louise

Worried about her health, Napoleon advised Marie-Louise to ask Corvisart whether she could follow him to the isle of Elba, and whether she could endure its climate.

[162]

Fontainebleau, 11th [April 1814], 7 p.m.

My Darling, I have just received your letter of the 11th this morning. Your anxiety and the state of your health wrings my heart. Tell me whether the plan of going together to Parma suits you; you could go from there to the spas at Lucca or at Pisa. Enquire of Corvisart which of these spas is more likely to agree with you. Bausset will deliver this letter; you will receive another which I will write to you when I have seen Caulaincourt, whom I am expecting tonight. My health is very good. I am full of courage; why is yours not like mine? I would willingly share it with you. Your letters are crowded with the emotions that fill your heart; they touch me profoundly and comfort me; I wish I could do as much for you. I am having Méneval written to. Good-bye, my dearest Louise, my misfortune vexes me more for your sake than for mine. All my love.

[Napoleon]

Corvisart, 'that low-down dog Corvisart', whom the Emperor was later to call the family oracle, examined the Empress and gave it as his opinion that a long and difficult journey would be beyond her strength; nothing but the waters of Aix-en-Savoie could cure her. The climate of Elba was out of the question both for her and for her son. Marie-Louise, naturally enough, accepted the reasons he gave.

[163]

[Orleans] 11th April [1814], 11 p.m.

I have just this moment seen General Fouler,[1] who has brought me your sweet letter; believe me, Darling, all my happiness will consist in comforting you and proving to you that I love you most devotedly. I don't know yet whether Mme de Boubers wishes to come with us, I should be delighted if she did, as she is an excellent person. I am waiting for you to give the word for me to join you, I hope I shall be strong enough to bear the journey, if you will just allow me to stop a few days in the middle, as my chest is not very good. M. Corvisart still thinks I need to exercise great care and to take the waters, but I shall not do so until I have seen that you are quite contented and happily settled somewhere.

I shall write to my father tomorrow, meanwhile I am going to bed, as I am very tired and not at all well. Mme Brignole will come with me if you will be good enough to let her. I shall try and arrange to see my father on the way. Good-bye, my Dearest, I love you and kiss you with all my heart and soul.

Your true and loving Louise

[1] Equerry to the Empress.

Full of anxiety, Napoleon reassured his wife about the hardships and discomforts of the journey to Elba.

[164]

Fontainebleau, 12th [April 1814], 10 a.m.

My Darling, I have received your letter in reply to the one Fouler delivered to you. I am very much concerned at hearing you are so dejected and in such bad health. I hope my care for you, and the expression of the love I bear you, will do you good and restore your health. I am expecting Caulaincourt. I will write to you immediately. They offer to give me back a battalion of my Guard, 1,100 strong, in Provence, and thence to the isle of Elba. We will travel as slowly as your health requires. Good-bye, my dearest Louise, the change in my fortune only affects me on your account. Love me well, and never doubt your

Nap

I fancy we might meet at Briare or Gien, whence we would proceed by way of Italy or Provence.

The Emperor was relying on Marie-Louise herself to find a way of escape, but by 12th April time was already running out. On that very day, Sainte-Aulaire, who had been dispatched from Blois, returned from Paris bringing Marie-Louise a letter from Metternich. Whilst seeking to reassure her, he invited her to go to Rambouillet, there to await the arrival of the Emperor Francis. Metternich had already commanded Prince Esterhazy and the Prince of Liechtenstein to call upon her in Orleans.

Faced with this dilemma, the Empress began to waver in her resolve.

[165]

[Orleans] 12th April 1814, [morning]

My Darling, I have this very moment received the letter you sent me by M. de Bausset. I promise you I will be brave, I am hoping that in a few days I shall feel strong enough to rise above circumstances, and show myself worthy to be yours. But just now, when I am receiving so many tokens of devotion and attachment from those who are leaving me, my heart cannot help but be most cruelly torn.

M. de Sainte-Aulaire has just brought me a letter from M. de

Metternich, in which he says they guarantee me an independent future, and the same to my son, and that whilst waiting for the details to be settled I had best go to Austria until everything is in order; at the same time he told M. de Sainte-Aulaire that even if I did not go (which you can well imagine) my father was extremely anxious to see me; don't you think I had better wait here until he says I may go and see him, then join you immediately afterwards, as it seems impossible for me to see my father on the way? M. de Metternich writes that my father will arrive in Paris tomorrow, so I shall wait here for your reply to this letter, I beg you to let me have it without delay.

Meanwhile I have made all my plans for the journey, I shall take more than five millions with us in the coaches, and as I had certain expenses to pay out, I have drawn the March and April allowances together, I am sure you would approve; besides, I was glad to be able to send a little money to those of my women and staff who are left behind in Paris with nothing to eat.

I am not at all well, but nevertheless I hope I shall be able to bear the journey as far as Parma; I shall rest there, if you agree, and afterwards go and take the waters. Corvisart says that the baths both at Lucca and Pisa are equally unsuitable for me; as he will be with me for some time, he proposes to talk to you about it himself on the journey, but he still insists that I rest at Parma and follow a course of treatment there. So before joining you, I shall wait here for your courier to bring a reply, I do beg you to let me have it immediately.

Prince Esterhazy is due at any moment, I will write and tell you what he has said. I send you a kiss and love you with all my heart.

Your true and loving Louise

Marie-Louise did her utmost to dispel those suspicions about her conduct which she felt to be awakening in Napoleon's mind.

[166]

[Orleans, 12th April 1814, afternoon]

My Darling, I have sent you one letter this morning by a courier, and am writing you this second note just as I am about to get into the carriage to go to Rambouillet. Prince Esterhazy and the Prince of Liechtenstein have just arrived to beg me, on my father's behalf, to leave at once for Rambouillet, because your interests and those of your son were at stake; even the Duc de Vicence said so; I told them I could not leave without your consent, they said there was no time to wait for it, and that even if I wanted to go away with you without having seen my father first, they would do all they possibly could to prevent it. Consequently, I thought it wisest to yield with a good grace, I am in black despair at being compelled to leave like this without seeing you, the very thought of it plunges me into such depths of misery that I don't know what will become of me; but please, Darling, don't be angry with me; I really can't help it, I love you so much that it breaks my heart in two; I am so afraid you might think it is a plot I and my father have formed against you. However, when I have seen him, I shall come and join you, it would be sheer barbarism to prevent me, and even if they wanted to, I assure you they could never do it. I long to share your misfortune, I long to care for you, comfort you, be of some use to you, and charm away your cares. I feel that if I don't do that, I can't go on living, and shall succumb to this last blow.

Your son is the only happy one here, he has no idea of the full extent of his misfortune, poor little soul; you and he alone make life bearable for me. I am taking him with me, I think he will touch my father's heart, and I shall be able to bring him back to you afterwards, for I'm determined to live with you; the more they want to part me from you, the greater need I feel to be near you, so that I can care for you. In the meantime, try at least to arrange for me to see you soon, and for me to write to you every day; I need it more than anything, I am so wretched and so ill that I feel I shall never survive all the misfortunes they are threatening to bring down upon us; but whatever happens, you can be sure that no one loves you and cherishes you as tenderly as I do, and I still live in hopes of being able to prove it to you before long. In the meantime, think of me sometimes, and spare a little love for the one who sends you an affectionate kiss.

Your true and loving Louise

I am leaving someone behind here to forward my letters to you, and to send yours on to me, and I feel sure that quite soon I shall be passing on some good news, or better still, bringing it you myself.

With the greatest reluctance Marie-Louise left Orleans on the evening of 12th April, since she could not, in conscience, refuse her father's request, when for a whole week and at the urgent instance of her husband she had been pleading for an interview with Francis I, now her only hope. In Orleans she left Joseph, who was to escape to Switzerland on the 18th. Of the convoy which had left Paris a fortnight before, only six coaches now remained.

A troop of Guards commanded by Cambronne had been sent by the Emperor to fetch the Empress away. By the time they reached Orleans Marie-Louise was already in Rambouillet.

Then began a *via dolorosa* which might have called forth heroic qualities from Marie-Louise if the stuff of greatness had been in her; but her soul was not cast in the mould of Corneille. The following note, hastily scribbled in pencil during the night of 12th April, folded in four, and entrusted to a loyal officer, betrays her fears and forebodings; she is answering the note written that same morning by Napoleon.

[167]

[Halfway between Orleans and
Rambouillet, 12th–13th April 1814]

I am sending you a few lines by a Polish officer who has just brought me your note to Angerville; you will know by now that they have made me leave Orleans and that orders have been given to prevent me from joining you, and even to resort to force if necessary. Be on your guard, my Darling, we are being duped, I am in deadly anxiety on your behalf, but I shall take a firm line with my father, I shall tell him that I absolutely insist on joining you, and that I shall not let myself be talked into doing anything else. We have brought away as much of the treasure as we could, I will get it through to you by every possible means, but I think it much more likely that I shall bring it you myself.

Your son is fast asleep at the moment, I myself am not at all well. I shall be quite firm about not going further than Rambouillet, you can rely entirely on my love and my courage when the times comes. I love you and send you a fond kiss.

Your Darling Louise

On that same tragic day, Caulaincourt brought from Paris to Fontainebleau the final draft of the Treaty of Fontainebleau. Realising at

Je t'écris un mot par un officier
polonais qui sort de me porter
à Angerville la lettre tu sauras
déja qu'un bon on a fait près de
d'Orléans et qu'il y avait des
ordres de m'empêcher de venir
te rejoindre même à raison
a la force. Sois sur te garder
mon cher frère on nous jure
je suis dans des inquiétudes
mortelles pour toi mais j'aurai
du caractère en voyant mon
père je lui dirai que je
veux absolument te rejoindre

Letter 167

last that he was to be separated from his family, Napoleon entrusted to the Grand Equerry a letter for Marie-Louise, in which he gave his consent to all that had been done, so that no blame should fall on her after his death, for he had made up his mind to commit suicide.

[168]

Fontainebleau, 13th [April 1814], 3 a.m.

My dearest Louise, I have received your letter. I approve of your going to Rambouillet, where your father will be joining you. That is the only consolation left to me in the midst of our misfortunes. For the past week I have been eagerly looking forward to the moment of your meeting. Your father has been led astray, and has behaved badly towards us, but he will be a good, kind father to you and your son. Caulaincourt has arrived. Yesterday I sent you a copy of the arrangements he has signed for ensuring a safe future to your son. Good-bye, my sweet Louise. I love you more than anything else in the world. My misfortunes only affect me in so far as they grieve you. As long as you live, you will be lavishing your affection on the most devoted of husbands. Give my son a kiss. Good-bye, my Louise. All my love.

Napoleon

Napoleon called for a small, red morocco portfolio, in which he had kept all the Empress's previous letters, and asked Caulaincourt to look after them so that he might hand them over to his son (soon to become Prince of Parma) when he was grown up. He then drank the poison prepared for him some time before, and which he always carried in a sachet around his neck. For several hours he was in agonising pain, then was overcome by attacks of vomiting. At about 11 o'clock on the morning of the 13th he began to recover. 'I am condemned to live', he remarked.

His letter of farewell was never seen by Marie-Louise—a fact which was not without consequences. As for the portfolio, it appears to have been returned to the Emperor by Caulaincourt and may perhaps be the one he was later to entrust to Joseph on 11th June 1815. (See p. 16.)

The deciding factor in Napoleon's renewed desire for life was the letter written him by Marie-Louise on the afternoon of 12th April, and which hitherto has been presumed lost. It reached him during the afternoon of the 13th.

The Prisoner

After travelling all night Marie-Louise reached Rambouillet at 9 o'clock on the 13th, and when she had written a note to her father, went to bed. Méneval reported that she was 'overwhelmed by the saddest thoughts as she came in here through the garden gates. . . . Her situation is that of a prisoner.'

Then began a confused exchange of letters, a welter of conflicting news, hesitations on the part of Napoleon, indecision on the part of Marie-Louise, which 'were to end in that final separation which neither had foreseen or desired'.

The following letter is not taken from the Bernadotte Archives; it has been published by Jean Hanoteau, in his commentary on the *Mémoires de Caulaincourt* (edit. Plon).

[169]

[Rambouillet] 14*th* [=13*th*] *April* 1814

My Darling, I wrote you a few lines yesterday by the Polish officer you sent me. Nevertheless I am writing again today, although I fear it may not reach you, but I just cannot bear the thought of not being able to keep in touch with you. I only hope you don't crave for my letters as much as I do for yours. I am bitterly unhappy and very sad, but am trying my hardest not to give way, so that I can comfort you the better, for my sole desire is to share your misfortune and to be able to help you in some way.

My father has not arrived yet. They say he is coming tomorrow. I am eagerly awaiting his arrival, so that I can join you immediately afterwards, wherever I may happen to find you.

Your son has borne the journey remarkably well. He really is a sweet child, and is growing more delightful every day. He has no intention of welcoming the Emperor of Austria very kindly, and I'm afraid he is quite set on this, no matter what we say to him.

I am still far from well. I am so unhappy away from you that I feel I shall only regain my full health and strength when I see you again. In the meantime I am dreadfully tired with travelling all night. The road was frightful. I went to bed the moment I got here. I do nothing but think of you. You are so kind, and so ill-fated, and you so little deserve to be. At any rate, if my warm, deep love could help you to look forward to some measure of happiness, you would still have plenty of it left to you in this world. My heart is torn by your sad plight. I must stop now. I feel I may be distressing you. I do beg you never to doubt the love and complete devotion of your own true

Louise

Napoleon's despair had given way to quiet resignation. He still cherished the hope that the Empress would accompany him.

[170]

Fontainebleau, 14th [*April* 1814], 1 *a.m.*
My dearest Louise, I am sending you General Flahaut, who will give you news of me, and bring back news of you. I know your health is not good and I fear travelling at night must have fatigued you. I myself am well, and longing for the time to come when we can set out. They tell me the climate is very fine in the isle of Elba. I am so disgusted with men that I am determined that my happiness shall depend on them no longer. You alone can affect it. Good-bye, my darling. A kiss to the little King, kind regards to your father; ask him to be good to us. All my love.

Nap

[171]

[Rambouillet] 14th *April* 1814, [*evening*]
My Darling, General Flahaut arrived at Rambouillet after dinner this evening, he has given me your welcome letter, you can

imagine how closely I have questioned him about you. I have been deeply moved to hear how bravely you are bearing your misfortunes; such courage is worthy of you alone. I tell you frankly that this crisis has made me too quite disgusted with the world and with mankind in general, as I have been witnessing such ingratitude and treachery for some time now. I think the isle of Elba is the only place which will suit us, and I could live happily there with you for company.

My father has not arrived yet, meanwhile I have had a letter from him dated the 12th, he said he was at Troyes and could not be in Paris before today, so I shall have to follow the advice of Metternich, who is his only real friend, and who in consequence will have some consideration for his daughter and his grandson. One thing disgusts me in all this—it is that he never says a single word about you, but I will pass on your requests, and you can be absolutely certain of this, that nothing in the world will persuade me to go to Austria, for my place is beside you, and both my duty and my inclination draw me there.

Besides, if they *do* want to force me into going to Vienna, I shall pretend to be ill, because I really have a dreadfully sore throat and a touch of fever, I only got up to see M. de Flahaut, and had to go back to bed afterwards, I don't know what can be the matter with me, red spots are coming out all over my skin, and I'm afraid it may turn out to be measles.

Your son is wonderfully well, he and I have been for a stroll in front of the house, he talked a lot about you, poor child, I assure you I am taking extra, special care of him just now. I am treating him like a grown-up, and having him to lunch with me, which delights him and cuts down expenses a little, for they are very heavy. I have put M. de Bausset in charge of the catering so that he can read them a few lectures on economy, for it seems to me essential that you should save money.

I beg you to tell me what is to be done with the treasure, I have more than two millions here; it is a source of great embarrassment to me and I wish I could transfer it to you in bills of exchange. Meanwhile fondest love from someone whose only happiness is that of being with you again.

Your true and loving Louise

The 'black' forebodings which had troubled Marie-Louise soon returned; her first reaction, on hearing the Austrian demands, was a violent one.

[172]

[*Rambouillet*] 15*th April* 1814

My Darling, I am sending you just a little note by M. de Flahaut, I have instructed him to tell you by word of mouth everything he has managed to pick up here. I am very much afraid that we are being tricked, and that they want to prevent me from joining you, but I shall hold my ground, because I feel it would be a blow from which I could never recover; I love you far too much for that.

My father, or rather M. de Metternich, has just sent the Comte Paar to tell me that my father is reaching Paris today, and would very much like me to go and meet him, or else go to the Trianon, I said firmly that I had made up my mind to wait for him today, or even for a week if necessary, and to wait *here*, as I was not at all well, and had such a bad throat that I couldn't possibly go out of doors. I am convinced they are doing all this to drag me off to Austria, but I have made up my mind, whatever happens, not to consent to such an arrangement, I shall absolutely insist on going to join you, for my whole heart is set on it, because I hope I shall be able to comfort you once I get there. It appears that since my departure they have captured that part of the treasure which was in Orleans; I'm very upset about it for your sake, you must be short of money just now.

Your son is keeping well, he is very cheerful and particularly glad to be at Rambouillet; how lucky he is to be so young, he hasn't a care in the world and I must say I envy him.

I am in rather a poor way, I was feverish all night, I hope it will pass off, but still it's a good excuse for not going to the Trianon. Meanwhile I am very miserable at not seeing you, my courage has completely deserted me. I kiss you and love you with my whole heart.

Your true and loving Louise

In feverish impatience, Napoleon waited for more detailed news from Rambouillet.

[173]

Fontainebleau, 15*th* [*April* 1814]*, 4 p.m.*

My dearest Louise, You must have met your father by this time.
They say you are going to the Trianon for the purpose. I wish
you to come to Fontainebleau tomorrow, so that we may set out
together for that land of sanctuary and rest where I shall be
happy, provided you can make up your mind to be so, and to
forget worldly greatness. Give a kiss to my son, and never doubt
all [my love.]

- Nap

Through the courier, news has reached me here from Flahaut,
whom I sent to you yesterday.

On 16th April, Marie-Louise went to meet the Emperor Francis at
the gates of the château at Rambouillet. The interview was anything
but affectionate, as students of the period (Bertaut amongst them)
have maintained. In the greatest agitation, and speaking in German,
the Empress reproached her father, and her eyes brimming with tears,
put her son into his arms. 'Maman Quiou' had experienced considerable difficulty in persuading the child to be civil to his grandfather: he
declared over and over again, 'He's Papa's enemy, and I won't see
him.' The following letter from Marie-Louise is the first known
account of the meeting, except for a note from Metternich to Talleyrand. It differs from the theories put forward by the historians, since
it proves how profoundly shocked Marie-Louise was to learn of the
veto imposed by Francis I. She was still far from complete acquiescence.
Metternich was present too; no further mention was made of
Tuscany.

[174]

[*Rambouillet*] 16*th April* 1814

My Darling, My father arrived just two hours ago, I saw him
straight away, he was most kind and affectionate towards me, but
it was all cancelled out by the most dreadful blow he could possibly have dealt me; he forbids me to join you, or to see you, he
won't even let me accompany you on the journey. In vain I
pointed out that it was my bounden duty to follow you; he
declared he did not wish it, and said he wanted me to spend two

months in Austria, then go on to Parma, and from there I could go and see you. This last blow will be the death of me, the only thing left to wish for is that you can contrive to be happy without me, for there can be no happiness for *me* apart from you.

M. de Flahault will bring you this letter, I implore you to send me news as often as possible, I will write to you every day and shall be thinking about you continually. Do try and take heart, I am hoping to be able to join you in the month of July, I haven't mentioned such a thing to these Gentlemen, but I've set my heart on it.

My health is going from bad to worse. I am so wretched that I just don't know what to say to you, I beg you again not to forget me and to believe that I shall always love you and that I am deeply unhappy. I send you a kiss and love you with all my heart.

Your true and loving Louise

Little by little, Marie-Louise began to accept the idea of going to Vienna instead of following Napoleon to his 'isle of rest', but not before she had shed many bitter tears. When 'the little King' asked her for news of 'Papa', her heart was 'near to breaking'.

[175]

[Rambouillet] 17th April 1814

My Darling, I have spent a sad and troubled night, the shock of being separated from you for several months is so painful that I cannot bring my mind to accept it yet, and I shall never be resigned to it. I am dreadfully sad at the thought of not seeing you, the Duc de Vicence will have been able to tell you how grieved I am, for I let him see the full measure of my sorrow; how dreadfully unhappy this must be making you too; I feel sure I should have been able to comfort you, that I should have soothed away your cares, and brought with me into your retreat that same disgust with mankind which you say you feel too, my only happiness would have been to make *you* happy, and now they have snatched from me this one and only consolation, so I'm desperately unhappy, but you simply must believe, Darling, that we shall be together again before four months have passed.

The Duc de Vicence has probably brought you money, I will keep back enough for my journey if you don't mind. I have just seen my father, who of his own accord showed every sign of promising to let me join you. I have told my father that once I get to Vienna, I want to go off into the country and receive no one at all, I said I was far too dejected and unhappy for him to insist on my seeing people; he has promised me I shall have my way, I want to avoid all the German Courts too, and would rather make a détour of several miles than be compelled to show myself in any of them. They tell me the Emperor Alexander is coming to see me the day after tomorrow, receiving him will be yet another sad experience; what further humiliations do you think we still have to suffer?

I shall be leaving here on Thursday, I don't know yet which route I shall take, I'll tell you tomorrow, because I want to write to you every day, and they are going to make it easy for me to get your replies, so if your letters don't seem to be reaching me, I shall ask you to send them by some other person, I simply must know that you are well and happy, it will help me to bear my misfortune.

Your son sends you a kiss, he is quite well, he has been very nice to his grandfather, he keeps asking about his Papa, and my heart comes near to breaking, and when he sees me crying, he asks me if I'm worried.

I am far from well, I still have a dreadfully sore throat, I'm afraid it may be turning into quinsies, I feel as if I ought to be longing for death when I'm parted from you. Believe, at any rate, that I love you most devotedly, and will remain my whole life long

Your true and loving Louise

Disappointed in the hope of taking his wife and son with him when he left France, Napoleon, in view of the health reasons put forward even by his father-in-law, resigned himself to a separation which he believed to be only temporary. He had, moreover, his own health reasons. Wishing at all costs to prevent her from going to Vienna, he directed Marie-Louise, in a letter sent by an orderly officer, the Marquis de Laplace, to proceed straight from Rambouillet to the spa at Aix.

[176]

Fontainebleau, 17th [April 1814], 6 p.m.

My dearest Louise, I have received your letter; it reveals the full extent of your distress, and thereby greatly increases my own. I am very pleased indeed to see that Corvisart is going with you. I am infinitely grateful to him; his noble conduct in this matter fully justifies the excellent opinion I had formed of him. Tell him so from me. Ask him to send me frequent short bulletins about the state of your health. Try to go straight to Aix to take the waters which I am told Corvisart has prescribed for you. Keep well, look after your health for the sake of your dearest love and of your son who needs your care.

I am about to leave for the isle of Elba, and from there I will write to you and will make all necessary arrangements for your reception. Write to me often, address your letters to the Viceroy, to the King of Naples and to your uncle if, as they say, he has been made Grand Duke of Tuscany.

Good-bye, my dearest Louise, my life will be wholly yours, and my feelings will never change. Give my son a kiss.

Your faithful Nap

In the Empress's entourage, talk turned again and again on the former infidelities of her husband. Bausset, in particular, took it upon himself to open her eyes.

[177]

[Rambouillet] 18th April 1814, [morning]

My Darling, I have just seen M. de Laplace, whom you have just sent with your very sweet letter, which touched me and moved me very deeply. He will tell you how much I long to join you, and how confidently I am expecting to find myself with you in the isle of Elba in a month or two. That is essential to my happiness. I am glad at least to know that your splendid courage has served you well in this crisis, it consoles me a little for the grief which possesses me. I promise to write to you every day, and if I can't send my letters off daily, I will send several at once by a different route. I do beg you too to let me have news soon and often. I will try again to persuade my father to let me go straight to the spa, but I fear I shall not be successful; however, I shall go on trying, and if I can't get my way, I shall go there in the month of June, then afterwards to the isle of Elba.

I have given your message to Corvisart, he was much moved, and begs me to tell you how grieved he is at the thought of not seeing you again, he is most sincerely devoted to you, and is giving ample proof of his attachment just now by staying with me when everyone is deserting you and abandoning me. He will send you a bulletin about my health at least once a week; in the meantime he says I am to tell you he is convinced that the Aix waters, and rest, will completely restore my health within a month or two.

Your son is well, he sends you a loving hug, you may be sure I shall take good care of him, and bring him back to you an exceedingly healthy and clever boy.

I am tolerably well, I have a touch of fever every night and again today, but it seems to be improving a little. I shall go on trying to get as much money through to you as possible, for I am sure you will be needing it. I am still expecting to leave on Thursday, but will write to you again before then. Believe me, my Darling, there isn't a single moment in the whole day when I am not thinking of you and sharing your troubles. I send you a loving kiss.

Your true and loving Louise

It has not previously been possible to date the following letter from Napoleon. From Marie-Louise's reply, written on the evening of 18th April, it is clear that it belongs to the same day. Anatole de Montesquiou, the governess's son, who had brought the letter from Marie-Louise, was immediately sent off again from Fontainebleau with the Emperor's reply, for Napoleon, expecting to leave on the 20th, had not a moment to lose.

[178]

[Fontainebleau, 18th April 1814]

My dearest Louise, Montesquiou has handed me your letter. The state of your health distresses me very much; try and bear up and take care of yourself for my sake and that of your son. Go direct to the spa, and try in that way to avoid Vienna. Méneval is being written to about money matters; have him show you the letter and give orders accordingly. My health is good. Laplace has doubtless delivered to you a letter from me; he left at 6 o'clock yesterday evening. I will write to you tonight. I do not think I shall be leaving before tomorrow [and then only] if everything is ready. Good-bye, dear Louise, love me, think of your best friend and of your son. Kiss him for me.

Nap

If what they say is true, the conduct of Aldobrandini and Beauharnais is frightful, and dishonours them and their heirs. Tell me about it very briefly; I cannot believe in such infamy.

Repulsed by the Bourbons, the Tsar Alexander made a point of showing a certain courtesy to the Bonapartes: he visited Joséphine, and wished also to see Marie-Louise and 'the little King'. In view of these advances, Francis I felt obliged to yield to the Tsar's wish to call on his daughter.

[179]

[Rambouillet] 18th April 1814, [evening]
My Darling, I have just this moment received your letter written today, it is *so* good of you to let me have news so often, it is such a comfort to me, and makes me very happy, if I can possibly be happy at a sad time like this, when we are being parted, but at least I need the consolation of knowing that you are well.

I still have a bitter experience in store for tomorrow, my father is sending the Emperor Alexander to see me; would you ever have believed I should still have to face meeting the man who is chiefly responsible for all the ill that has befallen us? However, I see now that I shall just have to resign myself to everything, but I shan't be happy until I am with you, far, far away from all mankind, that's where I shall be truly content.

My father has sent me his Grand Equerry today to show me a map of the route he has suggested I should take to Vienna, but all the same I shall try hard to persuade him to let me go to the spa; I have already mentioned it to him several times, but he won't let me do as I wish, and we are here under the protection of Austrian troops, who can do whatever they please with us. Nevertheless, I shall insist that I need to go to the spa, and immediately.

You told me to say something about the conduct of Pce Aldobrandini and Beauharnais; the latter took a long time to make up his mind, and did not leave Orleans until after I had gone myself, but the Prince left the day after I got there, without even asking to take leave of me, I know nothing of what they did afterwards, nor of what they said and did in society, for I scarcely saw anything of my attendants.

I have given instructions about the money, I fear it may be difficult to get as many bills of exchange as you want in Basle, but we shall do all we possibly can.

I am tolerably well, I tried to go riding for a few minutes so as to get a little fresh air, but it made me very tired.

Your son is well, all the Austrians who have seen him think he's wonderful; he had a slight cold this morning, but is fairly well tonight. Do, please, just give a thought to me tomorrow at the time when I shall be receiving the Emperor of Russia, the very thought of it makes my heart bleed. I send you a kiss, and love you with all my heart.

Your true and loving Louise

Napoleon endeavoured to reassure his wife about the climate of Elba.

[180]

Fontainebleau, 19th April [1814], 3 p.m.

My dearest Louise, I have received your letter of the 18th through Laplace; all he tells me has moved me deeply, and the hope that your health will overcome all the trials of fate bears me up. Isabey has brought me a portrait of you—the one in which you are holding your son in your arms. He has given me great pleasure by this gift of his. I think I shall at last be able to set out tomorrow and I hope to reach the *isle of rest* before 1st May. Have Méneval send an article on that island, written by an officer in the Engineers who lived there for 3 years. I am sorry to hear that people are indiscreet enough to weary you by untimely visits, in view of the condition of your heart. Good-bye, my Darling, love me, and never doubt the affection of your

Nap

Shocked by the news of the Tsar Alexander's visit, Napoleon urged Marie-Louise to 'uphold your rank, and face misfortune with steadfastness and courage'.

[181]

Fontainebleau, 19th [April 1814], 4 o'clock

My dearest Louise, Baillon[1] has just brought me your letter [dated the evening] of 18th April. I am sending him back for further news; he will join me at Briare, where I shall put up for the night tomorrow, and he will give me full particulars of your meeting with the Emperor Alexander. I pity you for having to receive such a visit, yet as he is devoid neither of tact nor of wit, I hope he will say nothing but pleasant things to you; but I do pity you if you have to receive the King of Prussia, who is as likely as not, albeit unintentionally, to say unseemly things to you. I am sorry to see you are not making direct for the spa, to which it would seem quite natural for you to go. At all events, I beg you to take care of your health and to be brave, so as to uphold your rank, and face misfortune with steadfastness and courage.

Good-bye, my dearest Louise. All my love. I will send you young Montesquiou tonight.

[Napoleon]

On the evening of 19th April, Napoleon again repeated the advice he had given that same afternoon. Raging and fuming like a wild beast in its cage, he returned again and again to the same subject; in the course of that one day, he wrote three times to Marie-Louise.

[182]

Fontainebleau, 19th [April 1814], 11 p.m.

My dearest Louise, I am sending back Montesquiou at his mother's request, and am entrusting him with this letter. He will give you news of me. I am leaving tomorrow at 9 o'clock in the morning, and shall put up for the night at Briare, where I hope to receive a letter from you before morning. I shall travel by way of Nevers, Moulins, Lyons and Avignon, I am sorry to think I

[1] The Palace Quartermaster.

shall be a few days without hearing from you. I hope you are in good health, that you will be brave, and uphold the honour of your rank, and of my destiny, without minding the hard blows fate has dealt us lately. Give a kiss to my son. Take care of him. Good-bye, my sweetheart. Yours as long as life shall last.

[Napoleon]

Two hours before he set out, Napoleon handed to Bausset the following letter for Marie-Louise. It was kept by the Prefect of the Palace.

[183]

Fontainebleau, 20th [April 1814], 9 a.m.

My dearest love, I am leaving to spend tonight at Briare. I shall set out from there tomorrow morning and shall not stop again until I reach Saint-Tropez. Bausset, who is bringing you this letter, will give you news of me, and will tell you that I am well, that I hope your health will stand the strain and that you will be able to come and join me. Montesquiou, who left at 2 o'clock in the morning, should have reached you by now. I had no news of you yesterday, but I am hoping the Prefect of the Palace will be with me this evening and will bring me some. Good-bye, my dearest Louise, you may ever and always rely on the courage, constancy and friendship of your husband.

Nap

A kiss to the little King.

In vain Marie-Louise implored her father to spare her a visit from the King of Prussia. These visits from the two sovereigns were deliberately intended by Metternich to draw public attention to the growing detachment of Marie-Louise from her French environment. Later, during the Congress of Vienna, there were even rumours of a possible divorce, followed by a marriage between Marie-Louise and the King of Prussia.

The Empress, however, was far from relinquishing her plan for a reunion. In her letter of 20th April—the longest, if not the most important, she wrote him—she confided to her huband what she described as a 'plan of campaign', a proof of the extent to which her trust in her father had been shaken. She would go so far as to consent to the actual journey to Vienna. Once permission had been given her to take the cure at Aix, there seemed, for the time being, no point in worrying her father about the return journey from Aix to Vienna. She was still determined to go direct from Aix to Parma, and from there to the isle of Elba. Napoleon was to make no mention of this in his reply, for she feared his letters might be opened on the way.

This plan of hers was the nearest she ever came to taking the initiative.

The account given by Marie-Louise of her interview with the Tsar clearly reveals the duplicity of Alexander, who was bending all his energies to the task of separating husband and wife. Her 'heart was dead' as she received him.

[184]

[Rambouillet] 20th April 1814

My Darling, I have just this moment received two of your letters brought by Bail[l]on; I am so grateful to you for sending me such frequent news, it gives me immense comfort, and you know how badly I need it just now when I am parted from you, perhaps for several months.

You can be quite certain I shall do my utmost to rejoin you, and I have already prepared my plan of campaign for doing so, and if you promise not to say a word about it when you write, I'll tell you all about it. I am going now to Austria, because my father has set his heart on it, and I can see that if I didn't go he would take me there by force. I have told him plainly that I want to go straight into the country, and that once there I shall see only my own family and no one else; my father said that in the month of June he would be entertaining all the German Princes, the Emperor Alexander and the King of Prussia, in Vienna; I told him in that case I should go immediately to take the waters, that they were most essential to my health, and that moreover it would give me a good excuse not to receive people the very sight of whom was bound to be disagreeable to me, and that I was expecting to go on from there to Parma and the isle of Elba.

My father said he didn't think I could go to Italy before the beginning of the winter, that nothing was planned and that I should have to go back to Vienna when I left the spa; he was most insistent about that; I didn't press the point, because for the moment I don't think it is any use opposing a plan which, in spite of everything, I shall never let him carry out when the time comes, but I don't want to seem too set on it just at present; so, *please*, don't say a word about it, because that would ruin the whole thing. I missed writing to you yesterday because I had no opportunity of sending my letter.

The Emperor Alexander has been to see me, he talked at great length about everything that has happened, to prove to me that it was through no fault of his that we were brought to our present situation. He made many fine professions of friendship, and asked me whether I was being taken to Vienna against my will, because if so, he would put a stop to it; I said I was quite content to yield to my father's wishes on this particular occasion, but that I had made up my mind not to stay there later on and to keep my independence, by which I set the greatest store, and that moreover I wished to go and join you.

This last statement displeased him, for he answered me very sharply, 'But, Madame, no one is going to prevent you, though you may possibly be making a mistake in going to the isle of Elba.' I said that duty and inclination alike impelled me to such a course of action, and that I was certain I should never regret it. He went out of his way to avoid mentioning your name to me; for the rest, he talked very volubly, especially during dinner, and afterwards he went to look at your son, whom he thought quite wonderful; he left at 4 o'clock. I tried to put on a brave face in front of him, but my heart was dead.

I hear that Baillon is coming to fetch the rest of the money; I shall hand it over to him as quickly as possible, but you really should leave me enough for the journey; it would be very hard for me to have to ask my father for it, especially at a time like this.

M. de Cussy[1] has asked to be attached to my personal suite, please tell me what to do about it, he has made up his mind to go wherever I go. M. de Bausset has asked to stay with me for 6 months. The Duchesse de Montebello, Mme Brignole, M. Caffarelli, Bausset, and St. Aignan are the only ones who have asked to accompany me on my journey [to Vienna].

Your son sends you a kiss and is very well indeed, he is full of

[1] Prefect of the Palace.

fun and in really good form, I am taking great care of him and am going to travel in short stages so that nothing shall happen to him.

My health is not very good; but that is the least of my worries at a time like this. I have asked them to send you that full-length portrait of me which used to be in your drawing-room at the Tuileries, as well as all the embroidered things I have made for you, I thought you would like to have them.

M. Anatole Montesquiou has just this minute brought me your letter, I have been plying him with questions about you, I was so grieved to see that Constant had deserted you; we've had ample opportunity of finding out which people are the ungrateful ones in this world.

I am just off to try once again to settle this business of the spa; I do hope I shall succeed, I should be so delighted if it could possibly be arranged, I can't think of anything more unbearable than spending the whole of my life in Austria; I will write and let you know the result of my negotiations; General Caffarelli, who is travelling to Paris this evening, will undertake to hand my father a letter in which I also ask him to arrange things so that I need not see the King of Prussia.

Do believe me when I say that I shall take every possible means of sending you news, meanwhile I love you and kiss you with all my heart and soul.

Your true and loving Louise

At 11 o'clock on 20th April, after a moving farewell to the Guard, Napoleon left Fontainebleau. Passing through Nemours and Montargis he reached Briare that same evening, and set out again on the 21st for Nevers.

[185]

Briare, 21st April [1814], *noon*

My dearest Louise, Laplace will deliver this letter to you. He is an excellent young man. He will tell you I am in good health. I am going to St. Tropez, I am leaving in an hour's time. I shall not stop on the way, I fancy I shall be there in 4 days. I am very satisfied with the disposition of the people, who are showing me considerable attachment . . . and love. I have had no letter from you since the 18th. The Palace Quartermaster has not arrived, which I put down to the lack of horses. Good-bye, my darling, keep in good health. Give my son a kiss, and never doubt

Nap

The Separation

Filled with mistrust, Marie-Louise began to number her letters from 23rd April onwards.

[186]

[Rambouillet], 23rd April 1814, *[morning]*

No. 1. My Darling, I did not write to you yesterday, as I no longer have any opportunity of sending you my letters, which makes me absolutely wretched, I still haven't got used to the idea of being quite a while, perhaps even more than a week, without hearing from you, it grieves me dreadfully, I expect you too will sometimes be just a little sorry at not hearing from me.

Thank you for the letter you sent me by M. de Turenne[1] and for the one M. de Laplace has just this moment brought me; I am delighted to hear you have reached Briare without mishap, your account of the love and devotion the people are showing you doesn't surprise me, they will soon come to regret you, and to realise what a loss they have suffered, and then they'll be sorry about it, but I won't go stirring up sad memories you are trying to forget, and which, since they are yours, are still most painful to me too. All I long for is to be able to join you soon in the *isle of rest,* and to reach the time when I can look back on all this as a painful dream—and may that be soon!—and I'm trying to keep up my spirits. I am numbering my letters, so that you can see whether any go astray.

This morning I had the promised visit from the King of Prussia, although I tried every possible means of avoiding it. He

[1] Comte Turenne, Master of the Robes to the Emperor.

only stayed half an hour and behaved fairly well; I was pleased
with the way he avoided all mention of subjects which might
have been displeasing to me.

Mme [Just] de Noailles[1] and her husband called on me yesterday, and didn't move me in the least, they came out of pure
curiosity, both of them looked radiantly happy and Madame had
lilies in her hat. Mme de Luçay,[2] the Duchesse de Plaisance[3] and
M. d'Andlau[4] have been to see me and behaved very handsomely.
They say M. and Mme de Beauvot[5] are behaving wonderfully
well.

I am leaving tomorrow for Grosbois, where I am to spend the
whole of Sunday with my father, and from there I shall continue
my long journey.

Your son is keeping well, he says I am to send you a kiss and
to tell you he loves you very dearly, he is charmed at the idea of
going on a long journey, and is full of chatter about the little bit
of it he has already done. What a happy age to be!

I have been tolerably well for the past two days, at least M.
Corvisart says I have. The poor man is in the depths of despair;
just imagine it, he has taken it into his head that you will think
him ungrateful because he didn't come to see you at Fontainebleau, and it's quite useless for me to insist that you think no such
thing, that on the contrary you would have been angry if he had
left me to go and see you at a time when I was ill, he is most
dreadfully upset about it, and sheds tears of remorse every single
day. He begs me to send you a letter, which I enclose.

I will finish this letter now, God knows whether it will ever
reach you, but I beg you to believe, even if you don't hear from
me, that I love you just the same and am full of despair at not
seeing you. I send you a kiss and love you dearly.

Your true and loving Louise

Corvisart who, during the stay in Orleans, was playing into Austrian hands by dissuading Marie-Louise from going to an Italian spa,
was slow to realise the fatal rôle he had played, more or less con-

---

[1] Talleyrand's niece.   [2] Lady of the Bedchamber.
[3] Sophie Barbé-Marbois.   [4] Equerry to the Empress.
[5] Prince Beauvau, whose wife, *née* de Rochechouart-Mortemart, was the
Empress's Lady-in-Waiting.

sciously, in thus facilitating the separation of husband and wife. His remorse is evident in the following letter which he wrote to Napoleon on the day after his departure for the isle of Elba:

Rambouillet, 22nd April 1814

Sire,

A grievous thought has arisen in my mind, discrediting that good opinion of myself which I had ventured to form, after receiving so many gracious tokens of Your Majesty's regard for me: it is that I have actually suffered Your Majesty to depart without expressing to You in person my bitter regrets and my profound sorrow! I should, Sire, be ungrateful and seriously at fault, where I not certain of finding, in the innermost depths of my conscience, an excuse which from its very motives will, I venture to believe, secure my pardon from Your Majesty's benevolent and understanding heart.

No sooner had a merciless fate constrained Your August Wife and Your illustrious heir to depart, than I hastened, Sire, to offer to them both every service that the most burning zeal and the most complete devotion could command from a body grown old before its time, and undermined by grief before its natural span of years. My presence and my ministrations, graciously approved by the Empress, made it incumbent upon me not to desert Her; and I have felt, Sire, as though I were in Your very presence, each time that duty has required me to attend upon her August person; I shall fulfil to the very end, Sire, this, the most absorbing and the most delightful of all my obligations, and the remembrance of fourteen years spent in Your Majesty's personal service, overwhelmed by innumerable proofs of Your kindness, and, I dare to say, of Your attachment, will be my only solace in the grief I shall bear with me even to the grave.

One word from You, Sire, one single word, and my fears will be dispersed, my uneasy conscience quieted, and my integrity, so sorely tried and shaken, restored again in its own esteem.

I remain, Sire, with the most profound respect, Your Majesty's most humble and most obedient servant,

Corvisart

On that same day Marie-Louise left Rambouillet, surrounded by an Austrian guard of honour. The journey proceeded by easy stages and two days were spent at Grosbois with the Prince de Neuchâtel. The Empress had one last glimpse of the domes of Paris. Berthier, all haste to reach the capital so that he might greet Louis XVIII, was somewhat cold in his manner towards her.

[187]

Provins, 26th April 1814

No. 2. My Darling, It seems an age since I heard from you, and for three whole days I have had no chance of sending you news; this time I am risking a few words through the post, quite possibly they will never reach you, but at any rate I shall have the consolation of leaving no stone unturned to get in touch with you.

Your son sends you a kiss, he is wonderfully well, the journey is doing him good, he is getting more and more intelligent every day, and is as fresh as a rose. He enjoyed himself immensely at Grosbois with my father, who seems passionately fond of him, which pleases me very much, but I shall only be truly happy on the day I can see you again.

My health is just about the same as usual, I caught a dreadful cold at Rambouillet, and simply can't get rid of it. We reached Provins in good shape yesterday evening; I shall be spending tonight at Troyes, which I am expecting to reach quite early. I hope you have had a good journey, and that I shall soon have the satisfaction of hearing that you have arrived safely. I send you a kiss and love you with all my heart.

Your Darling Louise

After leaving Nevers on 22nd April and passing through Moulins, Napoleon spent the night at Roanne. He set out again on the 23rd, and journeying all through the night in his travelling-carriage, as a safety precaution, reached Avignon at 6 o'clock on the morning of the 25th. To the south of the city he was insulted and threatened by the local population—it was the beginning of a most trying ordeal. On the 26th he found himself compelled to make for the Château Bouillidou, where he met his sister Pauline again. On the 27th, after an all-night journey, he arrived at Fréjus.

The Emperor was still troubled by the disturbing incidents which had occurred to the south of Avignon, but did his utmost to reassure Marie-Louise.

[188]

Fréjus, 27th April [1814], 3 *p.m.*

My dearest Louise, I reached Fréjus two hours ago. I was well-pleased with the disposition of France as far as Avignon; but from Avignon onwards I found people very much inflamed against me. I was very satisfied with the Commissioners, particularly with the Austrian and the Russian generals; tell your father this. I am leaving for Elba in two hours' time, and will write to you from there as soon as I arrive. My health is good, my courage undaunted; it could be weakened only by the thought that my darling no longer loved me. Give a kiss to my son. Princess Pauline, who is in a château 2 leagues from here, declares she is determined to come to the isle of Elba to keep me company, but she is so ill that I do not know whether she will be able to bear the journey. I have the Grand Marshal and my aide-de-camp Drouot with me.

[Napoleon]

The letter written by Marie-Louise on the 23rd was a great consolation to Napoleon; this was the first news he had received from the Empress since the 20th. He was even more reassured by Francis I's letter from Rambouillet, which gave him to understand that Marie-Louise, 'once restored to health and strength', would go to take possession of her estates, 'which would naturally bring her nearer to her husband's place of abode'.

[189]

Fréjus, 28th April [1814]

My Dearest, I have received your letter of the 23rd, informing me that you were going to Grosbois, and would continue your journey from that point. Your father wrote to me from Rambouillet a fortnight ago; I have just sent him the enclosed reply. I am expecting, in 2 hours' time, to go on board an English frigate which will take me across to the island in a very few days, and from there I will write to you by way of Leghorn, through the Viceroy. My health is good, the weather is fine and I shall have a smooth passage. I hope your health will remain good and that you will have the necessary courage. I shall be very glad to see both you and my son. Deliver the enclosed letter to Corvisart.

Good-bye, my dearest Louise. Pray give a very loving kiss to my son, and give my kind regards to all the ladies. All my love.

Your af[fectionate and] faithful husband

Napoleon

Marie-Louise drove through the enemy camps, passing burnt-out or ruined villages by the wayside. She stopped at Troyes and Châtillon-sur-Seine. On the 28th the procession reached Dijon, where Austrian soldiers were drawn up in line.

[190]

[*Dijon*] 28*th April* 1814

[No. 3] My Darling, I am seizing every possible chance of sending you a few lines, today I am sending my letter for my father to forward. It is really agonising not to hear from you more often, a week has gone by since I heard anything at all, I have spent the time in great sadness, my health is suffering from all this worry, and I've grown so thin that you would hardly recognise me, but don't worry about it; Corvisart says the Aix waters will cure me completely, but that if I were not to take them, my chest might become seriously affected, so I have decided to go there at the beginning of July.

Your son sends you a kiss, he is wonderfully well and is standing up to the journey quite marvellously; wherever he goes people go into raptures about his good looks, and I can tell you I vastly enjoy all the compliments that are being paid me on his behalf.

I reached Dijon yesterday, and saw the Mont Blanc in the distance, which greatly astonished your son. The weather is lovely, the countryside superb, but I'm not enjoying any of it, I shall only be happy when I know you have landed safe and sound. I send you a kiss and love you with all my heart.

Your Darling Louise

The letter never reached Napoleon. Another letter, however, written from Dijon by the Comtesse de Montesquiou, who was still in attendance on 'the interesting Child', did reach the isle of Elba. It throws an interesting light on the relationship between Marie-Louise and her son:

Dijon, 29th April 1814

Sire,

I have discovered an opportunity of sending Your Majesty news of Your interesting Child, and am hastening to take advantage of it. He is in the best of health, is standing the strain of his journey remarkably well, and is everywhere receiving proofs of the most touching interest. He has frequently asked for his Dear Papa and seemed disappointed that all this long journey he is making is not bringing him any nearer to him, I myself was most unhappy when I realised that we should have to forgo the pleasure of presenting him to you. I believed for some considerable time that the Empress would be going to see Your Majesty at Fontainebleau, and had I had the least idea that She would leave France without doing so, I should have asked Her permission to go instead of Her, so that I might bring him to You; unfortunately, however, my advice is not sought, and I often deplore that which is given, but am compelled to remain silent.

I beg Your Majesty to have no misgivings about the care I am taking of His dear Child. I wish I could have written to tell You that he was being taken to Parma, but it appears that the route we have taken leads in an entirely different direction. It was probably much more difficult to get the Empress to go to Vienna than it will be to keep her there. In Vienna, then, I shall spend the six months during which I am still to be with him. I dread the moment of our separation for the Child's sake, he grows more deeply attached to me every day, and proves it in a thousand different ways. Since he has noticed that a great number of people have already left him, he is terrified that I too shall do the same, and will not let me out of his sight for a moment. I very much hoped that these unhappy events would draw the Mother closer to her son, but there has been no change at all in that quarter. The friend is continuing to play her rôle to the very end, and is making full use of every moment and ... of every vestige of self-interest. I was delighted to see that the Emperor of Austria treated His grandson extremely well, I had some difficulty in persuading the Child to be civil to his Grandfather, he kept on saying to me, 'He's Papa's enemy, and I won't see him.' However, by dint of reasoning with him, I brought him to the point of being very nice indeed to him. It would, alas, take a good deal of reasoning to make me too accept all that has happened. I grieve and sorrow over this poor Child's misfortunes, and never shall I be reconciled to them.

I remain, Sire, with the most profound respect, Your Majesty's most humble and most obedient servant

Comtesse de Montesquiou

I enclose a lock of the Prince's hair in my letter. I thought it would give Your Majesty pleasure.

On 2nd May Marie-Louise crossed the Rhine, and her inmost thoughts, as she passed over the frontier, were reserved for her diary. She rested at Basle, where she received Napoleon's letter of 27th April. She found another, dated the 28th, waiting for her at Schaffhausen, and answered it immediately.

[191]

[Schaffhausen] 8th *May* 1814

[No. 4] My Darling, It is such a long time since I wrote to you, I can't think how to get my letters through, I can't even address them to the Viceroy, because he has gone to Munich. I have received your two welcome little notes of the 27th, one in Basle and the other today. You know how dearly I love you, so you can imagine what pleasure they have given me, but it was not un-mixed with sadness, the idea of your being exposed to the insults of the people has caused me deep distress, I have courage enough to bear my own personal misfortunes, but none at all for those endured by you.

I will write and tell my father that you were pleased with your Commissioner, he'll be glad about that. I wrote to him the other day [4th May] on the subject of money matters, you can be quite sure, Darling, that you are ever in my thoughts, that I want to settle your affairs in the best possible way, and that I long to prove how very devotedly I love you.

Your son sends you a kiss, he is keeping well, he has been just a little out of sorts for the past few days, but Corvisart said it was because he was eating too much cold meat during the day, so now we are stopping to let him take some soup. He is grow-ing extremely intelligent and talks wonderfully well, he is much admired by all who see him, they think him a very handsome child.

My health is tolerably good, though the journey is tiring me a great deal, but I am hoping the waters will restore me completely.

I have been marvellously well received everywhere, in France as well as in Switzerland. I have seen some lovely country, and the Lake of Zurich and Lake Constance, which are exceedingly beautiful, but just at the moment I am in no mood to enjoy the beauties of nature, I am far too sad, and quite insensitive to everything except the joy of getting your letters.

I was so glad Princess Pauline wanted to go with you, she has the kindest of hearts, but is exceedingly lucky to be able to follow you. I am waiting most impatiently for news of you, I do implore you to write to me very often; I am sending this letter by Pce Metternich, I can't think of any other way for the moment. I am staying here with the Pce de Waldsee, I shall leave tomorrow to cross the Tyrol and shall be in Vienna on the 20th, I will write to you at greater length from there; I will write again on the way there as well. I send you a kiss and love you with my whole heart.

Your true and loving Louise

This letter also was suppressed by Metternich.

Bulletin from Corvisart:

10th May 1814

H.M. the Empress is, up to the present moment, bearing fairly well the fatigue of a journey which is being made in comparatively short stages, interrupted by occasional periods of rest: Her appetite is keeping up well on the whole.

The cough, however, persists; it has been a dry cough for some time now: she is growing appreciably thinner every day: a kind of feverish diathesis (a condition which is not quite a true fever) comes on almost every evening, and ends before nightfall, or in the morning, with violent perspiration.

The time of her period will coincide exactly with the crossing of the mountains in the Tyrol: I do not know what effect this will have on its onset and course, which are usually fairly painful.

The young Prince's health is excellent.

Corvisart

On 29th April, Napoleon embarked in the English frigate *Undaunted* at Saint-Raphaël. The ship set sail at 11 o'clock. He landed in the '*isle of rest'* on 4th May, and at once sent off the following note to Marie-Louise.

[192]

Portoferrajo, 4th May [1814]

My dearest Louise, I have been 4 days at sea in calm weather, I did not suffer in the least. I have arrived in the isle of Elba, which is very pretty. The accommodation is but middling; I will have a home fitted up in a very few weeks. I have had no letter from you. It is a daily source of sorrow to me. My health is very good. Good-bye, my darling, you are far away, but my thoughts are with my Louise. A loving kiss to my son. All my love.

Nap

[193]

Portoferrajo, 9th May [1814]

My dearest Louise, General Koller, who has come here with me, and with whom I have been extremely pleased, is going back; I am sending this letter through him. Pray write to your father asking him to do something to show his gratitude to this general, who has been most considerate.

I have now been here 5 days; I am having fairly nice quarters fitted up, with a garden and in very good air, I shall be there in 3 days' time. My health is perfect; the island is healthy, the inhabitants seem to be of a kindly disposition and the country-side is fairly pleasant. All that is lacking is news of you and the reassurance that you are well; I have heard nothing from you since the letter you wrote me and which reached me at Fréjus.

Good-bye, my darling, give a kiss to my son and never doubt your

Nap

At the gates of Vienna, Marie-Louise found the Empress Maria-Ludovica waiting to meet her. This courtesy on the part of her step-mother, who was ailing, had been planned to refute any rumours of disagreement.

On 21st May, Marie-Louise at last reached Schönbrunn—the 'bad dream' was nearing its end. Since half-past two, two hundred and thirty carriages, crammed with spectators, had been waiting for her. Slowly,

like a funeral procession, the line of coaches entered the castle courtyard. At twenty past six, wearing a large travelling-hat, Marie-Louise
stepped from her carriage. A tremendous cheer greeted Francis I's
daughter. She withdrew at once to her private apartments, but was
obliged to appear for a moment at a window, pretending to read a
letter.

'What a heart-rending fate mine is!' she sighed in her diary, 'to
slip out of the Emperor's hands, and leave poor France! God alone
knows how great is my sorrow! How weak and powerless I am in this
whirlwind of plotting and treachery!'

Three days went by before she sent any news.

[194]

[Schönbrunn] 24*th May* 1814

No. 5. My Darling, I have not written to you for quite a long
time, which has distressed me very much, but don't reproach me
with forgetting you, that would be just about the most poignant
of all the sorrows I have endured up to now. I fear even this
letter may not reach you, but I keep on trying, and would rather
it went astray than have occasion to blame myself for missing a
chance of sending you news of my son.

How drearily the time goes by when I'm away from you! This
feeling of emptiness grows worse with every day that passes, and
I pray that I might see you again. Your welcome letter of the
24th [=27th April] was handed to me at Mölk, it was my father
who sent it on to me, I was delighted to hear that you had arrived
safely; the news took a long time to come through, and I can tell
you I was terribly distressed about it. I am glad too to hear that
you find the island pretty, I hope it has a good climate, and that
your health will be none the worse for it, I hope you will send
someone who can describe it all to me, I should simply bombard
him with questions; but there, I shall be putting you out of
patience by asking so many things. I want to embroider a piece
of tapestry for the furniture in your room, which I wish to be
beautified by no other hand than mine.

Your son sends you a kiss, he has never been better in health
than he is just now, he is growing and gaining strength in a
really amazing way, and is also becoming more lively and intelligent every day; people here think him very like you, and that is

one more reason why I love him so. I can't believe that the journey tired him so little, I have never seen him as rosy-cheeked as he is at the moment, he talks a great deal to me about you, and I to him even more.

I have been wonderfully well received here, and have been deeply touched by the way my step-mother and all my family have welcomed me, but I've been disgusted with myself because I haven't felt the slightest pleasure at seeing them again, I'm becoming quite indifferent to everything, I wish it could end in my having no feelings at all, it would be so useful.

My health is improving a little, I'm not quite so poorly, but am still not well, I'm so tired, but am hoping that the waters will restore me and that I shan't have to mention such a boring subject to you again, except to tell you that I'm perfectly well.

M. Corvisart asks me to convey his respectful greetings; he is obliged to go and stay in Paris for business reasons, but has promised to come back and join me at Aix in a month's time, in the meantime he is leaving M. Métivier [Mitwen] with me, and a surgeon named M. Hérault whom he recommends as being good.

The Duchess, General Caffarelli, M. de Saignan [=Saint-Aignan] are leaving on Monday too, so I shall be left alone with my melancholy thoughts, I like to commune with them, joy and happiness have gone out of my life for ever.

The Comte de Lobau[1] is arriving here today, he is to stay with me 3 days, I shall be glad to welcome him, he has been so devoted to you that I shall enjoy talking with him.

I beg you to send me some news of yourself, I am waiting for it with the utmost impatience, meanwhile I kiss you and love you very dearly.

Your true and loving Louise

Letters Nos. 6 and 7 from Marie-Louise are missing.

On 30th May 1814, peace had already been concluded in Paris. At Schönbrunn, Marie-Louise was installed in the left wing of the palace, surrounded once more by the familiar scenes of her childhood. She was still attended by a small French suite, and kept her French way of life. Openly professing her devotion to her husband, she endeavoured,

---

[1] Mouton, Marshal of France, who had been a prisoner of war in Hungary.

in her own way, to obey his instructions to 'uphold her rank and face misfortune with courage', but whenever criticism or complaint sounded too loudly in her ears, she did her best to give satisfaction. Thus, having heard derogatory remarks about the panels of her coach, which still bore the imperial arms of France, she ordered them to be replaced by her cipher.

From time to time Marie-Louise paid a visit to her grandmother, the aged Queen Marie-Caroline of Naples, sister of Marie-Antoinette. The implacable enemy of 'Buonaparte', who had formerly despoiled her of all her property, Marie-Caroline nevertheless reproached her granddaughter for having failed in her duty: 'Marriage', she said, 'is for life. If I were in your place, I should tie my sheets to a window and escape.' In spite of—or perhaps because of—these admonitions, the 'terrible' Queen won the heart of the less forceful Marie-Louise.

[195]

[Schönbrunn] 5*th June* 1814

No. 8. My Darling, At long last I have found an opportunity of writing to you again, God knows whether my letter will manage to get through. I am very upset at not having heard from you since the 4th [=3rd] May, I fear you are not getting the letters I write, that you will think I am forgetting you, and I assure you that would be the cruellest thought of all, but it is just as sad for me not to get your letters, and not to know whether you are well. I am very much afraid one letter has been kept back from me, General Koller simply must have brought one for me, and Pce Metternich has probably thought best to keep it on his table.

I am comforting myself with the idea that you do sometimes think about me, but perhaps I ought rather to want you to forget me, because then you would have nothing to worry about, whereas I, weighed down with care, and loving you more devotedly than ever, am spending whole days in despair because I can't see you.

The Duchess and M. Corvisart set out for Paris just three days ago, so now there are only two people left to whom I can talk about you, and even then I hardly ever see them.

I am rather better in health, but Corvisart insists on my going to take the waters, and once there, I hope I shall be left in peace, hearing no news of any kind and living as though I were not in the world at all. My father arrives on the 14th, I am expecting to leave on 30th June, and shall reach the spa on 10th July. M. Corvisart wants me to stay there two months so that I can take the two cures, but I am hoping to have finished in six weeks, and after that I shall go straight to Parma.

Your son will go there direct with Mme de Montesquiou, I can't take him with me to the spa as the accommodation there is very limited and it would add another 100,000 francs to our expenses straight away, and at the moment I am having to live very economically so as to have enough to set up my household in Parma, where there seems to be absolutely nothing, but all the same I shall go immediately. I don't mind having uncomfortable lodgings, if only I can get there. M. de Marescalchi has been appointed Imperial Commissioner.

I am leading a very quiet life here, and a very peaceful one; I go for walks in the park and am learning Italian and getting on quite well with it.

Your son, on the other hand, is delightfully gay, he has never been better in health and is greatly admired by everyone who sees him. People here think he is very much like you, which really delights me. The person here I find the most sympathetic is the Queen of Sicily, she has spoken so kindly to me and won my heart immediately. Your son talks about you a great deal, he's getting so sensible, he keeps asking me, 'when we shall see Papa', I should love him to have his wish granted soon, in the meantime I implore you to let me hear from you.

I kiss you and love you dearly, and beg you not to doubt my fond affection.

Your Darling Louise

Marie-Louise still clung tenaciously to the idea of going to Aix, having extracted a promise from her father that she might make the journey, but in a variety of ways the Viennese Court set itself to detach the 'Duchess of Parma' from 'Buonaparte'. They pointed out to her all the inconveniences of the journey, and affirmed that the waters at Carlsbad were equally efficacious, but on this occasion her passive resistance could not be broken down. Dimly apprehending their intentions, she bitterly reproached herself for having placed too great a trust in the promises of her father and of Metternich. She treated with reserve rumours current that the Bourbons were opposed to the idea of handing over the Duchy of Parma to Napoleon's wife. The following letter was taken to the Emperor by the Chevalier Wolodkowicz.

[196]

[Schönbrunn] 5th June [1814], 5 *p.m.*

No. 9. My Darling, Fortune is loading me with favours today by providing me with two different ways of sending you news. I only wish your letters could come by means which seem as safe as these, I need them so badly.

I wrote you a very long letter this morning, enough to re-assure you that I am tolerably well and that your son is in the best of health, so I would rather take advantage of this safe opportunity to give you some other details about certain things which are worrying me very much.

I am eagerly awaiting my father's arrival, which will calm my apprehensions as nothing else can, and will throw some light on my future and on my fate; they say the most dreadful things are being repeated about me at the Archduchess Marie-Béatrice's, that a plot is being hatched there to prevent me from going to the spa, and that they are even trying to wrest the Duchy of Parma from me so that the family can round off its own possessions; they say too that the ideal thing would be to find some way of preventing my son etc., etc., etc. I am desperately worried about all this, all the more so as they say that every word I utter is reported to them.

Nevertheless I am still determined to go to the spa, even if I'm feeling well I shall still say I feel ill, so as to have an excuse for going, and I think I shall take my son with me, otherwise I should be too distressed by all these wicked rumours. I assure you, Darling, I'm dreadfully unhappy about everything; if only I were near you I should at least find comfort in the happiness of your presence, and in telling you that I love you, but here in this prison-house, life weighs so heavily upon me.

I have seen M. Wonowitz,[1] who is to bring you this letter, he has actually seen me and your son too, I shall be so glad for him to give you news of us. I am delighted that I can keep M. Méneval with me, we often talk to each other about you, and

---

[1] Wolodkowicz?

grow most indignant at the things people are saying about you; however, I have discovered one of my young brother's tutors here who appears to be devoted to you, he thinks the way I am being treated here is disgusting, he's an excellent fellow, and I can tell you that if I had to take a German into my service, he is the only one I could accept.

Good-bye, my Darling, I love you and kiss you with all my heart.

Your true and loving Louise

On 15th June, Francis I returned to Vienna. Timidly he endeavoured to dissuade his daughter from undertaking the journey to which he had consented. It was essential to propitiate the Bourbons, and there was also the question of the boy: should she take him with her or leave him behind in Vienna? The Emperor, evasive as ever, suggested that the matter should be submitted to Napoleon for his advice!

Napoleon had sent to Parma, to attend on his wife, a detachment of fifty Polish Light Cavalry, and a hundred carriage-horses—an unwelcome attention.

Letter No. 10 from Marie-Louise is missing.

[197]

[Schönbrunn] 22*nd June* 1814

No. 11. My Darling, Yesterday I experienced a moment of intense happiness when M. Méneval came to bring me a letter from General Bertrand, dated 27th May, which gave me news of your health; although it was old news, it gave me immense pleasure, because I had heard absolutely nothing from the isle of Elba, and was most upset about it.

I am very happy to know that you are comfortably settled there, and are thinking of building yourself a pretty country house. Do, please, keep a little corner in it for me, for you know I am still fully expecting to join you as soon as ever I can, and I hope and pray it may be before long. If you are going to make a pretty garden, I hope you will let me be your agent for the plants and flowers; people declared it was most unjust of them not to let you have such things sent from Paris; they are not behaving at all worthily towards you, it simply disgusts me, it's

o   209

quite scandalous, though really not in the least surprising, for we are living in a world where high-minded people are extremely rare.

I have been very touched at the way my father has welcomed me, he has anticipated my every wish; he told me there was not the least difficulty about my going to the spa, but advised me to leave my son here for the time being, he said that as I was going on to the French frontier, it might be thought that I was wanting to disturb the peace, which might involve both me and my son in a certain amount of unpleasantness; I strongly opposed this suggestion, so then he said the best thing would be to write to you about it and tell you what he had advised me to do, and added, 'If he doesn't approve, he's the child's master, and you can take him with you', so I'm writing to ask your advice, and longing for your considered opinion to coincide with my own desire to have my son with me, I know that he couldn't be in safer hands than he is here, but you know how mothers worry when they are parted from their children.

I can't tell you often enough how good my father is being to me, he is deliberately setting himself out to make me forget all my past troubles, and they were very big ones because you had spoilt me so, for it was not the Empire I regretted, but seeing you unhappy and distressed, and worst of all deserted by all those who had served you when you were fortunate.

General Bertrand has written to say that you are sending carriage-horses and Lancers for me to Parma; I have told them to leave all that until I arrive, I'm afraid I may not be able to feed so many horses, but when I get there I shall choose out the best and sell the rest, they say the Duchy will bring in practically nothing the first year, so I shall live as economically as possible.

Your son sends you a kiss, nothing can quench his high spirits, and he's as fair as the day, he is winning golden opinions everywhere here, they think he's wonderful and say he looks very like you, which gives me great pleasure. He keeps on talking to me about you, and I talk to him about you even more, he says some really astonishing things for his age, it makes me tremble for him, they say that children who are so forward for their years don't live long, God grant I may not be called on to endure this final sorrow.

I am very much better in health, I am following a very strict
régime prescribed for me by M. Corvisart, and my chest has been
much better since; I am hoping the waters will cure it completely;
I am taking great care of myself, trying not to take walks that are
too tiring, riding a little, and doing my best to keep busy, but
not succeeding very well; I am a prey to the most terrible des-
pondency, which haunts me wherever I go, and the rest of the
time I spend thinking about you.

I shall leave for the spa on the evening of the 29th; I am expecting to go as far as Lambach on the 1st day, to Kaunstein on the
2nd, Mindelheim on the 3rd, Mörseburg on the 4th, Rasau on
the 5th, Berne on the 6th, where I shall stay one day, then to
Lucerne on the 8th, Lausanne on the 9th, Geneva on the 10th,
where I shall stay, and I shall reach Aix on the 12th day. I am
travelling incognito, receptions weary me so and are so boring,
and as I don't intend to receive anyone at the spa, I shall take
the name of the Comtesse de Colorno, after the country-
residence in Parma.

If you are so good as to reply, do please send your answer to
Aix, as it would no longer find me here; write to me often,
Darling, that is my sweetest consolation, and be quite sure that
nothing in the world will ever be able to change the tender love I
bear you. I kiss you and love you with my whole heart.

Your true and loving Louise

In the isle of Elba, Napoleon continued to speak of her with deep
tenderness. To her query about her son, he replied by proposing an
entirely different solution.

[198]

[Portoferrajo] 3rd July 1814

My dearest Louise, I have received your letters numbered 8 and
11, dated 22nd June, the rest have gone astray. The news you
give me of your health and of my son gives me great pleasure. I
think you should come as soon as possible to Tuscany, where
there are very good waters, much like those of Aix-en-Savoie.
It will have every advantage; you will be nearer Parma, I shall
hear from you more often, you will be able to have your son

with you and you will give nobody any trouble. Your visit to Aix has nothing but disadvantages. If this letter finds you there, remain only for the season and come on to Tuscany for your health. My health is good, my feelings towards you are ever the same, and my longing to see you and prove this to you is very great. Good-bye, my dearest, a loving kiss to my son. All my love.

Nap

Napoleon's chief worry was that in Aix Marie-Louise would find herself in a false position *vis-à-vis* the Bourbons. The Emperor may also have been apprehensive about the too close proximity of Joseph in Switzerland; the ex-King might be capable of involving Marie-Louise in some rash venture.

The Emperor Francis, for his part, wished his daughter to be accompanied to Aix by some trustworthy person. He asked Schwarzenberg to suggest a general who would be able to send him reports, and 'if need be, assist my daughter with his advice'. The choice fell on General Count Adalbert von Neipperg, at that time stationed in Pavia.

Born of a French father, Neipperg had been involved in every campaign against the Revolution. In 1813, he had collaborated with Bernadotte in Stockholm, and in Naples had also endeavoured to detach Murat from Napoleon. In 1813 he had married the former wife of one of his friends, Thérèse Pola, who bore him four children. In the entourage of Marie-Louise he was to act as spy, companion, escort and attendant.

On 29th June, Marie-Louise left 'this prison-house Vienna', with a retinue of thirty-three. At Munich she had supper with Eugène de Beauharnais and the Vicereine, who presented their children to her, amongst them Joséphine, then only seven. At Baden, Marie-Louise met Louis, and at Alaman lodged with Joseph, who arranged to send her a Spanish stallion to ride. Finally at Carouge, she joined Neipperg, who had come to meet her, and on 17th July reached Aix, where she settled at the Villa Chevaley in which at one time Queen Hortense had lived with her lover Flahaut.

Napoleon's letter of the 14th [= 13th?] July, and another which preceded it, are missing; the Emperor's letters were sent off by the Comtesse Bertrand.

Count Adalbert von Neipperg

From a lithograph by F. Lieder

Désirée

From a miniature by Isabey. (Royal Palace, Stockholm)

[199]

Aix-en-Savoie, 21st July 1814

My Darling, I haven't written to you for ages because there seems no way of getting my letters through to you; it worries me dreadfully, I'm afraid you may think me capable of forgetting you, and I confess that any such suspicion on your part would pain me extremely, because it would be as little deserved as well-founded, but what worries me even more is not having heard anything from *you*, I haven't had one single line since 10th May. Nevertheless, Darling, I feel certain that you *have* written, and that you think about me sometimes, but the idea of not being able to hear you say so is very hard to bear. Fortunately news has reached me through an intermediary that you were quite well on the 11th of this month; do try, if you can't write, to send me news by every available means, it does me a world of good, and is the surest way you can find of hastening my cure.

I heard from Prince Eugène that Pélard[1] had arrived in Paris, I was hoping you would send him to me as you had promised, but I've been told he had sent all his letters back to Portoferrajo, I'm really very angry with him. M. Méneval left yesterday for Paris, where private business required his presence, he begged me to tell you that during the five weeks he expects to stay there he will not be writing to you, as he can see no way of getting his letters to you.

When the season at the spa has ended, I expect to go back to Parma, if it can be managed, and I am thinking of writing to Parma to that effect, I think it essential to go there as soon as possible; in four months the Provisional Government has let me in for more than 15 millions in debts, and if it goes on there will be still more to follow. It really grieves me, as do many other things that have been done there, and which I should describe to you in greater detail if I knew my letters were reaching you intact.

I expect, then, to go to Parma for the month of September, about the 20th or 25th; I am determined not to go back to Vienna, the Congress has been postponed until 1st October, and my father will not think it fitting for me to be in the same city as the Allied sovereigns. If I do go to Parma, I shall send M. de Bausset to fetch my son as soon as I am settled there, I think

---

[1] The Emperor's valet de chambre.

213

it will be better to wait until I get there rather than have him come here. They write to say that he is wonderfully well and very cheerful and that his intelligence is growing more acute every day. My father is treating him very well indeed, he seems to love him devotedly.

I am keeping fairly well and have not been as wearied by the journey as I had reason to think I might be; I found M. Corvisart here, he had arrived two days before me, he has made me take the first bath today, and it has been fairly effective, I am expecting to drink the waters in a day or two. He begs me to present his humble duty.

I was so glad to see him again, he says such kind things about you, and that's a luxury I've enjoyed all too rarely for some time now, people have shown the greatest tact in not even mentioning the subject.

As I passed through various towns I was moved by the way people remembered you, and that is something which should comfort you in your great misfortunes; as for myself, I only know it made me cry, and that I just couldn't find words to thank those kind folk adequately, there are so few who can really appreciate you. I've had such amazing instances of that lately, but I won't tell you about them, it would only upset you to no purpose. I am living in the strictest incognito here, my father has sent me General Neipperg, he's quite nice and speaks well of you. I am taking plenty of exercise, as you have to do when you are taking the waters, King Joseph, whom I saw at Alaman, has given me some of his horses. I am finding plenty to do, I am sketching from nature, Isabey has come here, he wants to go and see you in the isle of Elba, and has told me that in the meantime, one of his pupils is going there.

Let me have news soon, my Darling, and spare a thought occasionally for her who, with a tender kiss, declares herself for life

Your Darling Louise

Napoleon's letter of 28th July 1814 *is missing.*

So life at the spa settled into its usual routine. There were trips on the lake, walks or rides, and above all, of course, the baths. A health bulletin, drawn up by Corvisart, is an indirect justification of the stay in Aix.

[200]

Aix-en-Savoie, 31st July 1814

My Darling, I am really distressed at not being able to send news more often, and even more worried at not hearing from you; this time I am taking advantage of the departure of M. de Bausset, whom I am sending to Parma, to try and get a short note through to you, and to assure you once again of all the love and tenderness which bind me to you. Try hard, Darling, to find a way of sending me your letters, I need them quite desperately, I feel that more urgently every day, I am so sad to think that, although I am nearer to you, I've had no letters since 10th May.

I have written to my father asking permission to be in Parma by 15th September, he can't refuse it, and my heart is quite set on it; I could get in touch with you more easily then, and really my presence there is absolutely essential, I don't believe anyone can ever settle into a new house properly unless they are there to arrange it themselves.

I have received good news of your son's health, the moment when I shall see him again can't come too quickly for me, they say he is growing more charming every day. I wonder when I shall be able to bring him to you, that *will* be a wonderful day, and your dear love will never have been so happy before.

I am sending you a bulletin about my health which M. Corvisart has drawn up here, I am infinitely better, the baths are doing me a lot of good, I have already had 3, and am going to start having one every day. I walk as much as the heat allows, for it's dreadful here, I don't think it could be hotter in the isle of Elba; I see no one, I am expecting the Duchess in three days' time, she is to stay with me for the whole of August, you will know I am speaking the truth when I say I am very pleased about it. I won't write any more, I'm afraid my letter will meet the same fate as the others. I send you a kiss and love you with all my heart.

Your loving and devoted Louise

Health Bulletin from Corvisart.

Aix-en-Savoie, 31st July 1814

Her Majesty the Empress, following the Advice I had the honour of giving her in Vienna, and which I pressed home in my letters, will proceed to Aix-en-Savoie in order to take the mineral waters there.

I should, so I believed, afford H.M. the Empress and Her illustrious husband a clear proof of my zeal and devotion by going myself to Aix, so as to judge the state of H.M.'s health on Her arrival, to direct and observe the taking of the waters, and to follow their effects.

On the actual day of departure, Her Majesty was feverish, and her general condition was low, so that the surgeons, or rather the one in attendance at the time, advised her not to set out. H.M. did, however, leave, and with every day of the long journey, Her health improved. On Her arrival here on 17th July, I found the Empress better than when I had left her at Schönbrunn.

Today, (31st July), Her Majesty's condition is very satisfactory: the Empress is coughing very little: her breathing is in general very easy, and consequently the feeling of suffocation, as well as the spitting of blood, have almost disappeared. Her complexion is good, her colour natural, her appetite quite regular, and her sleep would be sound were it not interrupted by hot flushes. The night sweating is no longer excessive and appears to be caused almost exclusively by the heat of this place. Her Majesty takes plenty of exercise, either on horseback or on foot, and bears the exertion well, without any recurrence of the cough or the troublesome breathing. After this brief report, we may trust that the health of Her Majesty the Empress will be perfectly restored unless grave and unforeseen causes arise to undermine a constitution naturally frail and delicate, and which, it should not be forgotten, is subject to a disease which at present appears to be quiescent.

Corvisart

[201]

Aix[*-en-Savoie*] *3rd August* 1814

My Darling, I have written you three letters in the last 5 days, I don't know whether you will have received them, I sincerely hope so, because then you will see that I love you very dearly, and that I am most uneasy at not hearing from you; do try, I beg of you, to send me news, I shall be in Parma about 15th September, I hope nothing will prevent it, and that once there, I shall have frequent and really up-to-date news.

I wrote telling you that I had good news of your son's health, I had still more yesterday, he has never been better than he is just now; except for the toothache, which often bothers him, he is always full of high spirits and very charming.

My health is improving too, I don't feel at all ill, I have been slightly indisposed the last few days, but it was nothing much, the baths are doing me a great deal of good, I have already taken 8.

I am very pleased with General Neipperg, whom my father has appointed to attend on me, he talks about you so pleasantly and in a way which goes straight to my heart, for I *need* to talk about you during this cruel absence. When, I wonder, shall I be able to see you again and embrace you? I long for it so much, and shall only be happy and contented when I can tell you with my own lips that I love you very tenderly.

Your true and loving Louise

The distractions of Aix, however, did not succeed in dispersing the cares which tormented Marie-Louise. Her natural inclination led her to join her husband; her respect for the Head of the House of Habsburg, and for the authority of her father, forbade her to do so. At the same time Neipperg, to whom she was at first indifferent, who even seemed rather tiresome, became more and more indispensable to her. 'I am', she confided to Méneval, whose advice she sought, 'in a very critical and unfortunate position. There are times when it puts my head in such a whirl that I think the best decision to take would be to die.'

For 15th August, Napoleon's birthday, she sent him, in great secrecy and by one of Joseph's servants, a lock of her hair.

[202]

Aix[-en-Savoie] 10th *August* 1814

No. 15. My Darling, I have safely received your letter of 4th July, which came by Vienna,[1] where it will certainly have been opened and commented on; it has given me such sweet satisfaction, it is so long since I saw your beloved handwriting, and I am delighted to see that your feelings towards me have not

---

[1] Transmitted by Bellegarde, an Austrian field-marshal in Italy.

changed. You know mine too well, my dearest, ever, ever, to be able to doubt either them or my longing to see you again.

I wish I could have wished you a happy birthday in more fortunate circumstances, and above all could have been there to kiss you. At least I am praying earnestly for your happiness, and I venture to say that no one's prayers are more sincere. I am sending you a lock of my hair, I am very upset at not being able to offer you anything better, but you will take the intention for the deed.

I am delighted to know you are keeping well, I do hope you will find that the climate suits you, I wish I were in a position by now to sample it for myself, I hope I shall be very soon, I can't live without that sweet hope.

The waters are doing me a certain amount of good, I am halfway through the first cure, I've had ten treatments and have to take ten more, afterwards I shall do my very best to follow your most congenial advice and go to Tuscany; I shall send for my son, because I shouldn't like to be parted from him for so long. In any case, I am expecting in a day or two to get a letter or a reply of some kind from my father, in answer to one I wrote him about my visit to Italy, and as soon as I get to Parma, my son will join me there. Moreover, I shall send your reply on to my father, and as he urged me to ask your advice about my visit, he can't object to my going to take the waters at Pisa. M. Corvisart says he thinks they are good, but not so good as those at Aix. I have a mass of things to tell you, and a host of problems about which I want your advice, but I can't put them in writing until I have some perfectly safe means of communication, if you think you can find me one, you will be giving me great joy.

My visit here is no longer causing any anxiety, I am leading an exceedingly quiet life and finding plenty to do, I should be wretched if I had to see a lot of people, I can't summon up enough cheerfulness for that sort of thing, and how can I when I'm so far away from you? I am spending my time embroidering tapestry covers for the furniture in your study, or for a small drawing-room, there will be a sofa, an armchair, a stool and four chairs, so arrange a place for them somewhere, you will have them in 4 or 5 months.

Isabey is asking to settle near me in Parma, but as you've had some objections to him, I told him I couldn't give him a definite answer until I had consulted you, so do please tell me what to say to him. M. Méneval is still in Paris, I have sent him General Bertrand's letter which came yesterday at the same time as yours. Hubert and Pélard[1] too have already reached Paris and have given me news of your health.

I do beg you to write to me very often, it's one of the few pleasures left me to enjoy at the moment, and above all, Darling, never doubt the warmth and completeness of my devotion, no one loves you, or ever will love you, better than I do. I kiss you and love you with all my heart and soul.

Your loving and devoted Louise

[*On the back*: To His Majesty the Emperor Napoleon at Porto Ferrajo.]

[*Red seal*]

This reply must have been sent through Vienna. In spite of the 'sweet satisfaction' with which Marie-Louise had received the brief note of 3rd July, it must have caused her pain. To make matters worse, on 15th August she received a letter from Metternich enjoining her to return to Vienna at the end of her cure. If Marie-Louise were to take immediate possession of the Duchies of Parma, as she fully intended to do, it would constitute a *fait accompli* with which no one would dare to confront the Congress. Moreover, the Cabinet in Paris had taken strong objection to her residing on the very threshold of France. To obtain Parma at all, it would be essential to deal tactfully with the Bourbons—and with Talleyrand.

Napoleon, however, furnished a home for Marie-Louise in the isle of Elba. He ordered the drawing-room ceiling to be painted with doves, separated by clouds, but joined by a ribbon with a knot which was drawn ever more tightly the further they moved apart. It represented Marital Fidelity. In his letters, of which at least one, that of 6th August, is extant, he did not cease to importune his wife.

[203]

The Isle of Elba, 18*th August* [1814]

My dearest Louise, I have written to you frequently. I presume you have done the same, yet I have received none of your letters

<hr>

[1] The Emperor's valets de chambre.

219

since the one written within a few days of your departure from Vienna. I have had no news of my son. Such conduct is exceedingly stupid and atrocious. Madame is here and in good health; she has good accommodation. My health is good. Your apartments are ready for you, and I look forward to seeing you in September for the vintage. No one has any right to stand in the way of your coming. I have written to you on this point. So mind you come. I am awaiting you with impatience. You are aware of all the love I bear you. I will write nothing more today, as this letter may not reach you. Princess Pauline will be here in the middle of September.

This is your Saint's Day. I send you my best wishes. Complain of their behaviour to you in preventing a woman and a child from writing to me. Such behaviour is despicable. Adio, mio bene.

Nap

At the end of his patience, Napoleon sent three emissaries to Aix, of whom two are known to us by name: Colonel Teodor Lanczinski, probably the brother of Marie Walewska, who landed on the isle of Elba on 27th July, and Captain Louis-Marie-Charles Hurault, the husband of Marie-Louise's lectress. Their messages, as well as the dispatching of one of the Emperor's brigs to Genoa, make it clear that he had decided to play his last card. He demanded that Marie-Louise should come to him at once, alone even, and in the meantime he gave her several addresses to which she could send letters.

The following letter of 18th August was to be the last in which Marie-Louise wrote with complete frankness and candour.

[204]

Aix[-en-Savoie] 18*th August* 1814

My Darling, I have just received your letter brought me by a Polish officer. I was delighted to get it, as I've been without news for a long time except for one letter dated 28th July, which was sent me, all unsealed, from Vienna. I believe all my letters are being stopped, such strict orders have been given all round the coast, and they are being so efficiently carried out, that not a single letter is being allowed to get through, but all the same I am writing to you regularly [more] than once a week.

How happy I should be if I could join you the moment I have my son with me! I had given orders for him to be sent here when I received a letter from my father asking me to go back to Vienna for the Congress, where my son's interests are to be discussed; it appears that the Bourbons are actively campaigning to have Parma taken away from me, they have a powerful following in the country,[1] and it is being seriously suggested that I should be given instead the three Legations,[2] which bring in twice as much, but I don't yet know anything about this officially. I wanted to go to Parma, they refuse to let me. Here I am surrounded by police and by Austrian, Russian and French counter-police, and M. de Fitzjame[s][3] has orders to arrest me if I attempt to go in the direction of Elba.

In spite of all this, you can trust my determination to get there, it will make me brave all obstacles, and unless they use force, I shall most certainly be with you soon, but I don't know yet what they will resort to.

I am most miserable at not being with you by now on your happy island, it would be just heaven to me. Do trust me, won't you? I should tell you quite frankly if *I* were the one putting difficulties in the way of my going, you know me well enough for that, and I beg you not to believe everything they may tell you on that score. I shall attempt to leave at the earliest possible moment, in the meanwhile I am not giving your officer one moment's respite. If they knew he was here, they would be quite capable of arresting him, and I feel sure he will be searched; you can't imagine how rigorously orders are being carried out, even the Austrians are shocked by it; General Neipperg told me he had in his pocket the order to intercept every letter I might write to you.

Your son is very well indeed, I met someone yesterday who saw him a week ago, he left him cheerful and very happy, the Emperor of Austria is crazy about him, he goes to see him every day, I feel sure you'll think it a good idea to try and encourage him to be fond of him. He can already read fluently, and

[1] Italy.
[2] Papal Legations.
[3] The Duc de Fitzjames, emissary of Louis XVIII and brother-in-law of General Bertrand.

is growing so charming, I can hardly wait for the moment when I shall be able to bring him to you.

Taking the waters has improved my health most wonderfully, if only I had a little peace of mind I am sure I should be perfectly well especially if I were with you.

The officer is asking me for this letter so that he can hide it in his kit, and I shall have to stop now, it's such a pity, I've told him to tear the letter up if he is arrested. Remember me to Madame.

I send you a kiss and love you dearly.

Your loving and devoted Louise

[*On the back*: To His Majesty the Emperor Napoleon
At Porto Ferrajo.]

'I shall have to stop now, it's such a pity . . .' The calamity which Marie-Louise had foreseen actually happened: Hurault was denounced to Neipperg by Mme de Brignole, the close friend of Talleyrand, and arrested by the Aix gendarmerie. The Empress found herself compelled to pledge her word never to undertake the journey without the sanction of Francis I. She even begged him to tell her what answer she should give to her husband.

On the following day, Marie-Louise yielded completely to her father's 'advice'. In order not to offend the French Government, she promised—and this marked her final defeat—to return to Vienna at the beginning of October, or in any case after the departure of the Allied sovereigns. She wished Neipperg to accompany her on the journey, 'he may be extremely useful to me on various occasions'.

'Madame Mère' had arrived in Elba on 2nd August; Princess Pauline was to follow in November. From the hermitage at Marciana Alta, where he had taken refuge from the excessive heat, Napoleon sent a short letter noticeably resigned in tone.

[205]

La Madonna di Marciano, 28th August [1814]

My Dearest, I have received your letter No. 15 dated 10th August. I presume you have received mine since then. I was glad to hear Corvisart was with you. I am here in a hermitage, 3834 feet above sea-level, overlooking the Mediterranean on all sides,

and in the midst of a forest of chestnut trees. Madame is staying
in the village, 958 feet lower down. This is a most pleasant spot.
My health is very good, I am spending part of the day shooting.
I am longing to see you, and my son too. I shall be glad to see
Isabey. There are some very fine landscapes to draw here. Good-
bye, my dearest Louise. All my love. Your

Nap

Many thanks for what you sent me.

On hearing that Marie-Louise was at last to return home, Metternich advised Francis I to let her stay for some time at a halfway stage
in Switzerland. He suggested a further reward for this proof of
obedience—a letter of thanks.

On 5th September, Marie-Louise set out on her return journey to
Geneva, where she received Napoleon's letter of 18th August. With
only one thought in her head—to conciliate the Allies so that she might
at last obtain her Duchies of Parma—the Empress confessed to the
Duchesse de Montebello on 8th September that she 'would never go
to the isle of Elba', 'but really the Emperor is so casual, so un-
reliable . . .' To the letters he wrote her during August, she did not
reply direct, but through Neipperg and Vienna.

In Switzerland, Marie-Louise went on expeditions, often alone with
Neipperg, the only man she could now trust, since her father's promises
had proved so false, and on one of these excursions, on 24th September,
she arrived at the chapel of William Tell. A storm compelled her to
put up for the night at the Golden Sun inn, and there she became
Neipperg's mistress.

On 4th October, Marie-Louise and her lover returned to Vienna.
She no longer waited for the departure of the Allied sovereigns—her
last stipulation had been withdrawn.

At Schönbrunn, from now onwards, Marie-Louise spent her time
almost exclusively with her son and her lover. She had returned just
as the Congress of Vienna was in full swing, but she took no part in
all the international festivities; she longed for rest and peace far away
from all the worldly bustle and tumult. 'In her son's interests', however, it was essential that she should receive the sovereigns, from the
Tsar down to the King of Denmark and the German princes, amongst
whom was Eugène Beauharnais, henceforth to be Duc de Leuchtenberg.

Notwithstanding the victory he had just won, Metternich was anxious to sever any communications which Marie-Louise might have with the outside world; her actions and movements were closely watched by day and night; spies prowled around her apartments, her letters were read—she was now literally a prisoner.

Napoleon's letters reached her only at rare intervals, and through the agency of the Grand Duke Ferdinand of Tuscany; they were held back, and only brief summaries were sent on to her. To a note of 20th November handed to her by Francis I, who had received it from Tuscany on 6th December, she did, however, reply, on 3rd January 1815, sending the letter through her father. It was phrased in conventional terms.

[206]

Schönbrunn, 3rd January 1815

My Darling, It seems a hundred years since I was last able to write to you, or received any letters from you, then suddenly my father produced your dear letter of 20th November. I felt a great weight lifted from my heart when I heard that you were well and did not doubt all my love for you. I can imagine how troubled you must have been at not getting news of your son or of me for such a long time; I know just what it feels like, from the anxiety which fills my own heart when I am left for months at a time without a single scrap of news from you, and without knowing whether you are well. I hope this year will be a happier one for you, at least you will be at peace in your island, and will live there happily for many, many years, to the joy of all who love you and who are, as I am, deeply devoted to you.

Your son sends you a kiss and begs me to wish you a happy New Year, and to tell you he loves you with all his heart; he often talks about you, and is growing taller and stronger in the most astonishing fashion. He has been rather out of sorts this winter, I at once consulted Frank, who completely reassured me by saying they were only passing bouts of fever; indeed he recovered almost immediately. He is beginning to know Italian fairly well, and is learning German too, my father is treating him with the greatest kindness and affection, he appears to love him devotedly and spends a great deal of time playing with him. He is heaping kindnesses upon me too, in fact all my family are treating

224

me with the utmost affection and going out of their way to make me forget all our misfortunes.

Hardly a day passes without my going to see my father, who often asks whether I have heard from you, it is he who has undertaken to send this letter to Portoferrajo, with the help of the Grand Duke of Tuscany. If it reaches you safely, I do most earnestly beg you always to use this channel of communication, I will take advantage of it too, then at least I shall know how you are.

My health is completely restored, the waters, the Swiss climate and the mountain air have had a really wonderful effect on it, I've put on a lot of weight and feel none the worse for the bitterly cold weather we've been having for some time now. I am living an extremely secluded life at Schönbrunn, befitting my personal inclinations and my position so long as the Allied Sovereigns remain here. I hardly ever see more than 3 or 4 people in the evenings, we have a little music, or I chat by my fireside. Please remember me to Madame and to Princess Pauline, write to me soon; once again I wish you a happy New Year and send you a loving kiss.

Louise

[*On the back*: To His Majesty the Emperor Napoleon
At Porto Ferrajo.]

Marie-Louise was chiefly concerned with the course of events in Italy, where her right to the Duchies was to be contested by Spain, supported by France. Talleyrand requested that Parma should be handed over to the Queen of Etruria, Marie-Louise receiving in exchange a large sum of money. That, however, was precisely what she wished to avoid: she was convinced that Parma was her only chance of escape from prison. She deluged her father and the whole of the Viennese Court with letters—she was fortunate in having Neipperg to direct her efforts.

On 9th March, amidst all this intrigue, the Comtesse de Montesquiou brought her the news that Napoleon had landed in France. Marie-Louise locked herself in her room and burst into tears. What trials, she wondered, did this return hold in store for her—was the Duchy of Parma to be snatched away from her, and would she be compelled to rejoin her husband if he were victorious?

At the instigation of Neipperg, Marie-Louise signed a letter which was to be shown to the members of the Congress. In it she declared that she placed herself and her son under the loving protection of her father, that she would recognise no other wishes than his, and that she expressed to him in advance her unbounded gratitude.

The Allied declaration of 13th March, which proclaimed Bonaparte to be an outlaw, reassured her about her own future. The information divulged to her by Viennese courtiers about the disease from which Napoleon had most probably been suffering since the winter of 1814, certainly strengthened her in her refusal.

On 11th March, however, there arrived from Grenoble and from Lyons messages from the Emperor, inviting her to join him with the 'Prince Imperial'. The actual letters were not passed on to her, she was merely told their contents. The letter sent her by Napoleon on 28th March, after his triumphal return to the Tuileries on 20th March —her son's birthday—aroused varied reactions amongst the members of the Congress. There was open talk of double-dealing; it was implied that the return from Elba could never have been accomplished without the consent of Austria. Metternich, anxious and uneasy, asked Marie-Louise to pledge her word that she would read no more of her husband's letters and would hand them direct to the Emperor Francis. With relief, she signed the required renunciation.

In vain, on 1st April, Napoleon addressed a message to Francis himself: the prey would not be allowed to escape again. When, a fortnight later, Parisians realised that 'the rose and the rosebud' were not returning, consternation prevailed: their absence could mean only one thing—war.

The small French Court which still surrounded Marie-Louise now at last began to break up. The rumour spread through Schönbrunn that Napoleon intended to kidnap his son, and that Colonel Montesquiou had been instructed to plan out the various stages of the journey. Metternich ordered Marie-Louise to dismiss the governess: the child was taken to the Hofburg. The departure of 'Maman Quiou' was heart-rending. On 1st April, Neipperg was back in Italy; on 5th May the Austrian army began its march.

The last Frenchman to leave the ex-Empress was the faithful Méneval. When he went to take his farewell of her, she begged him to assure Napoleon of her sincere and unbounded good wishes for his welfare: she hoped he would understand the unhappy position in which she had been placed. She would at no time take steps to obtain a divorce, venturing to hope that he would agree to a friendly separation, 'which had now become a necessity'. The regard she still felt for him, and the gratitude she bore him, would remain unchanged.

Once again, on 4th April, Napoleon wrote urging her to return to him. She did not read the letter, nor had she any wish to do so. On the eve of Waterloo, Napoleon entrusted to his brother Joseph these letters from his wife, which had become little more than mementoes. For Marie-Louise, however, the future held Parma, with its charming, intimate Court given over to love intrigues and gallantry, and not, as before, the stately Empire, with its dull and wearisome victories.

The bad dream had ended for ever.

Additional Letters from the Bernadotte Archives

Amongst Queen Désirée's papers in the Bernadotte Archives are to be found thirteen letters from the young Napoleon, of which only one is in his own hand. All the others, the originals of which have been lost, exist only in the form of copies made by Désirée herself. Only the signed letter from General Bonaparte to his fiancée, written in 1795 during that journey to Paris which was to prove so decisive for his future career, is included below. Désirée's replies have already been published in part by Baron Hochschild and in the biography of Marshal Canrobert by Bapst.

[1]

Avignon, 20th Floréal, noon, [1795]

To Citizeness Eugénie Clary
Marseilles.

To Eugénie,

I have reached Avignon very cast down at the thought of being parted from you for so long. The journey has seemed most tedious to me. The hope that my dear Eugénie will often be thinking of her darling, and will go on loving him as she has promised to do, can alone lighten my sorrow and make my situation bearable.

I shall not get any of your letters before I reach Paris; that will be a great incentive to me to hurry; see that news is waiting for me the very moment I arrive.

The overflowing of the Durance has prevented me from reaching this place earlier.

I have not managed to carry out . . . your Mamma's request

228

for the simple reason that I was fool enough to forget the petition and the letters of reference in support of it.

Tomorrow evening I shall be at Lyons. Good-bye, my dear, sweet love. Don't forget, and go on loving, him who is yours for life.

N.Bp.

From General Buonaparte, commanding the artillery of the Western Army, now in Paris, poste restante.

The Napoleonic Empire was at the height of its splendour. From his capital, Joseph Bonaparte, King of Spain, addressed several letters to his sister-in-law, the Princesse de Ponte-Corvo. They show how thoroughly he was deluding himself about his new kingdom.

[2]

Madrid, 27th September 1809

My dear Désirée,

I have received your letter, I do not doubt the sincerity of your friendship towards me; mine for you, as you well know, is affectionate and already of long standing, but has remained as fresh and young as you yourself; my love to Oscar too, I hope he is as well as when I left him.

Your affectionate brother Joseph

[3]

Seville, 6th February 1810

My dear Désirée,

I have received Your letter with the greatest pleasure, much has happened, and long years have gone by, since the name of Désirée first came into my life, but my heart is ever the same towards you, and will never change. I am very pleased with the Andalusias; the people are kindly, and hot-blooded, like myself, the clergy are reasonable and the nobility well-meaning and energetic.

I send you an affectionate kiss.

Your loving brother Joseph

On 4th September 1810, the Princesse de Ponte-Corvo informed the Emperor that her husband had been elected Prince Royal of Sweden. Napoleon returned a very stiff and formal reply.

229

[4]

My Cousin,

I have received your letter of 4th September. You have long known the regard in which I hold Your family. I have no doubt that the excellent sentiments you will instil into your son will render him worthy of the high destinies to which he is being called. Therefore, my Cousin, I pray God that He may have you in His holy and blessed keeping.

Napoleon

To Madame the Princesse de Ponte-Corvo.

On the 25th of the same month, a Sunday, Désirée and her husband were allowed to join the Emperor's family dinner-party—an unprecedented mark of favour.

King Joseph, who was also informed of the promotion, replied less pompously. Charles XIII, the aged King of Sweden, had just conferred on him the decorations of his Order of the Seraphim.

[5]

Madrid, 26th September 1810

My dear Désirée,

I have received your letter and am really delighted at the great event you announce. I can imagine how painful it will be for you, and for Julie too, to be parted, nor will Oscar be willing to leave his cousins behind, but they will be more likely to meet again than we shall; long years and many adventures lie ahead of them, such as already lie behind us; whatever may happen, rest assured of my warm and unchanging friendship, and impress upon your husband that time and events have only served to strengthen my feelings for both of you; give Oscar a hearty kiss for me, and I kiss you too as I used to long years ago.

Your affectionate brother-in-law Joseph

On 9th January 1811, Désirée, with her son Oscar, arrived in Sweden from Paris. A letter from the Grand Duchess of Tuscany, Elisa Baciocchi, had been sent on to her from there.

[6]

Florence, 12th January 1811

My dear Désirée,

I have received the letter you wrote me, and I thank you very much for your kind remembrances, you know how devoted I am to you, and my love for you is deep and sincere.

My health is good. My daughter has remained in Pisa, as this bitterly cold weather, which is nothing much compared with that in the North, made me nervous of the fog in Florence.

The Prince sends you his respectful greetings; when next you write to the Prince Royal, don't forget to remember me to him. Good-bye, dear, kind friend, and remind yourself sometimes that you have a friend in Florence who is very, very fond of you.

Your affectionate Elisa

From Stockholm the Princess Royal wrote to congratulate Napoleon and Marie-Louise on the birth of the King of Rome.

[7]

Stockholm, 7th April 1811

Sire,

Will Your Majesty graciously permit me to join my congratulations to those being addressed to Him from every quarter on the happy delivery of Her Majesty the Empress? Today, as never before, I regret that I am so far away from France. It would, indeed, have been pleasant to offer in person to Your Majesty the tribute of my good wishes. I beg Your Majesty to believe how sincere are the prayers I offer up for the speedy recovery of Her Majesty the Empress and for the safe preservation of Her Illustrious Child who, from birth, is called to the most brilliant destiny.

Be pleased to accept, Sire, this expression of my most respectful devotion.

I have the honour to remain, Sire, Your Majesty's very humble and obedient servant,

Désirée

Marie-Louise sent Désirée a letter of thanks written in her own hand:

[8]

[April 1811]

I have been much moved by the interest Your Royal Highness has so kindly shown in the Birth of my son, I beg you to
accept my grateful thanks. The sentiments you express in your
last letter have touched me deeply, and I beg You to believe that
the affection I have professed for You will never change or alter,
in spite of your absence, and that I shall always take a lively interest in all that concerns you. I hope and pray that the waters
may prove beneficial to your health, as well as to that of the
Queen of Spain. I hope soon to be able to express in person those
feelings of esteem and regard with which I remain

Your Royal Highness's
Most affectionate Cousin Marie-Louise

Désirée did not enjoy her first visit to Stockholm. As early as the
4th June 1811, she returned to Paris leaving Oscar in Sweden. Jérôme
Bonaparte, King of Westphalia, wrote to her as soon as she was back
in France.

[9]

Cassel, 11th January 1812

My dear Désirée,

I am delighted to hear from you direct, you have long been
aware of the warm friendship I feel towards both you and your
husband; it will never fade, and *you may always* rely on me to
seize *with alacrity* any and every opportunity of proving it to you.

I could ask you, dear Désirée, to promise me one thing—
namely to call and see me on your way back to your Estates;
however, I won't ask you to give a definite pledge, since I feel
certain that affection and friendship will bring you quite naturally
in this direction, if that is at all possible.

I do wish, my dear Désirée, that this year may be a happy one
both for you and for all those you love. Such are the prayers I
offer up for you, and with which I shall ever remain

Your affectionate friend Jérôme Napoléon

When Paris capitulated, Désirée was still in her town house, 36 Rue
d'Anjou, where she was living under the name of the Duchesse de

Gotlande. In a letter to her husband she describes the entry of the Allies, his brothers-in-arms, ending with a positive military communiqué.

This document was found amongst her own papers, proof that Bernadotte, who was in Liège at the time, never received it, since the route was closed by the French.

[10]

Paris, 31st March [1814]

My Dear,

Comte Loveriel [Löwenhielm] is doubtless writing to give you full details of the Allied entry into Paris. It was carried out in a most orderly manner. I deeply regret that you did not come with them . . . it might have influenced your prospects considerably, as well as those of the people we love. It is for you to decide whether you are in a position to come quickly with your army, your presence here would carry great weight. The Faubourg St. Germain has come out with the white cocade, and seems to be gaining adherents. . . .

M. de Talleyrand has already seen the Tsar, [?] and has even dined with him, he is sufficiently ingratiating to inspire confidence [?] . . . The entire family of the [Emperor] N[apoleon] has left for Tours, my sister was the last to go. She was very upset at leaving me, you can imagine how completely I shared her grief, one of her great regrets was to give up all hope of seeing you again soon.

I am longing to hear from you, look after yourself, my darling, don't do anything rash,

Your loving and devoted
Désirée

All the family send you a thousand affectionate greetings, I've been asked to send you this letter, make use of it if you wish.

N.B. I am not very well-versed in military matters, but will repeat what seems certain, namely that L.N. appears to have followed the Allied advance and is at this moment somewhere in the neighbourhood of Montereau. A general engagement may develop, the Allies seem to be expecting it, and indeed if the French Army marches on Paris, it is inevitable. The French Corps involved in the fighting before Paris was occupied were those of the Duc de Trévise [and] the Duc de Raguse, in the last encounter which took place beneath the walls of Paris, these two Corps together could only muster 20 to 25 thousand men.

After the abdication of Napoleon, Désirée had no thought of deserting her sister and brother-in-law, and Joseph wrote expressing his gratitude.

[11]

[Blois] 8th April 1814

My dear Désirée,

Julie has let me read your letters, and I am more touched than surprised by your sympathy and affection for us, I am so very anxious not to be parted from my wife, and for her not to be parted from you, that I beg you to continue your efforts, I feel certain they will succeed in the end because they are so obviously right and their aim so justifiable—I am sending you a letter from the Emperor Alexander, he has shown a certain amount of concern for me on several occasions.

If Morfontaine were not too near Paris, we should prefer a more distant part of [the country], or at the worst, Switzerland.

I wrote yesterday to Bernadotte, I won't say any more, it would be abusing your very real friendship.

A kiss to you.

Your affectionate brother-in-law Joseph

The following letters from Prince Eugène de Beauharnais were found amongst the papers of Joseph Bonaparte. They were probably entrusted by Napoleon to his brother on the 11th June 1815.

[12]

Malmaison, 25th May 1814

Sire,

At last I have found an opportunity of getting in touch with you, and am hastening to take advantage of it.

I have, however, no wish to worry Your Majesty with talk of my own grief, I flatter myself that Your Majesty well knows the disposition of my heart, and will realise the full extent of my distress when I heard news of the many and varied misfortunes which have befallen You.

I came to Paris a fortnight ago to see my mother and sister, to make sure of a peaceful future for them, to secure French citizenship for myself, and so prove that I would not willingly renounce such a claim.

I am expecting to leave again in a few days for Munich, where I have left my wife and children. There I shall wait quietly for whatever fate it pleases the Allied Powers to assign me under the terms of the treaty of 11th April.

My numerous family makes it incumbent upon me to accept this fate, no matter what it may be, and furthermore I shall feel I am still conforming to Your Majesty's wishes, since it was with You that the treaty of 11th April was concluded.

Sire, take care of your health; do not, I beg you, forget me, or cease to think kindly of me. Wherever I may be, Your Majesty may always be certain—if You do justice to my feelings —of finding in me the most respectful of sons, the most devoted and grateful of friends.

I have the honour to be, Sire, Your Majesty's very humble and most affectionate son,

Prince Eugène

As he was about to leave for Bavaria to take possession of his territories of Eichstädt and Leuchtenberg, he was compelled to remain in France by the sudden death of the Empress Joséphine. Contrary to the generally accepted belief, Prince Eugène immediately sent news of it to his exiled stepfather. This letter, written with all a son's affection and regard, was almost certainly known to Queen Hortense—which explains why she did not, herself, write to Elba.

[13]

Saint-Leu, 31st May 1814

Sire,

I write to fulfil a most painful duty which lies heavy on my heart. I have the honour to inform Your Majesty that on the day before yesterday, at noon, you lost the best of friends, and my sister and I the most devoted of mothers.

235

A malignant and putrid disease ended her life within 4 days. She died with the courage, serenity and resignation of an angel. Everything she said to us about you in the last moments of her life showed us clearly how sincerely she was devoted to you.

When, a few days ago, I had the honour to send you a letter through the kind offices of Mme Bertrand, I was far from suspecting the calamity which overwhelms me today.

I am, Sire, with deep respect, Your Majesty's very affectionate son

Pce Eugène

Since the Prince's letter was delayed by Mme Bertrand's confinement, he wrote again to the Emperor.

[14]

Saint-Leu, 11*th June* 1814

Sire,

For the past twelve days I have been making vain attempts to obtain passports for a courier who was to have brought you the two enclosed letters. Today I learn that the C^sse Bertrand has not yet left [for the isle of Elba], so I am sending her this letter with all possible speed. I entreat Your Majesty to believe that I am in no way to blame if You have not heard from me until today.

My sister and I hope that when Your Majesty learns of the irreparable loss we have just suffered, and of the deep sorrow which overwhelms us, You will feel You are sharing it with us.

I expect to leave for Munich in 6 or 8 days' time, I should be happy to have news of Your Majesty's health whilst I am there.

I beg you to believe in my unfailing devotion.

I have the honour to be, Sire, Your respectful and affectionate servant and son,

Pce Eugène

On hearing of Joséphine's death from Comtesse Bertrand when she reached Portoferrajo, Napoleon is reported to have said, 'Ah, now she is indeed happy.' This sudden and unexpected death influenced the future of Marie-Louise. Learning that the divorce of 1809 had never been considered valid by the Vatican, she had, perforce, to accept her own marriage as null and void, in which case she herself was no more than a concubine, and the little King a bastard. This revelation, in no uncertain way, encouraged her liaison with Neipperg.

Désirée's vast circle of correspondents included also the Emperor's untrustworthy brother, Lucien Bonaparte, whose most unsuitable marriages provoked Napoleon's disapproval. Leaving England, Lucien had arrived in Rome on 27th May 1814, and settled there for good.

[15]

Rome, 29th July 1814

Madame,

I have received your kind letter; it means a great deal to have you remember me; nothing would ever cause me to forget you; moreover, the help and sympathy shown me by the Prince Royal [Bernadotte] have drawn me even closer to you. I beg you to write and tell the P[rince] R[oyal] how deeply I appreciate all he has done for Boyer [Lucien's brother-in-law] and how interested I am in everything that concerns him. If I can be of any use to either of you in Rome, I am entirely at your service.

Your affectionate relative

Lucien Bonaparte

The Emperor's miraculous return to France at the beginning of March 1815 closely affected his family, and repercussions of it are to be found in the papers of Joseph Bonaparte. Julie, who was living with her sister in Paris, wrote frankly to her husband, who was still in Switzerland.

[16]

[Paris] 3rd March 1815

Your letter of the 3rd only reached me today, darling; as you will see, there was no point in making any further plans for your stay in Prangins, everything has changed so completely since I made those arrangements about which I sent you word through Mme Magnitot, I don't suppose you are worrying about them any longer; I haven't been given any answer yet, the Government here is in a state of the wildest alarm, you must have seen from the papers all that is happening here. The Emperor's affairs are going exceedingly well, the army seems to be for him, and if any of the commanders want to make a show of resistance, they are threatened by the soldiers. So far the people and troops in Paris have not committed themselves, and the nation in general seems quite indifferent, only those in the upper reaches of society are afraid their fortunes will be compromised by this change of government.

I feel sure you have a fairly good idea how things are, all the same I thought I ought to send Pauline to give you even fuller details and set your mind at rest about your position in Prangins. The chief thing, in fact the only thing to do is to play for time, and our uncertainty won't last very long. If the Emperor does not succeed, our main difficulty, it seems to me, will be for me to obtain permission for us to stay on in Prangins, but no matter where we go we shall still have a good music-master and drawing-master for the children, they will go with us everywhere for very small salaries; I had fixed things up with them before these recent developments.

There seems something miraculous about all that is happening, it's amazing how everything has changed, for the day Mme Magnitot left I was tormented with anxiety, and I must admit that I was afraid your brother was dead, but two days have altered the whole situation and quite reversed it, and now I'm as calm as can be. Good-bye, dearest, and darling children too, I send you all a kiss.

Just as I was sealing this letter, I heard that there are doubts about your brother's entry into Lyons and that people here are feeling hopeful; before this letter reaches you, you will almost certainly know more about the true state of affairs than we do, and if in the meantime they urge you to leave the Canton of Vaud, you should insist on waiting to hear what the French Government has decided about your new place of residence, and demand a guarantee that you would be well-received and protected there, you know I have made a firm request for this, and only the pressure of recent events has prevented me from getting an answer by now, it wouldn't surprise me to receive one at any moment. Good-bye, darling, don't worry about me, as I'm with Désirée, I don't think I have anything at all to fear. Good-bye, good-bye, I simply must stop as it's time for the courier to go. I wrote by the post yesterday to Zénaïde.

[Julie Bonaparte]

Joseph hastened to get in touch with Napoleon once more, and both he and his wife begged Marie-Louise to return. From Lyons, Napoleon sent Joseph orders which also concerned the Empress.

[17]

I have received your letter brought by your valet de chambre. Keep the Empress fully informed of all that happens, and send someone to her by post-stage, making out that he is travelling on business. More than 30,000 men, the whole lot already drawn up under my command, and the entire population around Lyons and in the Dauphiné, are wild with enthusiasm. I am sending you my proclamations, and everything that has been printed about the present state of affairs. Have a large number of copies printed and send them with all possible speed—to Alsace via Basle and into Franche Comté via Porentruy. In 3 days' time I shall be at Châlons. I see no objection to your going to Zurich, you fully realise that a request must be made for the Empress and my son to be returned to me immediately, and for Austria to send someone to see me, and you can understand that I am particularly anxious that France should remain calm. If the Austrian Minister could come to you, I should prefer that. Write and tell him to come, he can hardly refuse. I am hoping to be in Paris from the 20th to the 25th. Chambéry is in my hands, and the Prefect, a man named Finon, Maret's nephew, is devoted to my cause. I am giving orders for the printed proclamations to be sent to you by that route. Your courier told me that the King of Naples was on the march with 80,000 men. This news conveys nothing to me. You yourself can have heard nothing in 10 days, and I have had news more recently than that. He was not even informed of what I had done. I landed with 600 of my Guard, and did not meet a single foreigner.

[Napoleon]

Lucien Bonaparte, who had recently acquired the Papal title of Prince of Canino, exchanged views with Joseph about the tremendous change which had just taken place. He was particularly worried about the conduct of their brother-in-law Murat, who was threatening the States of the Church.

[18]

[*Rome,* ... 1815]

My dear brother,

I have received your letter of 20th February; I am writing at once to tell you what information we have here.

The Emp[eror] left the island on the 26th; he landed at Cannes on the 28th; on 4th March he was at Digne, marching on Grenoble. Murat left for Ancona, and has declared his intention of supporting the Emperor with all the resources at his command; here we are afraid of being invaded by the Neapolitans. Mamma is at Portoferrajo, where the tricolour has been hoisted; she wrote on 5th March to tell us she was in good health and that the Emp[eror], who had written to her from France, had been welcomed everywhere with open arms. Caroline, who is still rather an invalid and very uneasy at these unforeseen developments, is staying in Naples with her children. Louis, Fesch, my family and I are all quite well. Jérôme and his wife have written to Louis from Trieste saying they are all well. Elisa is at Bologna, and Pauline at Viareggio in a country-house and from there she wants to go to the baths at Lucca; it seems that the Tuscan Government has advised her to stay where she is until fresh orders come through, but it's not true that either she or Elisa has been arrested.

In all this fresh upheaval, I have given up all thought of going to England. Circumstances make it imperative for me not to leave the Pope, to whom I owe so much, and for whom I would give my life a thousand times over. If the Holy Father stays quietly in Rome, I shall stay here with him. If the Neapolitans come and disturb him and invade the provinces that have been allotted to him, then the Holy Father has made up his mind to leave; in that case I shall follow him, leaving my family here. But I have written to the King of Naples, and I am hoping he will respect the actual State of Rome and take his troops through the Marches.

I will write to you frequently, and you do the same. I am writing to the Abbé Charpentier to whom your letters should be addressed. Let me have news of what is happening at your end: I will keep you informed about what goes on here.

The Emp[eror] has done the right thing in plunging straight

into the midst of danger: he will either have to die in a blaze of glory or win back his [lands].

Lucien Bonaparte

However, Napoleon's second abdication, after Waterloo, completed the downfall of the Bonapartes. On 29th June 1815, having entrusted his papers to his sister-in-law Désirée, Joseph slipped away in the direction of Rochefort, and on 25th July set sail from Royan for America. From New York he carried on a somewhat difficult correspondence with his wife and sister-in-law, making out that his more fortunate relatives in Sweden were enjoying something of a gilded exile.

[19]

New York, 28th January 1816

My dear sister-in-law,

It will soon be three months since I heard any news of Julie or of my Children; I have just read in the Moniteur of 9th December about the decree which will compel them to leave France and sell our possessions, so I am sending off M. Pelletran[1] with all speed to give her my letters and bring hers back to me; I have told him to seek her out wherever she may be, and I am urging him to set out at once in the hope that She may not yet have left Paris. Julie has had my power of attorney for quite a long time now, so she is perfectly free to do whatever She wishes, I shall consent to everything: I am telling her it is my most earnest wish that She should come and join me with my Children in the month of May, which is the best time of year for the voyage, I don't imagine they will refuse her this delay so that she can wait for the most favourable season. She will be able to use it to prepare for the voyage and to put our affairs in order.

I had started this letter with the intention of thanking you for all your kindness to my Children, but I was on the verge of forgetting all about it, because your warm heart so continually showers kindnesses upon them, and because I myself so readily take for granted all that your friendship for me, and your affection for their mother, have led you to do for all of us over so long a span of time—if I am fortunate enough to have them here with

---

[1] Pelletan, former surgeon to the Emperor?

me, I shall be able to forget a whole host of misfortunes, and I hope my wife and Children will share my own attitude to life. I shall probably feel as sad as they do at being so far away from so many loved ones, I imagine you yourself will decide to join Prince [Bernadotte]. The prosperity and good fortune which both he and your son Oscar are enjoying will console you for many of the anxieties you have suffered, and my Children will live in hopes of seeing you again one day in your Kingdom, where I hope to hear that you are very firmly established and as happy as I could wish you to be.

One thing in particular attracts me about this country in which I am living, and that is the extreme freedom enjoyed here, people live as they please, go into society or not just as they feel inclined, and seem generally disposed to look kindly on us; the climate is mild and you can be as warm as you wish by going further south.

I am not writing to the Prince, but beg you to remember me to him in your next letter; you know, my dear Désirée, that my friendship for you has long been warm and devoted.

Your affectionate brother-in-law

Joseph

[20]

New York, 11th July 1816

My dear sister-in-law,

I have received your last letter, this of mine will be handed to you by Mr. David Parish of Hamburg who knows your husband, he is a friend of mine and so, I am convinced, you will make him doubly welcome, he is a fine person, rich and capable, he will give you news of me; I expect Julie will have left by now, I hope she will be as happy here as it is possible for her to be away from you.

I am growing more attached to this country every day. It is the land of liberty, peace and happiness. Rest assured, I beg you, of my warm and continuing friendship.

Your affectionate brother-in-law

Joseph

APPENDIX

Note on Baron Dudon

M. Jean Savant has supplied a note, a résumé of which is given below, on the theft of the Empress's jewels by a 'certain Dudon', an incident related by several historians.

Frédéric Masson (*L'Affaire Maubreuil*), Madelin (*Histoire du Consulat et de l'Empire*, XIV, 356) and Maurice Garçon (*La Tumultueuse existence de Maubreuil*, 91) have given an account of this incident. The two latter drew on the work of Frédéric Masson, who in turn drew his information from the *Indiscrétions, souvenirs anecdotiques* reputed to be by Réal (Vol. II, pp. 70 et seq.). Masson failed to make due allowance for the evidence against the story which is to be found in this book. The chapter ends with the following statement: 'M. le Baron Louis . . . had been informed that the Imperial Treasure was in Orleans and had sent M. Dudon there. But on the very night of M. Dudon's arrival a riot . . . broke out in Orleans. M. Dudon, seized with panic, returned with all possible speed to Paris, without even having attempted to fulfil his mission.' Lacour-Gayet (*Talleyrand*, II, 396) affirms also that 'Dudon arrived too late'.

Who, then, was the 'certain Dudon', brought out of prison by Talleyrand to retrieve the Empress's jewels? He was an official who had enjoyed a brilliant career as an administrator from the moment the First Consul had appointed him auditor to the Council of State. He held in succession the offices of Secretary-General of the *Conseil du sceau des titres*, Baron, Master of Requests to the Council of State, Attorney-General to the *Conseil du sceau des titres*, Comptroller-General of the Army of Northern Spain with a monthly salary of 1,350,000 francs. In 1812, Dudon was imprisoned at Vincennes for 'disobedience to His Majesty's orders' by Savary, Minister of Police, but his arrest was most probably an error, since Baron Dudon was released, not in 1814, but forty-eight hours after being put in gaol.

The part played by Dudon is quite clear: the Provisional Government of 1814, faced with empty coffers, had its attention drawn to the fact that the Imperial Treasure was rumbling through Loir-et-Cher and the Loiret in the wake of Marie-Louise. The Minister of War dispatched one agent; the Minister of Finance, Baron Louis, sent off another, Dudon, who turned back without having approached the Empress.

Had he completed his mission, he would almost certainly have been at once rewarded by the Provisional Government and the Restoration. In August 1814, however, Baron Dudon had no job, and was applying for a Prefectship; Baron Louis, recommending him for the post, mentioned all his qualifications, but the recovery of the Crown diamonds was not amongst them. (Arch. Nat. F. I b. I., 158, 32.)

A study of the *Letters of Marie-Louise* disposes of the legend once and for all. The Empress, who kept nothing back from her husband, makes no mention whatever of this theft in her letters from Orleans (Nos. 158 et seq.).

Biographical Notes

BY M. JEAN SAVANT

ALDOBRANDINI. Prince Aldobrandini Borghese, brother of Pauline Bonaparte's second husband, had married on 12th April 1809 a young Mademoiselle de la Rochefoucauld, daughter of the Empress Joséphine's Lady-in-Waiting. He was First Equerry to the Empress Marie-Louise.

ANDLAU or ANDLAW. Napoleon's entourage included two men named Andlaw.

1. Armand-Gustave-*Félix*-d'Andlaw (1779–1860), Count of the Empire, Chamberlain to the Emperor, married to Pauline-Marie-Joséphine d'Hennezel (1813). His descendants continued to write their name ANDLAW.

2. Hardouin-*Gustave* d'Andlaw (1787–1850), Baron of the Empire, Equerry to the Empress, Colonel, married to Aglaé Tourteau d'Orvilliers. His descendants wrote their name ANDLAU.

ARCHBISHOP OF AIX, *v.* JAUFFRET

ARCH-CHANCELLOR, *v.* CAMBACÉRÈS

AUGEREAU. Charles-Pierre-François Augereau (1757–1816), Marshal of the Empire, Duc de Castiglione, was in command of the Army of the East or of the Rhône, in Lyons in 1814. His first wife, Gabrielle Irach, born in Smyrna, had died on 21st August 1806 at the Château de la Houssaye (Seine-et-Marne), and on 22nd February 1809 he married again, also at La Houssaye, Adélaïde-Joséphine de Bourlon de Chavanges, who is the 'Duchesse de Castiglione' mentioned in the letters of Napoleon and Marie-Louise.

BACIOCCHI (Princesse), *v.* BONAPARTE (Elisa)

BAILLON. The Palace Quartermaster-Sergeant.

BARY. Archivist to the Secretary of State's Office, under the direction of Maret, then private archivist to Napoleon.

BASSANO (Duc de), *v.* MARET

BAUSSET [BEAUSSET]. Chamberlain and Prefect of the Palace, the Baron de Bausset was one of Napoleon's 'go-betweens'. (It was he who, after the abdication, revealed the secrets of his master's private life to Marie-Louise.) He had helped Bonaparte to carry Joséphine to her room after the scene following his announcement of a divorce. Author of *Mémoires sur l'intérieur du palais impérial.*

BEAUHARNAIS (Claude de). Comte Claude de Beauharnais mentioned in letters 154, 179, etc., a relative of the Empress Joséphine, was First Gentleman Usher to the Empress Marie-Louise and a Senator.

BEAUHARNAIS (Eugène de) (1781–1824). Eugène-Rose de Beauharnais, son of General Alexandre de Beauharnais (guillotined 23rd July 1794) and of the future Empress Joséphine, had been adopted by Napoleon, appointed General, Chancellor of State, Prince of Venice, Viceroy of Italy, etc. His attitude during the 1814 campaign has been severely criticised. He had married Princess Augusta, daughter of King Maximilian-Joseph of Bavaria, to whose Court he retired with the titles of Duc de Leuchtenberg and Prince d'Eichstädt.

BEAUHARNAIS (Hortense) (1783–1837). Daughter of Joséphine, sister of Eugène de Beauharnais, wife of Louis Bonaparte (and thus stepdaughter and sister-in-law of Napoleon), Hortense lived apart from her husband (*v.* BONAPARTE, Louis). She had already given birth to the future Duc de Morny. She continued to be known as 'the Queen of Holland', or simply 'the Queen'. Mother of Napoleon III.

BEAUPOIL. Louis de Beaupoil, Comte de Sainte-Aulaire (1778–1849), married a Mademoiselle de Soyecourt (died 1806), then a Mademoiselle Du Roure (1809). Napoleon's Chamberlain from 21st December 1809, Prefect of the Meuse in 1813, he returned to Paris in January 1814 and followed Marie-Louise to Blois.

BEAUVAU (Comte de). Napoleon's Chamberlain.

BELLEGARDE. Austrian General and Marshal, Member of the Supreme War Council, often opposed to Napoleon. With Eugène de Beauharnais, Viceroy of Italy, he signed the treaty handing over Italy to Austria.

BELLUNE (Duc de), *v.* VICTOR

BERNADOTTE (Mme), *v.* CLARY (Désirée)

BERNADOTTE. Jean-Baptiste-Jules de Bernadotte (1763–1844), General, Minister, Councillor of State, Ambassador, Marshal of the Empire, Prince de Ponte-Corvo, elected Hereditary Prince of Sweden (1810), commanded the Army of the North against Napoleon, defeated his former comrades-in-arms Oudinot and Ney, King of Sweden and Norway in 1818. Brother-in-law of Joseph Bonaparte. (*v.* CLARY, Désirée.)

BERTHIER. Louis-Alexandre Berthier (1753–1815), Prince de Neuchâtel, Duc de Valengin, Prince de Wagram, Marshal, Grand Chamberlain, Master of the Hounds, Prince Vice-Constable of the Empire, Major-General of the Grand Army, Minister of War, etc. 'The army', Napoleon used to say, 'is accustomed to obey him as it would myself.' Through his marriage with a German princess, he became brother-in-law and cousin of the King of Bavaria.

BERTRAND. One of Napoleon's companions during his captivity on St Helena. General Henri-Gratien Bertrand (1773–1844), Count of the Empire, Major-General, had assumed the duties of Grand Marshal of the Palace several months after the death of Duroc (1813). He had married Fanny Elizabeth Mary Dillon, who was the last person Napoleon expressed a wish to see on St Helena.

BLÜCHER. Gebhard-Leberecht von Blücher (1742–1819), Prussian General and later Marshal. He won a great reputation for himself (thanks to his Chief of Staff) during the French campaign, and completed the defeat of Napoleon at Waterloo.

BONAPARTE (Elisa). Sister of Napoleon, wife of Félix Baciocchi, Maria-Anna-Elisa Bonaparte (1777–1820) was Princess of Lucca and Piombino, and Grand Duchess of Tuscany.

BONAPARTE (Jérôme). The Benjamin of the Bonaparte family, Jérôme (1784–1860), naval officer, General, King of Westphalia (1807–1813), had married Princess Cathérine of Württemberg. His conduct during the 1813 campaign, and his desertion of his kingdom, brought him into disgrace. Napoleon III created him Marshal of France.

BONAPARTE (Joseph). Elder brother of Napoleon, Joseph Bonaparte (1768–1844), reaped a rich reward from his young brother's good fortune. Ambassador, General, Councillor of State, Grand Elector of the Empire, Prince of the Empire, King of Naples (1806), King of Spain (1808), he had abandoned Spain after the defeat at Vittoria. Napoleon had appointed him Lieutenant-General of the Empire (January 1814). Brother-in-law of Bernadotte. (*v.* CLARY, Julie.)

BONAPARTE (Létizia). The 'mother of kings', widow of Carlo Buonaparte, had received the official title of Madame Mère. She was more generally addressed as Madame (as in this correspondence).

BONAPARTE (Louis). Louis Bonaparte (1778–1846) was for long Napoleon's favourite brother. General, Constable of the Empire, King of Holland, he had abdicated to avoid being associated with the requirements of the Continental Blockade, so prejudicial to the interests of the Dutch. Husband of Hortense de Beauharnais, but separated from her.

BONAPARTE (Pauline). Napoleon's favourite sister, Pauline Bonaparte (1780–1825), widow of General Leclerc, had married Prince Camille Borghese. Famous for her numerous love affairs and for her devotion to her brother whom she joined on the isle of Elba.

BONAPARTE (Zénaïde). One of the daughters of Joseph Bonaparte and Julie Clary.

BOUBERS (Mme de). Under-governess to the King of Rome. (The other under-governess was Mme de Mesgrigny.)

BOULAY. Antoine Boulay (de la Meurthe), (1761–1840) an accomplice in the 'coup' of the 18th Brumaire, Councillor of State, etc.

BRIGNOLE (Mme de). Anne-Marie-Gasparde-Vincente Fieri, widow of M. de Brignole-Sale, Countess of the Empire, Palace Lady, a native of Genoa, friend of Talleyrand.

CADORE, *v.* CHAMPAGNY

CAFFARELLI. General Marie-François-Auguste Caffarelli Du Falga (1766–1859), Napoleon's aide-de-camp, had been appointed Palace Governor to the Empress in 1813. He accompanied Marie-Louise and the King of Rome to Vienna.

CAMBACÉRÈS. Jean-Jacques-Régis de Cambacérès (1753–1824), Minister, compiler of the Civil Code, Second Consul, Arch-Chancellor of the Empire, Duke of Parma, etc., second only to Napoleon in the hierarchy of the State.

CARNOT. Lazare Carnot, former member of the Directory, victim of Napoleon Bonaparte on the 18th Fructidor, an opponent of the Empire, nevertheless offered his services in the hour of disaster.

CASTIGLIONE (Duc and Duchesse de), *v.* AUGEREAU

CAULAINCOURT. Armand-Augustin-Louis de Caulaincourt (1773–1827), closely concerned in the affair of the arrest of the Duc d'Enghien, General, Grand Equerry, Senator, Duc de Vicence, Minister Plenipotentiary, Minister of Foreign Relations, etc.

CHAMPAGNY. Jean-Baptiste-Pierrefitte Nompère de Champagny (1756–1834), successively naval officer, deputy, Councillor of State, Ambassador to Vienna, Minister of the Interior, Minister of Foreign Relations, Comptroller to the Crown, and finally Secretary to the Regency. He had been created Count of the Empire, then Duc de Cadore.

CHASSELOUP-LAUBAT. François de Chasseloup-Laubat (1754–1833), General in the Engineers, Count of the Empire, placed on the retired list in 1813, Senator, appointed director and supervisor of defence work on all bridges from Nogent to the Loire (1st February 1814). Voted for the deposition of Napoleon.

CHATEAU (General), *v.* HUGUET-CHATAUX

CLARKE. General Clarke (1765–1818) had thrown in his lot with Napoleon Bonaparte during the campaign in Italy (whilst supposedly keeping him under observation). He was rewarded by the appointment of Minister of War (1807), and the titles of Comte de Hunebourg (1808) and Duc de Feltre (1809). Louis XVIII made him a Marshal (1816).

CLARY (Désirée). Engaged to Napoleon in 1795, Désirée-Eugénie Clary married General Bernadotte, who became a Marshal, Prince de Ponte-Corvo, Prince Royal of Sweden, King of Sweden and Norway under the name of Charles XIV John. Her sister had married Joseph Bonaparte. After she had become Mme Bernadotte, Désirée Clary would often point out, in her drawing-room, a magnificent carved box containing love letters from General Bonaparte, whom she referred to as '*mon illustre ingrat*'.

CLARY (Eugénie), *v.* CLARY (Désirée)

CLARY (Julie). Sister of Désirée Clary, wife of Joseph Bonaparte, Queen of Naples (1806), then of Spain (1808). Sister-in-law of Bernadotte.

COMMISSIONERS. They were: Schouvaloff, Koller (*q.v.*) and Waldburg-Truchsess (for Prussia).

CONSTANT. Constant Wairy, known as Constant, first valet de chambre to Napoleon. He laid down his duties at the time of the abdication and of Napoleon's attempted suicide, obviously fearing to be implicated in the incident. Constant has been reproached for this defection, but the secretaries, doctors, etc., who refused to accompany Napoleon to the isle of Elba are more deserving of censure.

CORVISART. Chief Medical Adviser to Napoleon, Baron of the Empire, (1755–1821).

CUSSY. Baron de Cussy was one of the Palace Prefects.

DARU. Pierre-Antoine-Noël-Bruno Daru, Count of the Empire, Comptroller-General of the Grand Army, Minister, etc., who, Napoleon used to say, was 'a plough-ox' for work. He had a brother Martial-Noël-Pierre Daru (1774–1827), Baron of the Empire (3rd February 1813), Comptroller of the Imperial Crown Lands in Rome, Inspector-General of Reviews, etc. The latter had married, on 29th September 1806, Charlotte-Marie de Froidefond Du Chatenet, of whom Marie-Louise makes mention.

DECRÈS. Denis Decrès (1761–1820), Admiral, Minister of Marine, Count of the Empire, then Duke. Having married a Mademoiselle Clary, he had thus become the nephew of Bernadotte and of Joseph Bonaparte. He had known Napoleon from the outset of his career, and in conversation with him never abandoned his forthright manner of speech.

DEJEAN. Jean-François-Aimé Dejean (1749–1824), General in the Engineers, Senator, had been Minister of War Administration, from which post he was dismissed by Napoleon in 1810. His second marriage was the subject of comment by Napoleon, as Dejean and his son (also a General), married two sisters; Dejean, however, retaliated by remarking that their situation was comparable to that of his own: a mother and daughter (Beauharnais) having married two brothers (Napoleon and Louis Bonaparte).

DENON. Dominique-Vivant Denon (1747–1825), Baron of the Empire, one of Napoleon's favourites, was Director-General of French Museums.

DROUOT. Nicknamed 'the Wise Man of the Grand Army', Antoine Drouot (1774–1847) was a General in the Artillery, Count of the Empire and Aide-de-camp to Napoleon, whom he followed to the isle of Elba but refused to follow to St Helena.

DUBOIS. Antoine Dubois (1756–1837), surgeon, had attended Marie-Louise at her confinement in 1811. His services earned him, amongst other pensions, titles, etc., a gratuity amounting to the equivalent of thirty million francs in modern currency.

DUCHESS (The), *v.* LANNES

DUDON, *v.* p. 243, 'Note on Baron Dudon'.

DURAND (Mme). 'Générale' Durand, authoress of several books on Napoleon and the Empire, and, at this time, one of the Empress's maids-in-waiting.

ELISA, *v.* BONAPARTE (Elisa)

FAIN. Agathon-Jean-François Fain (1778–1836), Baron of the Empire, private secretary and archivist to Napoleon. Married to Adélaïde-Louise-Sophie Lelorgne. His son, Camille, was private secretary to Louis-Philippe.

FELTRE (Duc de), *v.* CLARKE

FLAHAUT. Charles-Auguste-Joseph de Flahaut de la Billarderie (1785–1870), son of Talleyrand, lover of Hortense de Beauharnais (Louis Bonaparte's wife), General, Aide-de-camp to Napoleon, Count of the Empire, etc. He did not accompany his benefactor to the isle of Elba, and in 1815 exclaimed to Gourgaud, who was preparing to leave for St Helena: 'So you too are going to do this foolish thing!'

FOULER. Albert-Louis-Emmanuel de Fouler (1769–1831), General in the Cavalry, created Comte de Relingue in 1808, Equerry in charge of the stables, first of the Empress (1804), then of the Emperor (1810).

GOURGAUD. Gaspard Gourgaud, General, Baron of the Empire, First Orderly Officer to Napoleon, and one of his companions in exile at St Helena. His name is wrongly spelt GOURGAULT in the letters of Marie-Louise.

GRAND MARSHAL, *v.* BERTRAND

GRÉTRY. André-Ernest-Modeste Grétry (1741–1813), the famous composer, had just died at Montmorency, in the hermitage where Jean-Jacques Rousseau had lived.

GROUCHY. Emmanuel de Grouchy (1766–1847), a fine General (later a Marshal), Count of the Empire, who has long been held responsible, and unjustly so, for the result of Waterloo.

HARVILLE. Louis-Auguste Jouvenel des Ursins d'Harville (1749–1815), General, Senator, Count of the Empire, Equerry and First Gentleman-Usher to the Empress Joséphine and Governor of the Tuileries (before Caffarelli).

HOLLAND (King of), *v.* BONAPARTE (Louis)

HORTENSE (Queen), *v.* BEAUHARNAIS (Hortense de)

HUBERT. Auguste-Charles Hubert, one of Napoleon's valets de chambre.

HUGUET. Charles-Louis Huguet, Marquis de Sémonville (1759–1839), diplomat, Senator, and later Grand Referendary to the Chamber of Peers. Friend of both Maret and Talleyrand, and deliberately played several different parts. Later, Dambray was to say to Louis XVIII: 'Sémonville had always a purse and a passport ready for those who were exiled.' Maret's candidate for the portfolio of Minister of Police in 1810. Early in 1814 he was dispatched to his senatorial district (of which Bourges was the county town), as Special Commissioner. He had voted for the deposition of Napoleon Bonaparte.

HUGUET-CHÂTAUX. General Louis Huguet-Châtaux (1779–1814) had married the daughter of Marshal Victor. Seriously wounded at Montereau (18th February 1814), he was taken to Paris, where, notwithstanding the ministrations of Dubois, the surgeon, he died on 8th May.

ISABEY. Jean-Baptiste Isabey (1767–1855), the famous painter of the Directory, the Empire and the Restoration.

JAUFFRET. Comte Jauffret, Almoner to the Emperor, was Archbishop of Aix in 1814, and had previously been Bishop of Metz.

JOSEPH (King or Prince), *v.* BONAPARTE (Joseph)

KASTNER (Mme de). One of the maids-in-waiting to Marie-Louise.

KLEIST. Emil-Friedrich, Count Kleist von Nollendorf, Prussian General, then Marshal (1762–1823), victor of Kulm, and in command of the left flank at Leipzig. Unsuccessful on 14th February 1814 (Napoleon announces the news to Marie-Louise), he took his revenge at Laon on 9th March.

KOLLER. Austrian General, one of the Commissioners appointed by the European powers to accompany Napoleon on his deportation to the isle of Elba.

LA BESNARDIÈRE. Jean-Baptiste de Gouy de La Besnardière (1765–1843), Oratorian, entered the Foreign Office at the time of the Revolution, Count of the Empire, one of the two most senior officials in the Ministry of External Relations. (The other was Hauterive.) He was in charge of the second Political Section

(Switzerland, Holland, Austria, Prussia and the German States, Denmark, Sweden and Russia).

LA BOUILLERIE. Baron de la Bouillerie, Treasurer-General of the Crown and of the Extraordinary and Private Crown Lands. Napoleon could not forgive him for having restored the Crown diamonds to the Government in 1814; see p. 243, 'Note on Baron Dudon'.

LACÉPÈDE. Etienne de Lacépède, (1756–1825). Count of the Empire, scholar (he continued the work of Buffon), Grand Chancellor of the Legion of Honour, Member of the Privy Council and Senator.

LANGERON. General Count Andrault de Langeron (1763–1831), born in Paris of a Nevers family, had entered Russian service, in which he made a brilliant career for himself. He won renown at Leipzig, crossed the Rhine (1st January 1814), fought at Soissons, Laon, Craonne, and occupied first Le Bourget, then the approaches to Paris.

LANNES. Jean Lannes (1769–1809), General, Duc de Montebello, famous for his eccentricities and for his quarrels with Napoleon, which he would end by declaring 'that he was indeed to be pitied for having conceived such an unfortunate passion for *this harlot*'. In honour of his memory, and also of the army, Napoleon appointed his wife Lady-in-Waiting to the Empress. The Duchesse de Montebello played a lamentable part in the affairs of Marie-Louise, though perhaps a less blameworthy one than has generally been stated, or than Napoleon believed, for on St Helena he spoke of her in terms of withering insult.

LAPLACE. Charles-Emile de Laplace (1789–1874), Baron of the Empire, Napoleon's Orderly Officer, and later Inspector-General of Artillery, Senator of the Second Empire, etc.

LAVALLETTE. Antoine-Marie Chamans de Lavallette (1769–1830), threw in his lot with Bonaparte in Italy. Councillor of State, Count of the Empire, Postmaster-General, he had married Emilie-Louise de Beauharnais, whom his devotion immortalised after Waterloo.

LEBRUN. Son of the Arch-Treasurer (and ex-Third Consul) of the Empire, General Charles-François-Paul Lebrun (1775–1837), Comte de Lohra, Duc de Plaisance, had married Marie-Anne-Sophie de Barbé-Marbois.

LEUCHTENBERG (Duc de), *v.* BEAUHARNAIS (Eugène de)

LOBAU (Comte de), *v.* MOUTON

MACDONALD. Etienne-Jacques-Joseph-Alexandre Macdonald (1765–1840), General, Marshal of the Empire, Minister Plenipotentiary, Duc de Tarente, architect of Wagram, persuaded Napoleon to abdicate.

MADAME, *v.* BONAPARTE (Létizia)

MARESCALCHI. Italian Minister of Foreign Affairs, resident in Paris.

MARET. Hugues-Bernard Maret (1763–1839), a lawyer in the Burgundy *Parlement* before the Revolution, diplomat, Minister-Secretary of State to Napoleon, Minister of Foreign Relations (the successor of Champagny), Count of the Empire, Duc de Bassano. His wife, one of the beauties of the Imperial Court, found favour with Napoleon for some time.

MARMONT. Auguste-Frédéric-Louis Viesse de Marmont (1774–1852), a friend of Napoleon's youth, General, Marshal of the Empire, Duc de Raguse, victor of Champaubert. Engaged in battle with Mortier and Moncey beneath the walls of Paris, and capitulated at Belleville.

MARINE (Minister of), *v.* DECRÈS

MÉNEVAL. Claude-François de Méneval (1778–1850), Baron of the Empire, Master of Requests to the Council of State, Secretary to Napoleon, then to Marie-Louise, had married Anne-Virginie-Joséphine Mathieu de Mauvières, whose father, also a Baron of the Empire, was tutor to one of Napoleon's sons—Léon. Napoleon, on St Helena, said: 'Méneval was a clerk who could barely spell' (Gourgaud, *Journal*). He received innumerable favours from Napoleon. In addition to the 150,000 francs (45 million in modern currency) which Marie-Louise urged her husband to grant him (Letter No. 161), he had received from his master at the time of his marriage the modern equivalent of 90 million; his salary (including endowments) amounted to more than 12 million by present-day reckoning, and under the terms of Napoleon's will he stood to gain the modern equivalent of 45 million francs. (The letters patent of 26th April 1810 conferring a barony upon him corrected the spelling of his name: MÉNEVAL for MENNEVAL.)

MESGRIGNY. Under-governess to the King of Rome, the Baronne de Mesgrigny, *née* Marie-Antoinette-Eléonore Berthelot de Rambuteau, was the wife of one of Napoleon's equerries, Adrien-

Charles-Marie de Mesgrigny (1778–1849). At Fontainebleau on 2nd April 1814 he was present at a luncheon party which included Napoleon, Berthier and Lefebvre. 'The conversation turned on an old love affair which Prince Eugène de Beauharnais had once had with La Bigottini, a dancer at the Opera. Napoleon, who was holding a leg of mutton in his right hand, and with his left was peeling off its brown outer skin with a knife, did not appear in the least worried, and much enjoyed hearing the details of this affair related by the Equerry-in-attendance, M. de Mesgrigny' (Despatys, *Magistrats et criminels*, 20).

METTERNICH. Prince Metternich (1773–1859), Napoleon's adversary, had skilfully negotiated the marriage of Marie-Louise, and paved the way for Austria's revenge.

MOLÉ. Louis-Mathieu Molé (1781–1855), Count of the Empire, Councillor of State, Prefect, Director-General of Roads and Bridges, Minister, to whose conversation Napoleon was very partial.

MONTEBELLO (Duc and Duchesse de), *v.* LANNES

MONTELEONE (Mme de). The Duchesse de Monteleone, whose husband had been Neapolitan Ambassador in Paris.

MONTESQUIOU (THE YOUNGER). Anatole de Montesquiou-Fezensac, born 1781, son of Napoleon's Grand Chamberlain and the King of Rome's governess. Orderly officer to Napoleon (1809), Colonel (1813) and Chamberlain.

MONTESQUIOU (Mme de). Governess to the King of Rome, wife of the Comte de Montesquiou-Fezensac, Grand Chamberlain and President of the Legislative Council.

MONTMORENCY (Mme de). Palace Lady.

MORTEMART. *Casimir*-Lucien-Victurnien de Rochechouart de Mortemart, Orderly Officer to Napoleon, Baron of the Empire (later General, Ambassador, Senator), married 26th May 1810 to Virginie-Antoinette-Pauline de Sainte-Aldégonde.

MORTIER. Adolphe-Edouard-Casimir-Joseph Mortier (1768–1835), General, Marshal of the Empire, Duc de Trévise, signed the capitulation of Paris.

MOSKOWA (Princesse de la), *v.* NEY

MOUTON. Georges Mouton (1770–1838), General of whom Napoleon was wont to say: 'My *Sheep*, he's a lion.' Aide-de-camp to Napoleon, Count of the Empire, with the title of Comte de Lobau, later Marshal of France. Taken prisoner at the capitulation of Dresden (11th November 1813), and sent into captivity in Hungary, he returned to France only after the downfall of Napoleon.

NANSOUTY. Etienne-Marie-Antoine Champion de Nansouty (1768–1815), former pupil (as was Napoleon) of Brienne and the École Militaire in Paris. First Chamberlain to the Empress Joséphine (1805), General, Chief Equerry to Napoleon (1808), Count of the Empire, commanded the cavalry of the Imperial Guard in 1814.

NAPLES (King of), v. MURAT

NAPLES (Queen of), v. BONAPARTE (Caroline)

NEUCHÂTEL (Prince and Princesse de), v. BERTHIER

NICOLAÏ. Comte Christian de Nicolaï (1777–1839) was one of Napoleon's Chamberlains. From 1811 to 1813 he had served in Baden, then in Karlsruhe, as Minister Plenipotentiary. Later a Peer of France.

NOAILLES (M. and Mme de). Comte Just de Noailles, Napoleon's Chamberlain, had married Mélanie-Xavière de Périgord, niece of Talleyrand.

OSCAR. Oscar Bernadotte (1799–1859), son of the General and Désirée Clary. His Christian name was chosen by General Bonaparte, who at the time was fascinated by the poems of Ossian. King of Sweden and Norway, under the name of Oscar I, from 1844 to 1857.

OSTEN-SACKEN. Russian General, then Marshal, a native of Livonia-(1750–1837). Commanded a cavalry corps at Eylau and Friedland. In 1813, joining forces with Blücher, he defeated Macdonald (at La Katzbach) and forced Puthod to surrender. Distinguished himself at Leipzig, crossed the Rhine (1st January 1814), victorious at La Rothière, etc. He was not, in fact, killed during the French campaign, as Napoleon announced to Marie-Louise. He became Governor of Paris after its capitulation.

OUDINOT. Nicolas-Charles Oudinot (1767–1847), General, Deputy, Marshal and Count of the Empire, Duc de Reggio, commanded the 7th Corps of the Grand Army in Champagne in 1814.

PALLAVICINI. Auditor to the Council of State, sub-Prefect of Moulins.

PARAVICINI, v. PALLAVICINI

PARMA (Duke of), v. CAMBACÉRÈS

PAULINE (Princess), v. BONAPARTE (Pauline)

PÉLARD. Frédéric-Auguste Pélard, one of Napoleon's valets de chambre.

PLACE (M. de la), *v.* LAPLACE

PLAISANCE (Duchesse de), *v.* LEBRUN

POLICE (Minister of), *v.* SAVARY

PONTE-CORVO (Princesse de), *v.* CLARY (Désirée)

POZZO DI BORGO. Charles-André Pozzo di Borgo (1764–1842), private adviser to the Tsar, compatriot and adversary of Napoleon, and one of the authors of his downfall.

RABUSSON (Mme). One of Marie-Louise's maids-in-waiting.

RAGUSE (Duc de), *v.* MARMONT

REGGIO (Duc de), *v.* OUDINOT

REGNAUD (de Saint-Jean d'Angély). (1761–1819), Napoleon's brilliant collaborator in the Council of State, Count of the Empire, Attorney-General of the High Imperial Court, Minister of State, etc.

ROVIGO (Duc and Duchesse de), *v.* SAVARY

SACKEN, *v.* OSTEN-SACKEN

SAINT-AIGNAN. Nicolas-Auguste-Marie Rousseau de Saint-Aignan (1770–1858), Baron of the Empire, Orderly Officer, then Aide-de-camp, Equerry and Minister Plenipotentiary. Brother-in-law of Caulaincourt.

SAINTE-AULAIRE, *v.* BEAUPOIL

SAINT-PRIEST. Guillaume-Emmanuel Guignard, Comte de Saint-Priest (1776–1814), served with Condé's army, then entered Russian service, distinguished himself at Austerlitz (1805) and Borodino (1812), etc. In command of the 8th Russian Corps under Blücher, he captured Rheims, 'sword in hand', on 12th March 1814, evacuated his conquest on the following day, was mortally wounded and removed to Laon, where he died on 29th March.

SAVARY. Anne-Marie-Jean-René Savary (1774–1833), General entrusted with the execution of the Duc d'Enghien, Duc de Rovigo, Minister of Police (1810–14). His wife, Félicité de Faudoas, was for a time Napoleon's mistress. She was then (1814) the mistress of General Sébastiani.

SCHOUVALOFF. Count Paul Schouvaloff, Russian General, Aide-de-camp to the Tsar, one of the Commissioners appointed to accompany Napoleon to the isle of Elba.

SCHWARZENBERG. Charles-Philippe, Prince Schwarzenberg (1771–

1820), General and diplomat, had represented Austria in Paris at the time of the marriage of Marie-Louise. Commander-in-Chief of the Austrian Army during the French campaign.

SÉGUR. Louis-Philippe de Ségur d'Aguesseau, Marquis, Count of the Empire, General (1791), Member of the Institute (1803), Grand Master of Ceremonies at the Imperial Court (1804), Senator, etc. Father of the author of the famous *Mémoires*. At the beginning of 1814, he was sent to the 18th Military Division (Dijon) as Special Commissioner.

SÉMONVILLE, *v.* HUGUET

SPAIN (King of), *v.* BONAPARTE (Joseph)

SWEDEN (Princess Royal and Queen of), *v.* CLARY (Désirée)

TALLEYRAND. Former Minister of Foreign Relations, high dignitary of the Empire, whose decisive voice in the Senate ensured the deposition of Napoleon, and who was responsible for setting up the Provisional Government, was a member of the Regency Council. His policy at that time was to maintain the Regency after Napoleon's downfall, but the departure of Marie-Louise made this impossible.

TARENTE (Duc de), *v.* MACDONALD

TASCHER. Cousin and Aide-de-camp of Eugène de Beauharnais, Viceroy of Italy. Napoleon was not satisfied with the explanations brought him by the messenger. 'Where is Eugène? When is he coming?', he asked Tascher. Eugène was not worrying himself unduly about obeying the orders which Napoleon had given him —namely to cross the Alps with the Army of Italy.

TRÉVISE (Duc de), *v.* MORTIER

TURENNE. Henry-Amédée-Mercure, Marquis de Turenne, Marquis d'Aynac and de Pignan, (1773–1852), General, Count of the Empire, Chamberlain and Master of the Robes to Napoleon.

VALETTE (M. de La), *v.* LAVALLETTE

VICENCE (Duc de), *v.* CAULAINCOURT

VICEROY, *v.* BEAUHARNAIS (Eugène)

VICTOR. Victor Perrin, known as Victor, (1764–1841), Drummer, General, Minister Plenipotentiary, Marshal of the Empire, Duc de Bellune, dismissed from office 18th February 1814 because of his tardy arrival at Montereau, remained in the army, was wounded at Craonne, etc.

WAR (Minister of), *v.* CLARKE

WESTPHALIA (King and Queen of), *v.* BONAPARTE (Jérôme)

WITTGENSTEIN. General (later Marshal) Ludwig-Adolf-Wittgenstein (1769–1843) had entered Berlin, 11th March 1813, and had commanded the Russo-Prussian forces.

WINTZINGERODE. Russian soldier and diplomat, Baron Ferdinand Wintzingerode (1770–1818) had been taken prisoner during the Russian campaign, ill-treated by Napoleon and set free by the Cossacks. Distinguished himself at Leipzig. Beaten at Saint-Dizier by Napoleon.

WONOWITZ. Possibly WOLODKOWICZ or WONSOWITCH, Polish officer and interpreter who, amongst others, accompanied Napoleon on his journey across Europe after the retreat from Russia.

WORONTZOW. Michel Worontzow, Russian General (1782–1854), who had won distinction during the campaigns of 1812 and 1813. Later Prince, Minister, etc.

YORCK. General Johann-David-Ludwig Yorck, Prussian General (1759–1830), had acquired the title of Count of Wartenburg in 1813, had distinguished himself at Leipzig, and in 1814 was in command of one of the two Prussian Corps which, combined with two Russian Corps, made up the Army of Silesia.

ZÉNAÏDE, *v.* BONAPARTE (Zénaïde)

Bibliography

AUBRY, Octave. *Vie privée de Napoléon.* Paris, 1939.

BAINVILLE, Jacques. *Napoléon.* Paris, 1931.

BERTAUT, Jules. *Marie-Louise, femme de Napoléon Ier*, 1791–1847. Paris, 1952.

BESSARD, Raymonde. *La Vie privée de Marie-Louise.* Paris, 1953.

BOURGOING, Le Baron Jean de. *Le Cœur de Marie-Louise. Marie-Louise, Duchesse de Parme,* 1814–1821. Paris, 1939.

Marie Louise von Österreich. Kaiserin der Franzosen. Herzogin von Parma. Vienna, 1953.

CIANA, ALBERT. *Les Bonaparte. Autographes, Manuscrits, Signatures.* Geneva, 1941.

GACHOT, Edouard. *Marie-Louise intime,* I–II. Paris, 1911–12.

MADELIN, Louis. *Histoire du Consulat et de l'Empire, XIII–XVI.* Paris, 1951–4.

Lettres inédites de Napoléon Ier à Marie-Louise, écrites de 1810 à 1814. Avec introduction et notes par Louis Madelin. Paris, 1935.

MASSON, Frédéric. *L'Impératrice Marie-Louise,* 1809–1815. Paris, 1902.

Napoléon chez lui. Paris, 1894.

NICOLSON, Harold. *The Congress of Vienna. A Study in Allied Unity:* 1812–1822. New York, 1946.

RONCIÈRE, Charles de la. *The Letters of Napoleon to Marie Louise. With a Commentary by Charles de la Roncière and an Introduction by Philip Guedalla.* London, 1935.

SAVANT, Jean. *Tel fut Napoléon.* Paris, 1953.

Index

References to the Biographical Notes are printed in italics

Aix, Archbishop of, v. Jauffret
Aix-en-Savoie, 169, 183, 184, 185,190, 207, 211, 212, 216
Aix-les-Bains, 20
Albert, 82
Albertina, 13, 16
Aldobrandi, Prince, 144, 159, 165, 167, 186, 187, *245*
Alexander, Emperor, 23, 29, 50, 79, 80, 88, 90, 137, 156, 161, 183, 186, 187, 188, 190, 191, 223, 233, 234
Alfred, 14
America, 16, 17, 241
Anatole, Mme, 99, 100
Andlau, M.d', 195, *245*
Ange-Gardien, L', 109, 111
Antwerp, 35, 89
Arch-Chancellor, v. Cambacérès
Aubert, Mme, 166
Augereau, Duc de Castiglione, 32, 71, 83, 91, 92, 135, *245, 249*
Austria, 29, 92, 171, 179, 180, 182, 190
Austrian Army, 71, 76, 77, 160
Austria, Emperor of, v. Francis
Auxerre, 92
Arcis-sur-Aube, 135
Avignon, 197, 198

Baciocchi, Princess, v. Bonaparte, Elisa
Baillon, 188, 190, 191, *245*
Bapst, 228
Bar-sur-Seine, 88
Barbé-Marbois, v. Plaisance, Duchesse de
Barbier, Mme, 166

Barcy, 134
Bary, 21, *245*
Bassano, Duc de, v. Maret
Basle, 187, 201
Bausset, 168, 170, 179, 184, 189, 191, 213, 215, *246*
Battle of the Nations, 35
Bavaria, 31, 35, 77
Bayonne, 112, 113
Beauharnais, Claude de, 159, 186, 187, *246*
Beauharnais, Eugène de, 17, 43, 71, 72, 111, 121, 184, 201, 212, 213, 223, 234, 235, *246*, 258
Beauharnais, Hortense, 31, 43, 69, 72, 89, 103, 107, 123, 132, 140, 146, 212, 235, *246*, 252
Beaupoil, Louis, Comte de Saint-Aulaire, 162, 170, 171, *246*, 257
Beauvot, 195, *246*
Bellegarde, 72, 217, *246*
Bellune, Duc de, v. Victor
Bernadotte, Désirée, 16, 17, 161, 228, 229, 230–4, 237, 288, 241–2
Bernadotte, Prince, 31, 35, 212, 231, 233, 234, 237, 242, *247*
Bernardière, 45
Berry-au-Bac, 101, 105
Bertaut, 181
Berthier, Marshal, Prince de Neuchâtel, 32, 33, 34, 64, 157, 196, *247*, 256
Bertrand, Grand Marshal, 74, 155, 198, 209, 210, 219, *247*
Bertrand, Mme, 236
Bianchi, 76

261